MEMBER CENTERS OF THE NATIONAL COUNCIL FOR RESEARCH ON WOMEN

ARIZONA
University of Arizona, Southwest Institute for Research on Women

CALIFORNIA
Equity Policy Center
University of California, Berkeley, Beatrice M. Bain Research Group
University of California, Davis, Consortium for Women in Research
University of California, Los Angeles, Center for the Study of Women
University of California, Los Angeles, Higher Education Research Institute
University of Southern California, Center for Feminist Research
Stanford University, Institute for Research on Women and Gender

COLORADO
University of Denver, Higher Education Resource Services, Mid-America

DISTRICT OF COLUMBIA
American Association of University Women Educational Foundation
American Council on Education, Office of Women in Higher Education
Association of American Colleges and Universities, Program on the Status and Education of Women
Business and Professional Women's Foundation
Center for Policy Alternatives
Center for Women Policy Studies
General Federation of Women's Clubs International, Women's History and Resource Center
George Washington University, Women's Studies Program
Howard University, African American Women's Institute
Institute for Women's Policy Research
International Center for Research on Women
National Association for Women in Education
The Union Institute Center for Women
Women's Research and Education Institute

GEORGIA
Spelman College, Women's Research and Resource Center

ILLINOIS
Loyola University Chicago, Gannon Center for Women and Leadership
University of Illinois at Chicago, Center for Research on Women and Gender
University of Illinois at Urbana-Champaign, Office of Women in International Development

INDIANA
Girls Incorporated National Resource Center

LOUISIANA
Tulane University, Newcomb College Center for Research on Women

MARYLAND
Towson State University, Institute for Teaching and Research on Women
University of Maryland, National Women's Studies Association

MASSACHUSETTS
Five College Women's Studies Research Center
Radcliffe College, The Mary Ingraham Bunting Institute
Radcliffe College, The Henry A. Murray Research Center
Radcliffe College, The Public Policy Institute
Radcliffe College, The Arthur & Elizabeth Schlesinger Library
Smith College, Project on Women and Social Change
Wellesley College, Center for Research on Women
Wellesley College, Higher Education Resource Services, New England

MICHIGAN
University of Michigan, Center for Education of Women
University of Michigan, Institute for Research on Women and Gender

MINNESOTA

College of St. Catherine, Abigail Quigley McCarthy Center for Research on Women
Hamline University, Upper Midwest Women's History Center
University of Minnesota, Center on Women and Public Policy, Humphrey Institute

NEW JERSEY

Rutgers University, Center for the American Woman and Politics, Eagleton Institute of Politics
Rutgers University, Center for Women's Global Leadership
Rutgers University, Institute for Research on Women
Rutgers University, Douglass College
Rutgers University, Institute for Women's Leadership

NEW YORK

Barnard College, Barnard Center for Research on Women
Catalyst
City University of New York, Center for the Study of Women and Society
Columbia University, Institute for Research on Women & Gender
Cornell University, Institute on Women and Work
The Feminist Press at the City University of New York
Hunter College, Center for Family Policy Studies
NOW Legal Defense and Education Fund
State University of New York at Albany, Center for Women in Government
State University of New York at Albany, Institute for Research on Women
State University of New York at Binghamton, Women's Studies Program
State University of New York at Buffalo, Institute for Research & Education on Women and Gender
Women's Interart Center
Young Women's Christian Association of the USA

NORTH CAROLINA

Duke University, Women's Studies Program

OHIO

Kent State University, Project on the Study of Gender and Education
Ohio State University, Center for Women's Studies
University of Cincinnati, Center for Women's Studies

OREGON

University of Oregon, Center for the Study of Women in Society

PENNSYLVANIA

University of Pennsylvania, Alice Paul Center for the Study of Women

RHODE ISLAND

Brown University, Pembroke Center for Teaching and Research on Women

TENNESSEE

The University of Memphis, Center for Research on Women

UTAH

University of Utah, Higher Education Resource Services, West
Utah State University, Women and Gender Research Institute

VIRGINIA

The Feminist Majority Foundation
Virginia Polytechnic Institute and State University, Women's Research Institute

WASHINGTON

University of Washington, Northwest Center for Research on Women
Washington State University, Women's Resource Center

WISCONSIN

University of Wisconsin, Madison, Women's Studies Research Center

The Girls Report
Commissioned by
The National Council
for Research on Women

the
girls report

*What We Know &
Need to Know About
Growing Up Female*

Written by Lynn Phillips

With contributions from
Girls Incorporated National Resource Center
An NCRW Member Center

The National Council for Research on Women extends its grateful appreciation
to the following foundations for their generous support of this project:

William T. Grant Foundation

Lilly Endowment Inc.

Remmer Family Foundation

Valentine Foundation

Girl's Best Friend Foundation

Contents

the girls report

Foreword

THE NATIONAL COUNCIL for Research on Women (NCRW) is proud to issue *The Girls Report: What We Know and Need to Know About Growing Up Female,* its second report on adolescent girls in this decade. Much has changed in what we know about adolescent girls, how they are viewed, and how they view themselves since 1991, when the first report, *Risk, Resiliency, and Resistance: Current Research on Adolescent Girls,* was released. Today, researchers and activists increasingly perceive girls as smart, bold, and determined, and call on them to help shape programs and research that address their special concerns and needs. Although the findings in this report are anchored in the proliferating research on, and programs for, girls in the United States, the expanding attention to this age group—and the perception of girls as partners with important perspectives to share—has become a global phenomenon, as demonstrated by the active participation of girls at the United Nations Fourth World Conference on Women, held in Beijing in 1995.

The Girls Report provides an important baseline of knowledge on adolescence as we approach the new millennium. Lynn Phillips, its author, has done an admirable job of synthesizing the present state of research on this pivotal phase in girls' lives. In contrast to most research reports, which tend to focus on single issues, *The Girls Report* employs a holistic perspective, exploring adolescent girls' health, sexuality, education, experiences with violence, and economic realities and viewing them across the divides of race, ethnicity, class, and sexual orientation. In so doing, it also assesses how what we know can guide future research and programs. While the report identifies programs and achievements that engender a sense of vitality and empowerment, it also delineates the underbelly of girls' experiences, the many areas in which they remain victimized, harassed, and diminished, and the very real risks that still constrain their healthy development. Throughout, the voices of girls themselves provide a counterpoint to the analyses of researchers. These statements, drawn from interviews and focus groups, express girls' struggles and aspirations, and their views of how their situations could be improved.

The Girls Report reflects both NCRW's mission and the wide range of interests, concerns, and research capacities of its membership. The strength of NCRW—a collaborative of 77 research centers focused on women and girls—lies in its ability to draw on the rich resources and expertise of its members to synthesize cutting-edge research, policies, and practices and make this information accessible to diverse audiences. Thus, member centers' programs and research are cited throughout the report, as well as in the "Resource Guide" at the end. While many centers made invaluable contributions, NCRW extends special appreciation to Girls Incorporated for playing a pivotal role in the preparation of the report, and to the Wellesley Centers for Research on Women and the American Association of University Women (AAUW) for providing critical information and insights at key junctures.

The Girls Report also inaugurates NCRW's new Research for Action program. Its goal is to stimulate dialogue and collaboration among the worlds of research, public policy, and activism, and to shape the lens through which policymakers, the media, educators and other professionals, advocates, and the public view women and girls. In keeping with these objectives, each chapter in the report identifies current issues and debates on the topics covered and concludes with recommendations on what is needed to enhance the lives of adolescent girls and help them reach their potential. The report ends with "Looking Ahead: Developing a New Research Agenda," which is designed to guide future studies of girls' needs, experiences, and development. To enhance the report's impact on policies and programs, NCRW, in partnership with our member centers, will conduct roundtables and workshops in a number of locations across the country. These events will provide an opportunity for researchers, public officials, funders, and others with a vital interest in the lives of girls to discuss the report's findings and compare them with local conditions and experiences.

NCRW expresses its gratitude to the funders of *The Girls Report:* the William T. Grant Foundation, the Lilly Endowment, the Remmer Family Foundation, the Valentine Foundation, and Girl's Best Friend Foundation. Sharing our view of the importance of synthesizing past research and programs so as to shape future agendas, our funders generously underwrote the research that went into this report, as well as its preparation and dissemination. Some also read and commented on various drafts. We also extend great appreciation to the Ford Foundation for general support during the preparation of this report. Considering the rich input to this project from so many sources, we are convinced that *The Girls Report* will inform, enlighten, and inspire all those interested in making the world a better place for girls and women.

—*Linda Basch*
Executive Director
National Council for Research on Women

Acknowledgments

THE NATIONAL COUNCIL for Research on Women's *Girls Report* represents the vision and expertise of many people who have collaborated in the creation and evolution of this project. From its conception to its final form, the generosity and insights of both talented colleagues and of girls themselves have strengthened the report and brought it to completion.

In many respects, this has been a collaborative project, with various member centers of NCRW and other colleagues making important contributions. Heather Johnston Nicholson, Director of Research and Resources, Girls Incorporated, offered excellent feedback on several drafts, shared timely information, and helped sort through important issues and complex data. Her keen insights and wealth of information have strengthened *The Girls Report* immeasurably. Angela Lane, Research Assistant at Girls Incorporated, combed carefully and thoroughly through various drafts, updating research findings, providing important new sources, and pointing the project in helpful directions. Mary F. Maschino, Librarian and Information Specialist at Girls Incorporated, also worked with *The Girls Report*, adding new information and updating statistics. Their generosity with both time and resources, and their spirit of collegiality, are gratefully acknowledged.

Susan McGee Bailey, Executive Director of the Wellesley Centers for Research on Women, read through various versions and offered valuable insights and information in a number of areas. Her support and interest throughout are greatly appreciated. The insightful suggestions provided by Sumru Erkut and Nan Stein of the Wellesley Centers also strengthened the report in significant ways.

Michelle Fine, social psychologist at CUNY Graduate Center, was tremendously helpful throughout the project. She offered valuable insights while the report was still in its infancy, provided important information during the research process, commented on several drafts, helped locate sources of girls' writings, and offered much-appreciated support and encouragement. Her interest and enthusi-asm have been a constant source of inspiration. Priscilla Little, Associate Director of Research of the Association of American University Women Educational Foundation, also read various drafts and provided important insights and suggestions on both the writing and dissemination process.

Several people sent curricula, reports, and other information, and took part in extended conversations about their work. They include: Peggy Brick, Director of the Center for Family Life Education of Planned Parenthood of Greater Northern New Jersey; Linda Burnham, Executive Director of the Women of Color Resource Center in Berkeley, California; Susan Cote of Kent Place School in Summit, New Jersey; Fern Goodhart, Director of Health Education at Rutgers University; Janet Kahn, Senior Research Scientist at the Wellesley Centers for Research on Women; and Donna Shoenberg, psychologist and health educator at Rutgers University Department of Health Education. Several organizations, including the Melpomene Institute, the Ms. Foundation, and the President's Council on Women and Girls in Sports, sent helpful materials.

Lisa Handler, doctoral candidate in sociology at SUNY Stonybrook, and Katie Cumiskey, doctoral candidate in social psychology at CUNY Graduate Center, brought their excellent research skills to the gathering of important data for the report. They located vital information, combed through the Internet, tracked down citations, and lent their ideas as the project developed.

Special thanks are owed to the adults who helped to gather girls' perspectives specifically for this project and/or shared girls' narratives from their own studies. Thomas Ficarra, Superintendent of Mount Arlington School District in New Jersey, coordinated efforts to collect girls' writings in his district and generously gave permission to have them included. Thanks to Delores Gates of Mount Arlington Middle School, who took time out of her class to ask girls to write about their developmental experiences. Maria Torre, youth advocate, asked several girls to write their thoughts on the issues covered here, and her contributions are most appreciated. Lois Weis, Professor of Sociology of Education at the Graduate School of Education at SUNY Buffalo, graciously shared data she collected from young women for her study, "Voices of Urban Girls," which was part of a larger project on Intergroup Relations and funded by a grant from the Carnegie Foundation to Lois Weis, Michelle Fine, and Linda Powell. Thanks to Louise Yohalem, Director of the School-Based Youth Services Program in Plainfield, New Jersey, who, along with Danice Stone, Shauna Christian, and Amber Farnia, introduced the author to girls interested in lending their voices to *The Girls Report.*

Special thanks are due the many girls who shared their voices and wrote their thoughts about what they, as adolescent girls, want and need in order to thrive (girls' writings were collected by the sources above, and girls' interviews were conducted through focus groups by Lynn Phillips). Some of the girls chose to use their own names, while others chose to take a pseudonym; in either case, their own self-descriptions follow their names in the text. It is a pleasure to acknowledge the important contributions of: Adele, Amirah, Beth, Brandie, Carla, Carrina, Cassie, Cecilia, Charlene, Chee-Chee, Chrystal, Claudia, Debra, Donyelle, Edwena, Emily, Holly, Jacqui, Jeanine, Judy, Julia, Karan, Karayah, Kianna, Krista, LahToya, Laisha, Laura, Laurie, Louisa, Maggie, Mekeia, Mirasol, Myah, Myra, Natasha, Nikki, Penny, Rochelle, Rosa, Sara-Maria, Tamika, Tanzania, Tia, Vaseah, Violet, and Zakiyyah.

Special appreciation is also due to the National Council for Research on Women. Mary Ellen Capek, Executive Director of NCRW from 1989 to 1996, first conceived of this project, noting the need for a timely and accessible guide for those working across a range of domains to support the health and well-being of girls. Her vision and commitment to girls' needs launched the project and helped to guide it through its early stages. Linda Basch, Executive Director of NCRW since September 1996, also recognized the importance of the project. Helping to guide it through its final stages, she broadened the net of critical input and offered her insights and expertise at various points. Nina Sonenberg gathered information, edited early drafts, and offered critical suggestions on both content and form. Kendall Moore worked on the resources section and handled many of the technicalities of its final production with energy and skill. Mariam Chamberlain and Liz Horton also read and helpfully commented on earlier versions.

Consultants to NCRW also read more recent versions and offered important suggestions: David Merkowitz and Ellen Hoffman worked on the Introduction, Conclusion, and Executive Summary and advised us on strategies for dissemination, while Susan Lowes provided invaluable assistance during the production process and offered much appreciated perspective and insight during the project's final stages. Kristen Golden was an admirable copyeditor and Susan Foster has been a cooperative and imaginative designer. Roberta Vrona of Eisenman Associates, and Leslye Borden and Elizabeth Ely at PhotoEdit, were generous with their assistance on the cover photo.

Others who have read, commented, and offered valuable help include Mark Jackson, Faith Morningstar, Nancie Zane, and funders Ellen E. Remmer and Ann Remmer Cole of the Remmer Family Foundation and Robbin Derry of the Valentine Foundation. The financial support of these foundations, as well as the William T. Grant Foundation, the Lilly Endowment, and Girl's Best Friend Foundation, is much appreciated.

The generous input of each of these individuals and organizations is gratefully acknowledged, with the hopes that the final product does justice to their contributions and to the girls whose needs and aspirations we are all working to support.

Executive Summary

A DOLESCENCE CAN BE both a rich and challenging time for girls as they confront new ideas, explore life's possibilities, and navigate through the stormy seas of physical, social, behavioral, and emotional changes. How are girls meeting these challenges? The research and policy studies reviewed and analyzed for this report provide a mixed picture of progress and continuing struggles.

Several large-scale national studies suggest that girls are as likely as boys of the same age to smoke cigarettes, that they have inadequate access to sports programs that offer physical, social, and psychological benefits, that they are twice as likely as boys to be depressed, and that they often are the victims of violence.

On the other hand, new evidence identifies other, more encouraging trends. In school, girls continue to do well in reading and language, and their math achievement now almost matches that of boys. The teen birth rate has declined steadily since 1992, after rising by 25 percent between 1986 and 1991, and although access to contraception and abortion services has been restricted in many states, more teens appear to be using contraception than ever before.

These are some of the key findings of this report, which is a sequel to *Risk, Resiliency, and Resistance: Current Research on Adolescent Girls,* produced by the National Council for Research on Women for the Ms. Foundation in 1991.

The current report strives to present a balanced picture of the status of adolescent girls today. Its goal is to provide useful information about what we do and don't know about adolescent girls that can guide future research, policy decisions, and programs designed to improve the climate and life possibilities for all girls, regardless of where they live, their racial or ethnic background, or their social or economic status.

The report contains three additional sections that will be helpful to people who want to advocate for girls. "What Do Adolescent Girls Need for Healthy Development?" outlines specific actions that individuals and groups, including parents, teachers, and funders, can take to support girls. The "Resource Guide" includes descriptions of diverse programs created by NCRW member centers and related organizations aimed at improving the situation of girls, as well as publications that illuminate adolescent girls' development. "Looking Ahead: Developing a New Research Agenda" points to areas that need future research. These range from further investigation of girls' needs to the impact of programs and policies addressing those needs.

INTRODUCTION

What exactly do adolescent girls need for healthy development? What do we know about these needs? What can families, schools, other public agencies, and private organizations and communities do to ensure that girls thrive as they make the transition from adolescence to adulthood?

These are the basic questions addressed throughout this report. Its structure and findings should be interpreted with the following context in mind:

● Adolescent boys face many of the same issues and challenges that confront girls. The report focuses on girls because they and their issues traditionally are underrepresented in research and policy debates, but it also recognizes that measures to improve the climate for girls almost inevitably benefit boys as well.

● Girls face gender-related issues throughout their development, but many of these issues come into especially sharp relief during adolescence.

● Research on girls often has focused on risks and negative trends, rather than exploring positive aspects of their lives.

● Research often does not take into account the social and cultural context—for example, the availability of health care in inner-city neighborhoods—that influences girls' life experiences.

● The voices of girls are rarely heard in research reports or in discussions of policies that affect their lives.

FRAMING GENDER, IDENTITY, AND ADOLESCENCE

Adolescence traditionally has been characterized as a period of "storm and stress." However, recent research suggests that many of the difficulties associated with adolescence are due more to social factors such as poverty, family stresses, and societal ambivalence toward youth than to some inevitable, internal process or characteristics of adolescents themselves.

Discussions of girls' identity development are based too often on narrowly defined notions of self-esteem, tending frequently to emphasize overall gender differences without probing the interconnections among race, culture, social class, and sexuality. The structure of future research and of programs and policies devised to improve girls' lives must strive to understand and account for these complexities.

PERSPECTIVES ON GIRLS' LIVES

Health: Adolescence is a potentially healthy time for girls, but the leading causes of premature death among women– including lung cancer, other cancers, heart disease, and AIDS–are associated with behaviors that often begin during adolescence. Evidence that sparks concern includes the rise in the percentage of girls who smoke (from 13 percent of eighth graders in 1991 to 21 percent five years later); a report that 30 percent of adolescent girls have thought about suicide, compared with 18 percent of boys; and the fact that 90 percent of cases of eating disorders are found among girls and young women. Society must search for ways to encourage young women to take a holistic approach to their health, educate them to take responsibility for their behavior, and provide universal access to reliable information and health services.

Sexuality: National data exist on the age of first intercourse, but little or no data has been gathered on the prevalence of other types of girls' sexual experiences. The rate of births to teens is declining and teens' use of contraception is increasing, but many adolescents are still not using contraception or are having abortions. More quantitative information about sexual behaviors among adolescents, and more qualitative research on the nature of their experiences, is needed, as are affordable and confidential access to both sexuality education and health services.

Violence and Victimization: Girls are a proportionally higher percentage of victims of violence—including rape— than boys. Their perception that rape is committed by strangers may inhibit girls from reporting rape or other violence perpetrated by family members or acquaintances. Other causes for concern include the rate of arrest for violent crimes, which is rising more quickly for girls than for boys, and the inadequate preparation of the justice system to address the special needs of girls, especially those who are pregnant or who have children. Schools as well as parents need to play a role in educating children about violence, and schools must have strictly enforced policies against sexual harassment on the premises.

Schooling: As in other aspects of girls' lives in recent years, the record of change in schooling is mixed. Girls' performance has improved in math (on standardized tests) but not in science. Girls say that they like these subjects less than do boys and that they have less confidence in their abilities in these areas. In general, girls are less likely to drop out of school than are boys. However, female dropouts are much more likely than their male counterparts of the same race or ethnic group to live in poverty. Researchers need to explore further the positive and negative effects of single-sex schools, classes, and programs. Educators should create learning environments that practice gender equity and are peopled by strong female role models and mentors from diverse cultural backgrounds. Schools should offer sexuality education as well as opportunities for critical discussion of issues including racism, class distinctions, and sexism.

Economic Realities: Women and children account for more than three-quarters of households with incomes below the poverty level. Contrary to stereotypes, only 11 percent of mothers on welfare are teenagers. Children from racial minority groups are much more likely to live in poverty than are white children. Recent changes in the welfare system discourage some girls from continuing their education and becoming economically self-sufficient. Unmarried teen mothers should not have to live in a home situation that is dangerous to receive a benefit; they need access to day care, transportation, and other supports that will enable them to work and pursue their education.

CONCLUSIONS AND RECOMMENDATIONS

This review of an extensive body of recent work on key issues in the lives of adolescent girls leads to five overarching conclusions. These perspectives should underlie efforts by adults, communities, and all others working to meet the needs of adolescent girls and enrich their opportunities.

● Girls are multidimensional individuals with diverse perspectives, needs, and developmental contexts. Researchers, policymakers, and people who work directly with girls must be sensitive to the interactions of gender with other aspects of their identities—including race, ethnicity, social class, sexuality, (dis)ability, and the communities where they live—that influence girls' actions, attitudes, and, ultimately, their futures.

● Girls can benefit from programs and strategies that build on their strengths and encourage them to explore meaningful possibilities for their futures. In many fields, including education, health care, athletics, and juvenile justice, adults have worked successfully over the last decade to create school- and community-based programs that provide support to many girls and that could be replicated.

● Research must continue to play a role in deepening our understanding of girls' needs and how to respond to them. Researchers, advocates, public officials, and funders should collaborate to articulate, fund, and promote a research agenda.

● Girls require and deserve the awareness, attention, and commitment of a wide range of individuals and institutions to promote their healthy development. Parents should continue to play the primary role in supporting girls' development. However, educators, a range of professionals, public officials, and other members of the community should strengthen their efforts to create a safe and supportive climate that nurtures girls and encourages them to develop and pursue their goals.

● Adults should listen to what girls have to say about their own lives. Adults who want to help girls must collaborate not only with one another, but also with girls themselves. Adults should listen to girls' concerns and perspectives and include girls as partners in designing and implementing programs and research that address their needs.

Introduction

*I*F I COULD TELL ADULTS ANYTHING *that would make my life better, it would be to listen to young people and help them out. I'm young and strong and independent, but there is also areas where I need help, like at school and my neighborhood and at home. Kids need health care and good schools and safe streets and constructive things to do with ourselves. It's hard enough being young, but being a girl, and then there's where you live and the color of your skin, it can be really hard growing up. I wouldn't ever trade who I am, I'd just make society hear us better. Youth have a lot to offer this world, but sometimes girls aren't taken that seriously. But just watch me. Me and my girls are making something of ourselves.*

— TARA, AGE 15
SELF DESCRIPTION: "African American, female, student"

Tara's thoughts speak to the experiences of many adolescent girls. These young women are strong, capable, and wise, making strides in their worlds. Yet too often they must struggle to get their needs met, and to have their perspectives heard. While girls are competent and resilient, they also need the understanding and assistance of concerned adults to ensure their well-being throughout adolescence and into adulthood. The National Council for Research on Women's (NCRW) report, *The Girls Report: What We Know and Need to Know About Growing Up Female*, illuminates important issues and newly emerging debates about the needs and experiences of adolescent girls, and offers concrete suggestions to guide adults in their efforts to provide girls the support they deserve.

What do adolescent girls need for healthy development? How do they fare as they make their way through this challenging and exciting time in their lives? And what can adults do to help them thrive along the way? These questions frame the work of an increasing number of researchers, educators, families, advocates, and others who are dedicated to learning more about what promotes girls' vitality. The status of girls is of interest not only in the United States, but globally, as seen in the exciting focus on the girl-child at the 1995 United Nations Fourth World Conference on Women held in Beijing.

The Beijing conference sparked unprecedented

levels of attention to girls and their diverse needs, both in the United States and internationally. It also prompted new opportunities for girls to take an active stance in reshaping their worlds—from girls' participation at the conference, to their central role in subsequent international meetings, the development of new programs and curricula that focus on women and girls, and activism in such areas as health, education, and environmental issues. The Beijing conference cast a global spotlight on the concerns of girls like Tara, and girls around the world. It fueled girls' energies, and called adults to action to promote the health and well-being of girls.

The Girls Report sits within this global movement to support girls in their diverse developmental experiences. In this pivotal period of increasing attention to the needs and contributions of adolescent girls, NCRW brings home the inspiration that took flight in Beijing to examine what adults know, and need to know, about adolescent girls. This report provides a forum to share that information with others who are concerned about girls. Bringing together the voices of researchers, educators, policymakers, advocates, and girls themselves, the report examines important new trends in research, programming, and policy on adolescent girls living in the United States, and points the way toward fuller understandings of what girls need for bright and healthy futures.

In 1991, NCRW produced the report, *Risk,*

Resiliency, and Resistance: Current Research on Adolescent Girls, for the Ms. Foundation for Women. At that time, the academic community and the general public were just beginning to turn their attention to girls' particular concerns and developmental needs. The focus on girls was still relatively new, and much of the emphasis was on the risks girls faced as they made their way through adolescence. Since that publication, there has been a proliferation of research and programs that highlight girls' strengths, although this work remains scattered and diverse.

The heightened attention to girls and the new paradigms being shaped raise the need to take stock of the present state of research and programs on adolescent girls. The 1998 NCRW publication, *The Girls Report,* does just that. Based on these new insights, it offers concrete suggestions for researchers, educators, health practitioners, policymakers, funders, families, community members, activists, and others who wish to play informed roles in advocating for girls.

In recent years, adolescent girls have been moved to the center of the discourse on social programs and policies in a number of ways. The much-debated welfare reform law has provisions that specifically affect teen mothers and their children. Discussions of rape, battering, and harassment have expanded to include the experiences of adolescent girls. Research on the incidence and health risks of smoking, sexually transmitted diseases (STDs), and drug and alcohol use have identified particular risks for teen girls.[1] Researchers and educators have focused on the challenges to girls' development of a positive sense of self, the importance of sexuality education, and the merits and limitations of single-sex learning environments.

New research highlights girls' achievements and commitment to taking action on their own behalf. Organizers and advocates increasingly cast girls as strong, competent, and resilient, despite the many societal obstacles they may face. Programs have been developed and reshaped to encourage girls to explore new areas and develop new skills. More and more educators are focusing on girls' academic strengths and working to transform classroom practices and curricula in order to speak to girls' particular needs and perspectives. Girls themselves are venturing into new realms—developing new curricula, starting their own teen magazines, creating their own Web sites, becoming peer advocates, and engaging in political activity in their communities and beyond.

Several recent reports have helped to frame the growing debates about adolescent girls' experiences. Public discussion of gender equity in education has been fueled by a series of reports from the American Association of University Women Educational Foundation (AAUW), including *How Schools Shortchange Girls* (1992), researched and written by the Wellesley Center for Research on Women; *Hostile Hallways: The AAUW Survey on Sexual Harassment in America's Schools* (1993); *Growing Smart: What's Working for Girls in School* (1995); *Girls in the Middle: Working to Succeed in Schools* (1996a); and *The Influence of School Climate on Gender Differences in the Achievement and Engagement of Young Adolescents* (1996b). The Ms. Foundation's *Body Politic: Transforming Adolescent Girls' Health* (1994) and conferences such as Planned Parenthood's "Unveiling Reality: Teen Sexuality in Today's World" (1996) and "Teen Savvy" (1997) have focused attention on what is healthy in girls' development, while also grappling with the personal and social conditions that continue to threaten girls' physical, social, and psychological well-being.

The Wellesley Center for Research on Women and NOW Legal Defense and Education Fund opened an important national discussion of sexual harassment with their publication of *Secrets in Public: Sexual Harassment in Our Schools* (Stein, Marshall, and Tropp, 1993), as did the NCRW with the premier issue of its journal *IQ: Sexual Harassment. A Look at a Disturbing Trend Among Teens* (1994). The Center for Women Policy Studies has developed *Girls Talk About Violence* (1995), a national survey revealing important data on girls' experiences as both participants in and victims of violence. Girls Incorporated has put forth such compelling publications as *Past the Pink and Blue Predicament: Freeing the Next Generation from Sex Stereotypes* (1992); *Prevention and Parity: Girls in Juvenile Justice* (1996a); and *Responding to the Impact of Violence on Girls* (1996b). And *The Commonwealth Fund Survey of the Health of Adolescent Girls* (1997) identifies specific challenges to girls' healthy development as they navigate their teenage years.

The past decade of research and activism has led to new insights about the difficulties girls face, as well as promising indications of girls' resiliency and ability to thrive. This information is vital for concerned adults who want to support girls in their growth and help create a rich, nurturing environment for tomorrow's strong and healthy women. Unlike most publications, which focus on a single aspect of girls' lives, *The Girls Report* explores several interrelated domains—health, sexuality, violence, schooling, and economic realities—to give readers a fuller picture of adolescent girls' experiences. Providing a critical overview of recent debates and findings in research, policy, and programming on girls' issues, the report aims to foster conversation among a wide range of constituents, and highlight areas that need further research attention, educational and programming efforts, policy reform, funding, and family and community support. It draws on a variety of sources and voices: qualitative and quantitative research studies; government and agency reports; recent policy decisions; and interviews with educators, researchers, advocates, and girls. The synthesis offered in this report makes it a resource for those committed to the safety, justice, understanding, and optimism needed to ensure a healthy future for all girls.

In using this report, readers should bear in mind several points. First, it is important to note that boys face many of the same challenges that confront girls. In fact, as Cohen and Blanc point out in the AAUW report, *Girls in the Middle* (1996), reforms that are supportive of girls often benefit boys. Yet as researchers, advocates, and activists have noted, certain social and developmental issues may have different implications for girls than for boys. Given the traditional underrepresentation of girls and "girls' issues" in the research literature and in policy debates, this report devotes its attention to the needs, concerns, and experiences of adolescent girls.

Also, while girls and women deal with gender-related issues throughout their lives, many of these issues come into sharp relief during adolescence. Since adolescence sits on a continuum from birth to late life, early childhood experiences have an impact on girls' experiences during adolescence, and behaviors begun during adolescence often have lasting consequences (both positive and negative) throughout adulthood. Thus, while this report focuses on adolescent girls, it also addresses research on other age groups where relevant. In addition, since many girls face particular difficulties resulting from poverty, racism, homophobia, and anti-immigrant sentiment, the report looks at social, cultural, and economic issues affecting girls.

It is important to recognize that research is constrained by what and whom gets studied, and how research questions are framed. While many important issues need and deserve research attention, only certain topics become translated into research questions. Often those questions revolve around risks and negative trends, rather than exploring the good news—such as girls' strengths, their wisdom, their hopes, their accomplishments, and the important work that is being done on their behalf. Furthermore, many research studies treat girls as a homogeneous category, rather than probing issues of race, social class, culture, and sexuality, and the interplay of these with gender. The research literature also tends to study girls as discrete individuals, outside the diverse social contexts and relationships that inform their lives. This report highlights research

that moves beyond homogenized and isolated portrayals of girls' experiences. But the dearth of such studies points to the continued need for researchers to explore girls' lives in greater depth, and to present their findings against a backdrop of critical examinations of societal prejudices, inequities, and exclusions.

Finally, it is important to recognize that girls' social and developmental concerns take shape in the context of a larger culture that in many ways remains indifferent, and sometimes even hostile, to girls' and women's needs. In examining trends in girls' academic achievement and feelings about education, readers must bear in mind the lack, in many schools, of curricular materials that highlight women's achievements; the ongoing struggle for equity in financing public schools; and the continued effects of racism, sexism, classism, and homophobia in and on school environments. Trends in girls' health emerge in a social context in which the tobacco industry continues to glamorize smoking and to target young women; where athletic opportunities for girls, while growing in some communities, remain too few; where lack of access to quality, affordable health care constrains the health options of many girls and their families; and where girls and women face enormous social pressures to conform to unhealthy images of thinness and narrow standards of beauty. Similarly, trends in rates of teen pregnancy and births, abortion, and use of condoms must be understood against a political backdrop in which educators are often prohibited from discussing contraception, safer sex practices, or abortion; and in which only 16 percent of counties across the United States had abortion service providers as of 1992 (Henshaw and Van Vort, 1994).

In light of such societal constraints, the decline in adolescent pregnancy and birth rates (Child Trends, Inc., 1997), the tripling of condom use among girls since the 1970s (Abma, et al., 1997), and the rise in girls' math and science achievement (National Center for Education Statistics, 1997b) speak to the hard work and commitment of educators, health care providers, activists, and other advocates, as well as to the strengths of girls themselves. They also speak to the continued need for activism and support so that girls can achieve their goals, and make decisions from a full array of viable options.

The report begins with a general discussion of girls' development, examining trends in research on gender, identity, and adolescence, and identifying conditions that are supportive of girls' healthy development. The report is then organized around five key issues: health, sexuality, violence, education, and economic realities. It is important to note that several areas of concern to girls span across categories. For example, sex education is relevant to discussions of sexuality, education, and health. In order to avoid redundancy, issues are addressed in detail in one chapter, with references made to those issues, where relevant, in other chapters.

Each chapter includes an examination of current issues and debates; key findings; and what is needed to further research, programs, and funding on behalf of adolescent girls. Throughout the report, readers will find a discussion of practices, assumptions, and trends that have particular relevance for girls of color, immigrant girls, girls of low socioeconomic status, teen mothers, lesbian and bisexual girls, and girls with disabilities.[2] Readers will also find the voices of girls themselves as they describe their struggles with the social conditions that frame their lives, and reflect upon what they need to support their development. The report concludes with a call to action, including the identification of a new research agenda, and recommendations tailored to guide the endeavors of concerned constituents— researchers, educators, mentors, health care providers, policymakers, funders, family members, and activists and other advocates. Finally, the report offers a section on selected programs that work creatively and proactively with adolescent girls; many of which are sponsored by member centers of the NCRW.

CHAPTER ONE

Framing Gender, Identity, and Adolescence

A DOLESCENCE CAN BE both a rich and challenging time for girls as they confront new ideas, explore possibilities, and negotiate among the often conflicting expectations placed on them. Although anthropologists and cultural psychologists have documented wide variations in the significance, experience, and duration of adolescence across cultures, developmental research suggests that for young people in Western societies, adolescence is a critical life stage accompanied by physical, social, cognitive, emotional, and behavioral changes. Lacking uniform, clear-cut rituals and rites of passage to mark the transformation from childhood to adulthood, adolescence can be complex and ambiguous for many American youth.

Developmental challenges typically associated with adolescence include experiencing shifts in relationships with parents or other adult caregivers; dealing with emotional, social, cognitive, and sexual maturation; balancing priorities between families and peers; developing feelings of competence; questioning and refining values; thinking about and experimenting with sexuality and sexual identity; and developing a sense of one's own identity in relation to one's culture(s). No longer children, but not yet adults, adolescents are engaged in an often confusing struggle to cultivate feelings of independence while working through changing expectations, roles, and relationships.

In Western societies, adolescence has traditionally been characterized as a stormy and stressful period, and many adults have assumed that emotional upheaval and alienation are inherent to adolescent development. Several decades of social science research, however, suggests that this is not necessarily the case. Indeed, several researchers have claimed that the difficulties often associated with adolescence are more attributable to social factors—such as poverty, family stresses, and societal ambivalence toward youth—than to some inevitable, internal process or to characteristics of adolescents themselves.

TRENDS IN RESEARCH ON ADOLESCENT GIRLS

Despite the growing recognition of the importance of developmental contexts, researchers still tend to place insufficient emphasis on the social conditions that nurture or constrain adolescent development. Development is often studied outside the environments—including schools, families, communities, and workplaces—that help to shape adolescents' lives. Further, despite feminist critiques since the late 1970s, much of the mainstream research on adolescent developmental and social issues still presents findings for youth in general, without considering gender. This is problematic, since many of the issues that adolescents deal with (such as reproductive concerns; violence; access to sports, academic, and career opportunities; and certain health concerns) tend to affect girls differently from boys. Studies that do address gender too often treat "male" and "female" as monolithic categories, neglecting issues of race, ethnicity, social class, and sexuality, all of which intersect with gender in the construction of personal and group identity. Societal barriers often create even more difficult hurdles for girls of color and/or low socioeconomic status, immigrant girls, girls with disabilities, and lesbian and bisexual girls, who are marginalized within a society that confers privilege on not only maleness, but also whiteness, so-called middle class values, "able" bodies, and heterosexuality.

Equally problematic is a tendency in the research literature, policy debates, and popular discussion to portray adolescent girls one-dimensionally as either victims or villains. On the one hand, in discussions of victimization, girls are often pathologized as passive, helpless, or lacking the competence to "know better" than to be exploited and abused. On the other hand, adolescent girls are frequently vilified—portrayed as wild, selfish, irresponsible, and out

which adolescent girls are "at risk," some researchers and advocates have begun to focus on what is healthy in girls' development, highlighting girls' strength, resistance, and sense of entitlement. Countering flattened and inaccurate images, portraits are slowly emerging of adolescent girls as competent and active initiators in their relationships, schools, and communities. For instance, works such as Bonnie Ross Leadbetter and Niobe Way's 1996 book, *Urban Girls: Resisting Stereotypes, Creating Identities,* examine the intersection of gender with race, class, sexuality, and culture in shaping the personal and social experiences of girls and women. And in the AAUW's 1996 report, *Girls in the Middle: Working to Succeed in School,* researchers Jody Cohen, Sukey Blanc, and their colleagues from Research for Action, Inc. highlight girls' active choices and personal strengths as they negotiate the complex developmental struggles and school settings that contextualize their early adolescence.

I think kids my age need alternatives. We have this group in my building, where two women meet with us once a week and it's just girls our age, and we can talk about whatever we want, and sometimes we go on little trips and things. My mom likes it a lot, because she wants me to have good influences to stay out of the traps a lot of kids get into. It's taught me to have self-respect, like I have other girls who are struggling with the same things as me, and I don't have to cave to peer pressure.

— Carrina, age 15
SELF-DESCRIPTION: "African American girl"

---

of control—in discussions of such issues as welfare, teen pregnancy and motherhood, sexual "promiscuity," violence, and school failure. Rather than being seen as possible symptoms of gender, race, and economic inequities, these issues, and the girls who experience them, are often framed as the causes of social problems and the supposed breakdown of "family values." Whether ignoring, pathologizing, or vilifying adolescent girls, few traditional researchers or popular writers have done justice to the complexities of girls' lives.

Fortunately, since NCRW first published *Risk, Resiliency, and Resistance* in 1991, feminist researchers have focused increasingly on girls. Research and reports commissioned by the AAUW Educational Foundation, Girls Incorporated, the Ms. Foundation for Women, the Wellesley Center for Research on Women, the Center for Women Policy Studies, the Commonwealth Fund, NCRW, and others have devoted specific attention to girls, and more governmental and academic studies have begun to offer analysis by gender and/or race.

Furthermore, in addition to studying the many ways in

Such research offers promising evidence of girls' capabilities and strategies for resistance. Rather than promoting a "deficit model" of girls, new research is focusing on girls' assets, and analyzing the problems they face in the context of larger societal inequities and cultural power issues. A small but growing number of researchers are committed to conducting research with and for girls, rather than simply conducting research on girls (c.f. Pastor, McCormick, and Fine, 1996). These projects take seriously girls' voices and perspectives, involving girls deeply in the development of research designs, the collection and analysis of data, and the presentation of findings. They focus on girls' own priorities, rather than presuming that what is important to adult researchers is necessarily important to adolescent girls.

Researchers are also working increasingly in collaboration with program professionals, educators, and other advocates, studying questions that emerge from their work with girls. This type of collaborative, activist research—supported by such national organizations such as Girls Incorporated, and statewide organizations such as Girl's Best Friend Foundation in Chicago—can unearth important information about what is working to support girls' development, rather than merely focusing on what stands in the way of girls.[3] These research orientations should inspire those who study issues of importance to girls, and should guide them in designing projects that empower adolescent girls through both their processes and their findings.

HOW ARE GIRLS DOING?
AN OVERVIEW

Several large-scale, national studies suggest a mixed picture of struggle and progress for U.S. girls. Girls are twice as likely as boys to be depressed (Nolen-Hoeksema, 1990). Too few girls—especially girls of color and girls from low-income homes—participate in sports programs, which have positive physical, psychological, and social benefits (The Commonwealth Fund, 1997; Kann, et al., 1996). Girls are as likely as boys to smoke cigarettes, and smoking is on the rise for both sexes (although it is important to note that smoking rates for African American teenage girls are significantly lower than those for African American teenage boys, or girls of other races) (National Center on Addiction and Substance Abuse, 1996; Johnston, O'Malley, and Bachman, 1997). In a study conducted among 11 states and the District of Columbia, girls under 18 were found to account for two-thirds of all reported cases of rape (National Victim Center, 1992). In 1996, convicted rape and sexual assault offenders serving time in state prisons confirmed that two-thirds of their victims were under the age of 18—and 58 percent said their victims were 12 and younger (Bureau of Justice Statistics, 1997).

However, even as girls continue to face depression, violence, and pressure to engage in high-risk behavior, new evidence suggests more encouraging trends. For instance, the U.S. teen birth rate has declined steadily since 1992, after rising by one-quarter between 1986 and 1991 (Child Trends, Inc., 1996). A study by the National Survey of Family Growth indicates that even though access to contraception and abortion services has been restricted in many states, more teens seem to be using contraception than ever before: condom use at first intercourse increased from 18 percent in the 1970s to 36 percent in the late 1980s and 54 percent in 1995 (Abma, et al., 1997).

In school, girls continue to do well in reading and language, and girls' math achievement is now approximately the same as that of boys (National Center for Education Statistics, 1996; National Science Board, 1996). Reports from educators and advocates suggest that girls are increasingly exploring non-traditional realms through school- and community-based activities. Such changes demonstrate the success of education and community programs that provide resources, explore options, and foster the development of all girls.

Today, women's organizations and youth programs are increasingly committed to devoting space and resources to girls. Organizational support networks continue to appear and expand, despite continuing threats to funding. Girls are educating themselves, one another, and their communities through peer education programs in schools and volunteer organizations. They are speaking out through the publication of girl-centered magazines such as *Teen Voices: A Magazine By, For, and About Teenage and Young Adult Women; Blue Jeans Magazine: For Girls Who Dare; New Moon: The Magazine for Girls and Their Dreams,* and *HUES (Hear Us Emerging Sisters).*

They are increasing their cultural awareness and fostering global connections with other girls, both through the Internet and through participation in international activities and networks sparked by the Beijing conference. They are developing Web pages to communicate with other girls about a wide range of issues, including relationships, depression, eating disorders, sexuality, career aspirations, and participation in sports. Many Web sites for girls are sheer fun, offering pen pals, advice, puzzles, and a seemingly endless array of inventive and supportive amusement. (See the Resource Guide for some girl-friendly Web sites). Girls are taking the lead in causes ranging from environmental protection to the development and enforcement of sexual harassment prevention policies in their schools. Although girls still face pressures to silence their voices, temper their actions, and second-guess their points of view, they continue to thrive and to make a difference in their worlds.

EXPLORING IDENTITIES:
BEYOND SELF-ESTEEM

Navigating the transitions into and through adolescence, girls (and boys) are trying on new roles, exploring various strategies for managing social pressures, and carving out a place for themselves in their worlds. Perhaps more than at any other life stage, girls in adolescence are involved in the sometimes frustrating, sometimes exciting, but always complex process of exploring and developing their identities. Individual girls' identities are unique and often feel profoundly personal; yet they are never formed in a social vacuum. Rather, they are constructed in dynamic social contexts—including families, peer relationships, schools, and communities—that provide often contradictory messages about girls' proper roles, their entitlement, and the barriers and opportunities they can expect to face now and in the future. Since these messages may vary across the range of girls' cultural contexts, their senses of self are drawn from a collage of experiences and understandings about race, class, culture, and sexuality, as well as gender.

Research in the last two decades has helped raise consciousness about girls' struggles to maintain a strong sense of self and has sounded an alarm to warn adults that overall, girls, more than boys, face a decrease in self-confidence and positive feelings about themselves as they go through adolescence. Unfortunately, despite recent research showing compelling variations in girls' senses of self across race and cultural groups (AAUW, 1996a; Erkut, et al., 1996; Leadbeater and Way, 1996; Linn, et al., 1992; Pastor, McCormick, and Fine, 1996; Rotheram-Borus, et al., 1996; Ward, 1996), girls are often portrayed as a unified group of people who lack confidence and a sense of entitlement. In popular discussion, as well as in much of the research literature, the complex and dynamic process of identity development is too often collapsed into an oversimplified concept of self-esteem, which is typically framed as an internal, psychological phenomenon or a static entity—someone either has a lot or a little. Within this framework, adolescent girls are often characterized as coming up short.

Further, low self-esteem is often offered as an explanation for the problems girls may face, suggesting that if only girls could be made to feel better about themselves, these issues would essentially resolve themselves. Yet researchers and advocates for girls have increasingly noted that a focus on narrow psychological constructs, outside the context of analyses of broader social issues, can obscure girls' strengths, overlook important cultural variations, deflect attention away from institutionalized inequities, and contribute to a deficit model of girls' capabilities (Erkut, et al., 1996; Pastor, McCormick, and Fine, 1996; Rotheram-Borus, et al., 1996; Swadener and Lubeck, 1995; Swadener, 1995).[4]

Since Carol Gilligan's work on girls' self-esteem was first published, researchers have devoted considerable energy to studying the causes and implications of the apparently marked decrease in girls' overall confidence and self-esteem during adolescence. Gilligan and her colleagues at the Harvard Project on the Psychology of Women and the Development of Girls have found that while girls enter puberty feeling strong, capable, and wise, they undergo a transformation during which they take their true selves "underground" and experience a "loss of voice," emerging as adolescents with less confidence and more negative views of themselves (Gilligan, Ward, and Taylor, 1988; Gilligan, Lyons, and Hanmer, 1990; Gilligan and Brown, 1992).

Yet others, such as Harter, et al., (1997) have conducted research that questions and expands these findings. Admin-istering extensive surveys to 165 girls and 142 boys from grades 9, 10, and 11, Harter and her colleagues have studied "level of voice," i.e., expression of one's "true self" or true thoughts or opinions, as opposed to sharing one's intimate information or expressing one's wants and needs. Students responded to questions about level of voice across five relational contexts: relationships with parents, with teachers in their classrooms, with male classmates, with female classmates, and with close friends.

The researchers found that level of voice varied across relational contexts and was related to the students' perceptions of support for making their opinions known in specific contexts, as well as to the students' concerns that expressing their true opinions might jeopardize particular relationships. Unlike Gilligan and her colleagues, they found no general decline in level of voice among girls. In fact, they found that in their relationships with female classmates and close friends, girls reported higher levels of voice than did boys. Since their sample was primarily white (75 percent) and middle class, Harter et al. did not analyze their data by race or ethnicity, but their results offer a compelling critique to the notion that girls, in general, experience a "loss of voice" in adolescence.

Other studies have found important racial variations in girls' senses of themselves and feelings about school. For instance, the AAUW's national self-esteem poll *Shortchanging Girls, Shortchanging America* (1991) surveyed 2,374 girls and 600 boys between fourth and tenth grades about self-esteem, experiences in and attitudes toward school, gender roles, and career aspirations. (The survey polled different girls and boys at each grade level, rather than following individuals as they aged, so the results suggest trends rather than actual changes in individuals.) Overall, the study found that adolescent girls reported much lower self-esteem than girls in grade school, that the discrepancy was larger than that between adolescent and grade school boys, and that boys in high school showed higher self-esteem than their female peers.

Yet important differences appeared among girls when the data were analyzed by race. For instance, unlike Hispanic and white girls,[5] black girls demonstrated high self-esteem in high school. However, while older black girls reported high levels of personal feelings of self-worth, they experienced less positive feelings toward their teachers and schoolwork than black elementary school girls. Hispanic girls, on the other hand, showed the largest differences in self-esteem across grade levels. Although elementary school Hispanic girls expressed higher self-esteem than other girls their age, Hispanic girls in high school expressed less confidence about their talents, abilities, physical appearance, and family relations than their counterparts in elementary or middle school.

The findings of Harter, et al., (1997) and the AAUW (1991) survey suggest that girls' sense of self and expression of voice are less straightforward than popular discussions of gender differences in self-esteem would seem to suggest. Girls' identities are far more complex than overall high or low self-esteem scores can indicate. Indeed, a singular emphasis on gender differences may obscure other important facets of the intricate process of girls' identity formation and articulation of feelings of self-worth. While gender is certainly a central aspect of one's sense of self, gender identity is textured by one's race, class, sexual identity, and culture.

Indeed, they found that within race groups, diversity in girls' socioeconomic status and rural/urban residence were associated with varying responses as to what promotes a strong sense of self, as well as differences in why certain activities may help girls feel good about themselves. Their research calls for further investigation of the ways that

---

Sometimes teachers treat girls like they're fragile, and my grandmother treats me that way. They try too hard to protect me and they don't give me enough credit to take care of myself and know my own mind. Sometimes I just keep quiet, because I know what I'm doing, and it's just not worth the hassle to try to express myself to them. Other times, you know, I get mad and I start yelling, and they act like I'm unstable or something. But like I said, I feel good about myself and I'm confident about who I am and where I'm going. I try not to listen to people who either put you down or try to smother you with overprotection.

– Lahtoya, age 16
SELF-DESCRIPTION: "a strong, quiet, assertive black girl"

If adults focus only on overall comparisons of girls' versus boys' self-esteem, they may fail to appreciate important nuances in the ways girls construct their own identities. They may also mistake girls' useful, culturally learned strategies for a lack of self-esteem or a tendency to give up on themselves. For instance, as Eleanor Linn and her colleagues (1992) point out in their discussion of girls' responses to sexual harassment, some girls' cultural beliefs have taught them to speak out and affirm their power, while others' have taught them to keep quiet and avoid "making trouble" in order to survive.

As Sumru Erkut and her colleagues at the Wellesley Center for Research on Women (1996) found in their interviews with 362 African American, Anglo-European American, Asian Pacific Islander, Latina, and Native American girls, social class and race/ethnicity come together to inform girls' feelings about themselves in deeper ways not tapped by studies which analyze data only by gender and/or broad race categories. Stressing the importance of cultural context in the development of girls' self-regard, Erkut, et al. write, "The gender roles, expectations, and relations that prevail in one community do not necessarily map well onto roles, expectations, and relations in another community. . . . Attitudes, values, and behaviors that lead to survival and success for females in one context do not necessarily serve a girl's interests in another" (1996: 61).

gender is configured and experienced across diverse contexts, with particular attention to girls' national origins, sexual identities, religions, languages, and histories of immigration.

Research by Rotheram-Borus, et al. (1996) suggests that Western notions of self-esteem and identity development, with their focus on individualism, autonomy, and self-direction, fail to capture not only gender differences, but also important cultural variations in experiences and expressions of self. Based on their work with a large sample of black, white, and Latino/a working class adolescents in schools, they write, "Rather than a process of active seeking of individuation, the girls' interviews suggest that the losing of oneself and one's boundaries in a group identity or passively waiting for an unfolding of one's 'true' nature may be alternative routes to integrating one's personal identity" (1996: 50). The researchers also found that gender, race/ethnicity, school setting, and grade level interact to produce compelling variations in adolescents' types of ethnic identification, self-esteem scores, acceptance or rejection of traditional values, and vocational plans. Interestingly, within this sample, girls were more likely than boys to regard themselves as strongly ethnically identified, and those adolescents who considered themselves strongly ethnically identified scored higher on self-esteem than students who considered themselves "bicultural" or "mainstream."

As Pastor, McCormick, and Fine's (1996) qualitative, collaborative research with a small group of urban girls across a range of cultural backgrounds suggests, girls' interpretations and ways of dealing with alienation and injustice often defy straightforward categorizations of high or low self-esteem. They have found that girls may simultaneously resist, critique, and accommodate the oppressive social conditions that surround them. Whereas silencing one's own outrage might be interpreted uncritically as an indication of passivity or low self-regard, these researchers found that girls'

If I could have any change in the world that would affect me personally, it would be to have a safe place to feel comfortable. Growing up, I have noticed when people refer to "gay," they only think of men. With all the things lesbians go through, I feel there should be a place primarily for lesbians that has tutors and mentors and talk about health care. I feel it is hard to be black, female, and also be gay, so we need support.

– Brandie, age 17

SELF-DESCRIPTION: "gay black female—very outspoken, confident, intelligent, mature, independent"

---

silences (as well as their vocalized critiques) may be strategies for resistance and preservation of their dignity in contexts that threaten to erase their concerns and perspectives.

Pastor, McCormick, and Fine have also discovered that girls' interpretations of their identities, histories, and struggles may vary depending upon whether girls reflect on their life experiences individually or as part of a group. They write, "Within contexts of plain talk and conversation, trust and solidarity, among peers and even a few adults, with a sense of connection and a democracy of shared differences, the one-time "deficits" of young women shine through as strengths; their histories of oppression and victimization are reread as struggles and victories; their biographies of loss are reconstructed as archives of collective resilience" (1996: 32). Thus, Pastor and her collaborators advocate for increased opportunities for girls to come together in solidarity to explore their struggles, develop collective forms of resistance, and "reconstruct a world rich in the wonders of race, culture, gender, and social justice" (1996: 29).

While it is easy to presume that it all goes back to self-esteem, studies like those discussed above demonstrate that girls' identities and feelings of self-worth are highly complex and constructed in various cultural contexts. Thus, adults should not look for oversimplified, individualistic

psychological explanations for the difficulties girls may experience. It is important, of course, to help nurture girls' positive self-images, but it is equally important to understand that identity is shaped by and formed within dynamic and often problematic social contexts.

Beyond developing programs that help girls to feel good about themselves as individuals, concerned adults need to consider the impact of discriminatory social practices and limited resources on both girls' senses of self and their aspirations. Continued exposure to the effects of sexism, racism, classism, ableism, and heterosexism may diminish girls' positive feelings about themselves, and make it less likely that they will have access to the resources they need to prevent a pregnancy or STDs; have meaningful learning experiences and achieve high grades in school; avoid victimizing circumstances; and assume leadership positions in their schools and communities. In a society which in general provides fewer opportunities to girls than to boys, and which further restricts the options and supportive messages available to girls who are poor, of color, lesbian or bisexual, disabled, and/or immigrants, adults can press for social change that will break down barriers that constrain the psychological, physical, and social well-being of girls.

Given the nuanced findings of studies such as those by Linn, et al. (1992), Erkut, et al. (1996), Rotheram-Borus, et al. (1996), and Pastor, McCormick and Fine (1996), it is clear that rather than looking to self-esteem as a one-dimensional, causal, or catch-all phenomenon, future research in this area should frame girls' identity development in broader cultural contexts, and should examine social practices, rather than individual tendencies, that enhance or diminish girls' confidence, critique, and visions of self.

CONDITIONS THAT SUPPORT OR HINDER GIRLS' STRONG SENSES OF SELF

In light of the overemphasis placed on girls' self-esteem, adults may be tempted to search for straightforward factors that nurture or inhibit the development of a strong sense of self. Yet many of the influences on girls' self-regard are inseparable from the social contexts in which they develop. For instance, growing up in a male-dominated culture, many girls face enormous pressure to judge their self-worth based on narrow standards of physical attractiveness; to put boys and men ahead of themselves; and to conform to very narrow notions of femininity which promote passivity, compliance, and self-sacrifice, while discouraging strength, autonomy, and entitlement to pursue one's own desires.

Even if girls accept this model and work to achieve the roles, behaviors, and attitudes associated with "femininity," they will find that the larger society tends to devalue those very characteristics. Thus, girls (and women) face a double bind. If they fail to accommodate the expectations placed on their gender, they are often perceived as unfeminine, selfish, or "acting out." Yet if they do follow these gendered scripts, they may be dismissed as weak, dependent, and less competent than boys or men. As Linn, et al., put it, "[s]peak up and you'll be destroyed in one way; remain silent and you'll be destroyed in another" (1992: 110). Of course, these factors vary across cultural groups and in different communities. But given the importance of social acceptance during adolescence, it is easy to see how girls' senses of self might be challenged by the competing demands imposed on women in a society fraught with gender-based double binds.

In more concrete terms, girls are often perceived and treated differently than boys by the adults in their lives, and this different treatment begins long before adolescence. Several studies have found, for instance, that parents play differently with, and encourage different kinds of behavior in, their girl and boy children. Whereas parental interactions with boys tend to encourage independence, mastery, and self-confidence, their socialization and play activities with girls are more likely to foster proximity and dependence by restricting exploration, offering premature intervention in problem-solving tasks, and providing toys which emphasize beauty and nurturance over skill mastery and action (Block, 1984; Weitzman, Birns, and Friend, 1986; Miller, 1987).

Research suggests that African American families are less likely than white families to place gender-stereotyped expectations on their children, and more likely to socialize their daughters toward independence, strength, and resourcefulness (Reid, 1985; Lips, 1989; Ward, 1996). In light of these findings, it is certainly worth noting that black girls are the one group of girls who have been found to have high self-esteem in high school (AAUW, 1991; Rotheram-Borus, et al., 1996).

Studies in schools show similar patterns. Since Carol Dweck and her colleagues' work in the 1970s revealed marked differences in teachers' interactions with boys and girls, researchers have increasingly noted gender-based patterns in classrooms and schools (Dweck, et al., 1978; Dweck, Goetz, and Strauss, 1980; Sadker and Sadker, 1994; Thorne, 1993). For instance, in mixed-sex settings, when teachers pose a question to an entire class, boys tend to be more demonstrative in asking to be called upon, and are thus more likely than girls to be called upon to answer the question (Mann, 1994). Research by Myra Sadker and David Sadker (1994) has found that teachers are more likely to encourage active learning in boys, posing more complex, open-ended questions to them than to girls. Teachers also tend to address boys' wrong answers differently than those of girls. Whereas boys are more likely to receive prods to develop their answers more thoroughly, teachers are more likely to correct wrong answers given by girls or to ask the class to supply the correct answer. Girls are less likely than boys to advocate for themselves when they disagree with a teacher (AAUW, 1991). As with parental interventions, girls tend to be given less space to explore possibilities, and work through problem-solving tasks in school than are boys.

Both Dweck and Sadker and Sadker have found that girls' academic difficulties are often attributed to lack of ability (which may be perceived as a stable characteristic), while boys' difficulties are attributed to lack of effort (something that can be changed). These discrepancies become increasingly disturbing in light of findings that girls, in general, place more importance on their relationships with teachers than do boys (AAUW, 1991). If girls' sense of self is more dependent upon their perceptions of teachers' regard for them, then the gender-based differences in teachers' attributions and interaction patterns may have a particularly negative impact on girls' sense of confidence and competence.

Further, boys and girls continue to be encouraged to pursue different types of courses and school activities (Sadker and Sadker, 1994; 1986). Whereas boys are encouraged to explore activities related to math, science, and sports, girls receive much less encouragement in these areas (although, thanks to recent programming and curricular efforts, this is beginning to change in some schools). Girls and boys tend to be praised for different types of competence. While boys are often rewarded for action and problem-solving, girls are more often praised for neatness, courtesy, and verbal skills (Sorensen and Hallinan, 1987; Bennett, 1986). In addition, classroom and school activities are often based on competition, rather than on cooperative models of learning. Since boys may be more likely to be comfortable in competitive environments (through encouragement in sports and other extra-curricular activities), girls may feel more alienated and less likely to succeed in competition-based academic and social arenas that impact upon their sense of personal competence. Furthermore, many teachers continue to frame classroom competition as "boys-against-the-girls," a practice that researcher Barrie Thorne (1993) has found to foster gender antagonism.

In the midst of these conditions which threaten to erode girls' confidence and self-regard, there is also cause for hope. Indeed, just as certain cultural messages and social practices may inhibit girls' positive feelings about themselves, others can promote their feelings of competence and healthy entitlement. School contexts that embrace students' gendered and multicultural realities can support girls' growth, and foster their confidence in their own strengths (AAUW, 1996a). While some suggest that single-sex learning environments can offer girls these possibilities, and provide them the space to fully develop without being overshadowed by boys, researchers and advocates such as Susan McGee Bailey (1996) have stressed that the features that work well for girls in single-sex learning environments can, and must, be integrated into mixed-sex schooling. Such features include opportunities to assume leadership positions; access to women role models and images of women in positions of strength, leadership, and scholarship; explicit and ongoing discussion of gender and multicultural issues; engagement with curricular materials that reflect girls' realities; and opportunities to work creatively and collectively, as well as competitively.

Teachers, particularly, can have a positive impact on girls' developing self-concepts, and their senses of possibility for their futures. Although peers are often thought to be the primary influence on adolescents' attitudes and self-images, families and teachers have been found to be more influential in the development of girls' aspirations and self-esteem (AAUW, 1991). Indeed, girls' feelings about their own achievements are highly correlated with their relationships with their teachers. Further, according to the AAUW's study, *Shortchanging Girls, Shortchanging America* (1991), pride in schoolwork is the most important factor in elementary school girls' self-esteem. Unfortunately, that study found that only 49 percent of elementary school girls reported feeling proud of their schoolwork, and only 17 percent of girls in high school reported positive feelings about their academic performance (1991). However, since positive relationships with educators are associated with girls' feelings about their schoolwork, and their pride in schoolwork is associated with increased self-esteem, teachers are in a unique position to help increase girls' feelings of overall competence and satisfaction with themselves.

Educators who encourage young women's voices and invite their critique can help to nurture girls' strong sense of self. When adults in schools recognize and respect girls' diverse strategies for balancing school and social challenges, and developing a personal sense of pride and accomplishment, they can help girls feel valued, visible, and successful (AAUW, 1996a). Teachers who develop classroom practices that promote critical consciousness of gender and cultural issues can help girls across social, cultural, and economic backgrounds to develop their competence, and envision expansive possibilities for their futures. They can support girls' exploration of new subjects (especially those not traditionally thought of as "female"), encourage them to take healthy risks and allow them to make mistakes, and give them space to work through their own solutions (Bailey, 1996).

Teacher training and professional development programs also must encourage educators to probe issues of gender, race, class, culture, and sexuality; to challenge their own assumptions; and to cultivate practices that enable girls in their classrooms to explore a wide range of options and develop confidence in their abilities. All concerned adults can lobby mixed-sex schools to achieve full gender equity, so that girls and boys of all cultures can experience schooling as a safe and respectful environment that nurtures their intellectual, social, and emotional development (Quintero and Rummel, 1995; AAUW, 1996a; Bailey, 1996). As Swadener (1995) suggests, rather than deeming certain youth "at risk" and trying to get them ready for schooling, emphasis should be placed on making schools ready to understand, respect, and incorporate the strengths and needs of students from diverse social, linguistic, cultural, and economic backgrounds.

While teachers are particularly significant to adolescent girls, the importance of concerned and accessible adults goes well beyond the classroom. Girls trying to envision their futures—their careers, their families, their roles in their communities—deserve supportive communities. In his book, *All Kids are Our Kids,* Peter Benson of the Search Institute calls for all segments of the community, including "families, neighborhoods, congregations, employers, and youth organizations to unite around a common language and employ complementary strategies toward a shared goal: healthy children and adolescents" (1997: 27). Girls need safe spaces and engaging activities in their communities that encourage them to express their opinions, explore new realms, and pursue both learning and recreational interests.

Girls also need role models and mentors who affirm their strengths, and help them sift through the negative cultural images of women and "women's roles" which may constrict their sense of self and hopes for adulthood (AAUW, 1996a). Mentors from girls' own communities can help girls to grapple with the painful effects of sexist, racist, classist, ableist, and homophobic attitudes; negotiate among the sometimes competing gendered and cultural expectations placed upon them; and develop positive images of themselves and their communities. Women who are activists, professionals, community leaders, and/or parents need to spend more time with girls promoting their talents and possibilities, grappling with roadblocks, and debunking myths that perpetuate those roadblocks (such as the myth of the "superwoman").

As Amy Sullivan's research with adolescent urban girls suggests, mentoring must go beyond attempts to teach or socialize girls. She finds that "important and health-sustaining relationships with women are overwhelmingly characterized by women's ability to listen, understand, and validate the knowledge, experience, and feelings of the adolescent. Efforts at teaching without acknowledging and respecting girls' perspectives may discount rather than enhance their experience and knowledge; attempts at socialization can be similarly destructive if they enforce social conventions that are harmful to girls and women" (1996: 226). Rhodes and Davis (1996) have also found that the most effective and enduring mentoring relationships are typically formed with adults from the girls' own communities. Their research suggests that when mentors share girls' cultural experiences and are committed to their communities, they are better able to relate to the girls' struggles, and to offer feedback that is consistent with the girls' realities.

In addition to guidance and support from adults, girls also need space to come together without adult intervention to explore their ideas, develop social relationships, and find support from their peers. While all girls need such opportunities, this may be particularly important for girls whose needs and perspectives tend to be marginalized in organized social or academic activities. For instance, in her article "Sappho Was a Right-On Adolescent: Growing Up Lesbian," Margaret Schneider (1997) notes that lesbian girls often lack opportunities to gather with their peers to discuss issues of sexuality, to explore relationships, and simply to have fun. In her in-

depth interviews with 25 self-identified lesbian adolescents, Schneider found that lesbian girls want time and space to pursue leisure activities with other lesbian adolescents. She writes, "They want to go on short trips, go dancing, camping, or simply hang out in casual surroundings with other lesbian friends. Their recreational needs are much the same as those of heterosexual youngsters, with the additional need to spend a portion of time in a completely lesbian environment" (1997: 82). Girls need to find safe spaces and develop peer networks to work and play together in environments that honor their identities, and that promote interaction both within and across social groups.

Families, of course, are critically important as girls endeavor to form strong and healthy identities. Indeed, Rotheram-Borus, et al. (1996) found that girls perceived their parents and other family members as more influential in their identity development than media, church affiliation, or teachers. Parents and other caregivers can promote girls' confidence, encourage them to critique and resist negative stereotypes, and foster their strategies for developing a strong sense of self amid competing pressures and societal barriers. Caregivers, like teachers, must reflect critically on their own stereotyping assumptions and practices, and work to both model and encourage gender-fair behavior.

Drugs are really hard. I want to stay away from that stuff, 'cause I seen what it can do to you. But it's tempting on another level, 'cause sometimes you just want to forget your problems, you know, kind of escape from you life. It would help if there were other positive things kids could do, 'cause I think a lot of girls are like me. They want to make the right choices, but it's really hard to be a teen who doesn't have a lot of options and is just trying to get along and feel better.

– Myra, age 17
SELF-DESCRIPTION: "black urban teen woman"

Family members can help girls navigate the cultural and institutional barriers that threaten to constrain their sense of pride and efficacy. They can encourage the celebration of girls' overlapping gender, race, cultural, and sexual identities, and fortify girls to challenge practices that marginalize them, their families, their communities, and their peers. As Janie Victoria Ward (1996) notes in her essay, "Raising Resisters: The Role of Truth Telling in the Psychological Development of African American Girls," family members can understand the injustices and negative images that girls of color are particularly likely to confront. They are uniquely positioned to speak explicitly with their daughters about racism and race identity to help them to trust their own knowledge and self-worth. She writes, "Most importantly, black parents who engage in truth telling that is liberating allow for strong, often painful race-related emotions to surface. Parents, by teaching their children to cope with these emotions, refuse to allow them to equate their disappointments with psychological destruction" (1996: 97).

Families who embrace girls' sexual identities and challenge homophobic assumptions can also help girls feel acknowledged and affirmed as they grapple with relationships and sexual desire (Thompson, 1995). Family members must also support girls' achievement and aspirations by taking an active interest in their schoolwork, extra-curricular activities, and dreams for their futures. By encouraging girls to explore new arenas, celebrating their accomplishments, and supporting them in areas of struggle, parents and other caregivers can help girls to hone their survival skills and develop confidence in themselves.

Organizations can also make a difference in promoting girls' positive self-images, identity development, and senses of possibility. For example, Girls Incorporated and its nearly 1000 program sites across the United States provide space and opportunities for girls to explore their interests, gain leadership experience, and develop decision-making skills outside of school. Public education campaigns like the Ms. Foundation's "Take Our Daughters to Work Day" encourage girls to speak their minds, envision themselves as active and productive workers, and imagine a range of possible life choices as adult women. Agencies such as Planned Parenthood offer adolescents encouragement to discuss their feelings, and make empowered decisions about personal health and relationships. Sports programs promote not only girls' physical health, but also positive feelings about their bodies and confidence in their abilities across both physical and intellectual domains (President's Council on Physical Fitness and Sports, 1997; Erkut, et al., 1996; Feminist Majority Foundation, 1995).

Whether through national organizations such as Big Sisters of America, Girl Scouts of the U.S.A., the Junior League, the YWCA of the U.S.A., and the YWHA, or through informal community or personal contacts, individual adults can help girls to feel good about themselves through coaching, mentoring, role modeling, engaging in meaningful conversations with girls, or providing them space and opportunities to explore their experiences with one another. By showing an interest in girls, adults can help girls to confront negative stereotypes, expand their senses of possibility, and develop healthy self-concepts.

CONCLUSION

Girls' identities and senses of self are complex, fluid, and shaped by the various contexts in which they live. Girls construct their senses of self not only through their gender, but also through their experiences regarding race, culture, social class, sexual identity, and disability. A growing number of researchers are studying girls in such contexts as schooling, families, communities, and peer relationships. Yet much of the existing developmental research still extracts girls from these contexts and speaks of girls or youth in general, without probing the important intersections of race, social class, sexual identity, and so forth in girls' construction of their textured and multi-layered identities. Recent studies on girls' identity and senses of self reveal important variations both within and across girls' experiences. Some research shows that while black girls appear to have a strong sense of self during adolescence, many of their peers of other races seem to fare less well. Yet other studies suggest that girls develop diverse strategies for exercising their voices, cultivating their resiliency, and navigating the competing expectations placed upon them.

Girls' feelings of pride, confidence, and efficacy can be hindered by inequitable and restrictive social practices, both in their immediate environments and in their broader culture(s). These practices, often fueled by racist, classist, ableist, and homophobic stereotypes, may impact differently on girls of different social groups. But adults can help support girls' feelings of self-worth by attending to their needs; respecting their concerns; supporting their decisions and aspirations; offering them diverse images of strong, healthy, and fulfilled girls and women that counter cultural stereotypes; providing them opportunities to explore and exercise their talents; and ensuring that they have the resources they need to realize their dreams.

Rather than using reports of low self-esteem to explain problems affecting girls, concerned adults can explore and challenge social practices and ideologies that may hinder girls' development. Research and programs should focus on girls' many strengths, and seek to learn more about what is working for girls.

● In Western societies, adolescence is often viewed as a period of inevitable conflict and duress. Yet research on positive aspects of girls' development suggests that when encouraged and supported in their social contexts, girls can thrive during adolescence.

● Although girls' development takes shape in complex and dynamic social contexts, research often extracts girls from the meaningful contexts in which they are immersed. Research also often examines trends for girls in general, failing to consider the important interplay among gender, race, culture, social class, sexuality, and disability in the formation of girls' identities.

● Despite concerns about girls' self-esteem, research suggests that girls do not necessarily experience a "loss of voice" during adolescence (Harter, et al., 1997). In addition, studies show that girls use a range of strategies for exploring their identities, articulating their opinions, and developing and preserving their sense of self (AAUW, 1996a; Erkut, et al., 1996; Harter, et al., 1997; Linn, et al., 1992; Pastor, McCormick, and Fine, 1996; Rotheram-Borus, et al., 1996; Ward, 1996).

● Girls' positive feelings about themselves and their futures can be fostered by spending time with mentors from their communities; participating in activities that support and encourage them; interacting with educators who respect their diverse strategies for negotiating the competing demands of female adolescence; discussing the impacts of sexism, as well as racism, classism, homophobia, and ableism with families and other concerned adults; and finding support for their emerging identities.

SUPPORT AT HOME. Families should encourage girls to explore their strengths and embrace their competencies; challenge themselves in difficult or unfamiliar arenas; achieve in, and feel good about, school; respect their own minds and bodies; explore a wide range of roles and career possibilities; think critically about social inequities; and envision themselves as fulfilled individuals in healthy, chosen futures. Adults at home can model respect for women and girls, and support girls' aspirations.

SUPPORT IN SCHOOLS. Teachers, counselors, and administrators must recognize and combat discrimination in their schools. They should also respect girls' diverse strategies for self-expression and identity development. Teacher education programs should help teacher recognize and modify their gender-based assumptions and practices. Sensitive and well-trained educators can increase the frequency with which girls are called on; allow girls to explore solutions without premature intervention; provide more leadership for girls; encourage girls to pursue a wide range of academic and career options; encourage girls in school-based athletics; incorporate cooperative, as well as competitive, learning models; and develop and implement curricula that emphasize the achievements of diverse scholars and leaders.

SAFE AND SUPPORTIVE COMMUNITIES. Girls also need opportunities outside of school to become active, vocal, and valued members of their communities. Adults can support girls' development through programs that allow girls to explore their talents, exercise their creativity, find encouragement, and take on leadership roles. Committed adults can provide safe spaces for girls to study, talk, work on projects, and play. Athletic programs for girls should include both competitive and non-competitive activities.

POSITIVE IMAGES. Adults should promote positive images of girls and women and encourage girls to experience themselves as competent, entitled, and important members of their society. Images in curricula, program materials, and media must include women and girls of diverse races, cultures, classes, abilities, sexual identities, and body types making a difference in a wide range of roles. Adults can help girls and boys to critique traditional notions of femininity which emphasize passivity, deference to men, and narrow images of beauty.

MORE CRITICAL RESEARCH. Research should go beyond narrow notions of self-esteem, and instead examine variations in identity development and expression among girls of diverse social backgrounds. Researchers must recognize that while gender is an important facet of identity, girls' identities represent a complex interplay of race, class, culture, and sexuality, as well as gender. Rather than reducing girls' senses of self to internal, psychological concepts that imply strength or weakness, research needs to focus on social, cultural, and institutional practices that impact on girls' self-concepts. It must also recognize cultural variations across girls' priorities, strategies, and ways of expressing themselves. Researchers should collaborate with girls, and with adults who work directly with girls. New research should emphasize positive aspects of girls' development and investigate conditions that support their well being.

SUPPORTIVE PUBLIC POLICY. Constructive public policy discussion acknowledges the many interrelated factors that affect girls' developing identities and senses of self. Public policy should not look to raising girls' self-esteem as a cure-all for more complex social problems. Rather, it should emphasize the need to challenge inequities in social institutions and popular culture that may both constrain girls' options and diminish their self-regard. Policymakers and others can challenge restrictive policies such as punitive welfare reform laws, prohibitions against open discussion of sexuality in schools, and inequitable school funding.

SUPPORT FROM FUNDERS. Funding is needed to develop and implement curricula that stress the accomplishments of people across diverse social groups. Increased funding is needed for programs that offer girls opportunities to work and study together, share ideas, express their creativity, and have fun. Funding is needed to promote safety in girls' communities, to create well-paying jobs with benefits for girls' families, and to develop programs that confront social inequities. Funders should support research that stresses collaboration between researchers and adults who work with girls; that involve girls in the research process; and that highlights positive aspects of girls' development.

CHAPTER TWO

Health

HEALTH IS OFTEN viewed from a traditional medical model as simply an absence of illness. However, Fern Goodhart, Director of Rutgers University's Health Education Program, notes that many progressive health educators and advocates conceptualize health as extending well beyond a lack of physical disease or injury to include one's social, emotional, and cognitive well-being, as well as positive feelings toward one's body.[6] According to Benson, "[T]he avoidance of health-compromising or future-jeopardizing behavior . . . is only part of a fuller conceptualization of healthy development. Equally important . . . is locating developmental experiences that promote forms of thriving. Included here are school success, affirmation of diversity, compassion for others, leadership, and choosing a healthy lifestyle (for example, nutrition and exercise)" (1997: 29).

At the 1994 *Healthy Girls/Healthy Women Research Roundtable* sponsored by the Ms. Foundation, researchers and practitioners grappled with the question, "What is health?" Participants noted that little is known about girls' healthy development, since traditional research focuses on illness, pathology, and disease. Drawing from their work across a range of settings and disciplines, roundtable participants framed health as a culturally contextualized process, rather than a set of ideal behaviors, and stressed the importance of girls' relationships with themselves, others, and their social environments. The approach advocated by Goodhart, Benson, and the Ms. Foundation roundtable participants broadens the definition of girls' health, and underscores the need for refocused research, since most studies available concentrate on illness and risk-related behaviors.

Even as researchers, advocates, and educators continue the important work of grappling with more proactive definitions of healthy development, research on girls' behaviors and experiences suggests that their health is compromised in a variety of ways. Since many adolescent behaviors have health implications well into adulthood (Costello and Krimgold, 1997; Ms. Foundation, 1994), it is important to examine girls' health-related practices early on in their development. Early attention will contribute to a better understanding of girls' current risks and wellness, and allow predictions of the health concerns of tomorrow's adult women. Therefore, this chapter identifies several aspects of girls' health for more detailed examination. These include exercise and sports participation; body image and eating disorders; HIV/AIDS prevention; depression and related concerns; and use of alcohol, tobacco, and other drugs. While issues such as reproductive decisions, feelings about self, school and community experiences, and victimization also involve health issues, these topics are addressed in depth in separate chapters.

EXERCISE AND SPORTS

Regular exercise and participation in sports during adolescence have important health benefits, not only during girls' teenage years but throughout their adult lives. According to *Physical Activity and Sport in the Lives of Girls* by the President's Council on Physical Fitness and Sports (1997), recent studies show that girls derive clear health benefits from exercise. Exercise and sports participation can enhance both the physical and mental health of girls.

These benefits include:

- increased muscle strength and cardiovascular endurance;
- decreased likelihood of obesity and hyperlipidemia (high levels of fat in the blood), which, in turn, may lower girls' likelihood of develop-

ing coronary heart disease and certain cancers as adults;

- greater peak bone mass, which may reduce girls' risk for osteoporosis later in life;
- improved immune system, helping girls to fight off diseases such as cancer or those caused by colds or influenza (however, this applies only to moderate exercise; overtraining can actually lower a girl's resistance); and
- decreased likelihood of symptoms related to stress and depression among girls.

In addition to promoting these aspects of physical and psychological health, girls' participation in sports and exercise benefits them in other areas of their lives. In a series of surveys of high school students, young women who partici-

(Kann, et al., 1996) offers these discouraging findings:

- Only 52 percent of all high school girls surveyed reported exercising vigorously three or more times in the previous week, compared with 74 percent of boys.
- Among the girls, white, non-Hispanic girls were most likely to have exercised three or more times in a week (58 percent), followed by Hispanic girls (45 percent) and black, non-Hispanic girls (41 percent).
- The percentage of girls who exercise regularly declines considerably during high school, from 62 percent in ninth grade (compared with 80 percent of boys) to only 42 percent in twelfth grade (compared with 67 percent of boys).

Healthy means not being weighed down by a lot of worries. Worries about is my mom going to be okay, is my little sister okay, will we have enough for the rent and food and things. It means feeling safe and like things will be okay, not depressed and angry all the time. It means being healthy in the usual sense, too, like not being sick. But it means more about being in control of things, being able to do the things I want. Being able to be young instead of always feeling old.

– Chrystal, age 14

SELF-DESCRIPTION: "African American, heterosexual young woman"

---

pated in sports were 40 percent less likely than those not participating to drop out of high school, 33 percent less likely to become teen mothers, and less likely to smoke cigarettes. Young women who participated, however, were 27 percent more likely to have engaged in binge drinking (Girls Incorporated, 1997c, citing Zill et al., 1995).

U.S. girls now participate in a wider range of sports and exercise than ever before (President's Council on Physical Fitness and Sports, 1997), thanks in part to the 1972 passage of Title IX, which required that federally-funded schools provide equal athletic opportunity to students, without regard to gender. However, the number of girls who participate still lags behind the number of boys, who have not faced the same barriers to participation as girls. Although the importance of regular exercise has been stressed in both medical and popular literature in recent years, too few girls—especially girls of color, girls with disabilities, and girls from low-income families—currently exercise enough to receive these benefits. The Centers for Disease Control and Prevention's "1995 Youth Risk Behavior Surveillance"

The reasons for girls' low participation in physical activity are varied. In general, schools have not been helpful in encouraging girls to exercise. Indeed, only about half (57 percent) of the nation's ninth through twelfth grade female students took physical education classes in school, and only about one-fourth (24 percent) attended physical education classes on a daily basis in 1995 (Kann, et al., 1996). Significantly, although the percentage of high school interscholastic athletes who are girls rose from seven percent in 1972 to 37 percent in 1994, most of that increase occurred in the mid-1970s, soon after the 1972 passage of Title IX (National Federation of State High Schools Association, 1996).

Girls now account for approximately 37 percent of all high school athletes—this marks an increase from one in 27 girls who participated in 1971 (pre-Title IX), to one in three girls in 1994. During the 1994-95 school year, 2,240,000 girls took part in high school sports, compared with 3,554,429 boys—37 percent and 63 percent respectively (National Federation of State High Schools Association, 1996, cited in President's Council, 1997). In fact, while the percentage of male high school sophomores who participated in sports remained at 63 percent from 1980 to 1990, the percentage of high school sophomore girls participating in sports decreased from 46 percent in 1980 to 41 percent in 1990 (National Center for Education Statistics, 1993). At the current rate of overall increase, the Feminist Majority Foundation's Task Force on Women and Girls in Sports (1995) estimates that girls' athletic participation will not be comparable to boys' until the year 2033.[7]

According to the Feminist Majority Foundation's (1993) report, despite clear health benefits to young women, many girls are either overlooked or actively discouraged from participating in sports. The report cites several interrelated reasons for young women's underrepresentation in high school (and college) sports. Unfortunately, a common barrier is the homophobic belief that female athletes are, or will become, lesbians. This myth has put pressure on girls and women (whether heterosexual, bisexual, or lesbian) to avoid activities perceived as "masculine" for fear of being labeled lesbians, and thus facing harassment and discrimination. The report finds that parents, too, have discouraged their daughters from pursuing sports based on an unfounded, homophobic fear that athletics will influence them to become lesbians. Certainly, this myth points to the narrow understanding of "femininity" and sexuality in this culture, as well as an unfounded link between physical competence and sexual orientation, and a heterosexist belief that lesbianism is unacceptable.

A second barrier cited in the report involves the emphasis placed on "superstar" athletes at the expense of others. Since sexism in sports and media makes it less likely that girls and women athletes will be perceived as "superstars," they receive less attention and encouragement than their male counterparts. Finally, the report notes that young women may be discouraged from pursuing athletics by the relative lack of female role models as coaches and sports program directors. Consider that:

- only 25 percent of all high school athletic teams are coached by women;
- whereas 40 percent of girls' teams are coached by men, only two percent of boys' teams are coached by women; and
- women coaches still earn considerably less than men.

In fact, according to a recent survey by the Chronicle of Higher Education (Selingo and Naughton, 1997), the average salary for the head coach of a men's team at a median Division I institution in the NCAA was 44 percent higher than that of a women's team head coach at the same institution. Yet ironically, since the implementation of Title IX in 1972 led to an increase in salaries for coaches of women's teams, many female coaches of women's teams have been displaced by men (Acosta and Carpenter, 1996).

Other studies suggest additional reasons for girls' lack of participation in sports. According to the President's Coun-

cil on Physical Fitness and Sports (1997), girls' ability to participate may be hampered by economic obstacles that impact more notably on girls from poor or working class families. For girls who live in communities with high crime rates, a lack of safe public space may also discourage their participation in athletic activities. They note that continued prejudice and institutional barriers may further hinder the sports participation of girls of color and girls with disabilities. Unfortunately, participation is most lacking and resources are most scarce among the very girls who may need the benefits of physical activity and sports the most (President's Council, 1997).

Girls' lower rate of sports participation may also be related to the different amount of attention devoted to male versus female athletic activities. Indeed, a 1991 analysis of four daily newspapers found that while 85 percent of all sports stories covered men-only activities, only 3.5 percent were devoted to women-only sports coverage (Duncan, Messner, and Williams, 1991). Taken together, these studies suggest that although athletic activity is important to girls' physical and psychological health, girls face many barriers to active participation in sports.

Unfortunately, preconceived notions about gender and sports may be internalized and reproduced by children. In her 1993 book, *Gender Play*, Barrie Thorne found that when school-age children explained girls' lack of participation in male-associated playground games like soccer or basketball, they tended to point to girls' lack of skill (i.e., "Girls are not good at it"). Interestingly, however, they did not attribute boys' lack of participation in female-associated games like hopscotch or jump rope to a lack of skill. Rather, children tended to say that boys did not participate because they were "girls' games."

In the midst of these often disheartening findings, some recent developments suggest that public attitudes toward women in sports may be slowly shifting. For example, the advent in 1997 of the Women's National Basketball Association (WNBA) and the all-female American Basketball League is a promising step towards professional opportunity, and provides positive role models for girls and all sports fans. Early reports note that the WNBA games exceed predictions of popularity and interest, and that girls are finding inspiration in female sports figures (Gross, 1997). In addition, Olympics coverage of such sports as women's softball and volleyball has expanded, and the U.S. women's hockey team received extensive coverage during the 1998 Winter Olympics; two female referees have recently been hired by the men's National Basketball Association; and the major networks and newspapers have expanded their rosters of women sportscasters (although these women remain the distinct minority). Each of these steps towards fuller participation and coverage of women and girls in sports offers hope for tomorrow's female athletes—and all health-conscious women. Whether they choose to become athletes or not, these positive images of women's physical competence may help inspire more girls to develop strong and healthy bodies.

Ironically, while girls derive clear benefits from their own participation in sports, studies suggest that girls' and women's safety may, in fact, be threatened by practices and ideologies surrounding boys' and men's involvement in athletics. Studies indicate that male athletes (as well as fraternity members on college campuses) are often encouraged to develop negative views toward women, through rituals and chants that degrade women, and by coaches, team members, and others who assign such labels as "girls," and "sissies" as a form of ridicule to boys and men who are not aggressive or do not perform well. Beyond holding more hostile attitudes toward girls and women, male college athletes are more likely than male non-athletes to actually engage in sexual aggression against girls and women (Koss and Gaines, cited in Feminist Majority, 1993).

These findings highlight the importance of challenging misguided stereotypes and practices that demean women, and equate male athletic competence with sexual aggression. Adults who coach male teams must model respectful behaviors and attitudes toward women and girls, and they must not tolerate homophobic language or actions. Women should be encouraged to coach not only all-girls' teams, but also all-boys' teams and mixed-sex teams, so that both boys and girls develop an early respect for females as athletes and sports leaders. And coaches, parents, and students need to insist on equal playing time, publicity, equipment, and community/school support for girls' teams. Such actions can ultimately help girls to develop stronger senses of themselves as athletic and physically capable, which may enhance their overall psychological and physical health.

Finally, several cautions are in order for young female athletes competing at the elite level. While moderate to strenuous activity poses few risks to most healthy girls, and the evidence suggests no detrimental effects to the cardiovascular system from heavy exercise, a number of health hazards have been associated with excessive exercise (President's Council on Physical Fitness and Sports, 1997). Many of these dangers involve the musculoskeletal system. In addition to overuse injuries, girls training at the elite level can experience changes in reproductive system maturation and

functioning, some of which are related to a preoccupation with body weight and underconsumption of calories.

The three primary concerns to highly athletic girls are:

- osteoporosis, resulting from decreased peak bone density;
- amenorrhea (irregular or interrupted menstrual cycles), which may harm girls by decreasing peak bone density; and
- disordered eating, resulting from pressure to maintain an "ideal physique."

Girls participating in sports where appearance is considered an important component of performance, such as figure skating, gymnastics, and dance, are particularly at risk. However, the President's Council report emphasizes that eating disorders do not result from participation in sports; rather, they develop from "psychological issues in the lives of girls" (1997: 9). The negative health consequences of anorexia and bulimia will be explored in the next section.

Overall, it seems that a moderate to high level of physical activity in girls leads to far greater long-term health benefits than risks. As the President's Council report notes, "Regular physical activity during childhood and youth may prevent or impede the development of several adult conditions in which physical inactivity is only one part of a complex, multifactorial etiology (e.g., obesity, degenerative diseases of the heart and blood vessels and musculoskeletal disorders)" (1997: 10). These long-term benefits, coupled with the more immediate benefits of enhanced confidence, fitness, and positive body awareness, suggest strongly that girls should be encouraged to participate in sports and regular exercise to be healthier now and in their futures.

BODY IMAGE AND EATING DISORDERS

Among the health issues affecting adolescents, eating disorders are amost strongly associated with gender. Indeed, 90 percent of all cases of eating disorders are found among girls and young women (National Institute of Mental Health, 1993). Further, the National Institute of Mental Health (NIMH) states that among all types of psychiatric disorders, eating disorders are associated with the highest mortality rate (10 percent). These findings suggest the vital importance of understanding the incidence, contributing factors, and implications of eating disorders.

Given the societal emphasis placed on female attractiveness, it should come as little surprise that a girl's body image is often central to her sense of self (AAUW, 1991).

According to *Shortchanging Girls, Shortchanging America* (AAUW, 1991), adolescent girls were more likely than boys to experience physical appearance as central to their self-esteem. And yet, adolescent girls tended to view the changes in their bodies more negatively than did boys. Fueled by today's ultra-thin cultural ideals of female body type, girls are encouraged to diet at alarmingly young ages. Indeed, the heaviest users of diet pills are now girls 7 to 17 years old (Schupak-Nauberg and Nemeroff, 1993).

The lines between excessive dieting and eating disorders are often blurred. In a society which encourages young women to diet, and focus enormous amounts of energy on "improving" their bodies, strict dieting is often considered a normal part of female adolescence (Steiner-Adair, 1990). The Centers for Disease Control and Prevention's "1995 Youth Risk Behavior Surveillance" (Kann, et al., 1996) survey of ninth through twelfth grade students found that 34 percent of girls (compared to 22 percent of boys) perceived themselves as overweight, and 60 percent of girls—or nearly two out of three—were attempting to lose weight. Since dieting and body dissatisfaction are promoted and normalized through teen and women's magazines and other media, it may be difficult to detect girls with anorexia or bulimia before they have developed severe symptoms of the disorder. Yet it is critical to do so, since eating disorders have been found to be correlated with clinical depression, anxiety disorders, low self-esteem, and substance abuse in adolescent girls (National Institute of Mental Health, 1993).

According to the National Institute of Mental Health (1993), anorexia—characterized by self-imposed starvation, weight loss at least 15 percent below normal body weight, and distorted body image—is diagnosed in approximately one percent of adolescent girls. Bulimia, which involves binge eating followed by purging through vomiting, excessive exercise, or use of laxatives, is diagnosed in another two to three percent of adolescent girls. However, given both the secrecy surrounding these disorders, and the cultural prescriptions which "normalize" adolescent female dieting, it is likely that many more girls actually experience eating disorders than are diagnosed.

Indeed, based on questionnaires administered to 6,748 students (3,586 girls and 3,162 boys) in fifth through twelfth grade, *The Commonwealth Fund Survey of the Health of Adolescent Girls* (1997) found that 18 percent of high school girls (compared to 7 percent of high school boys) reported having binged and purged, and 8 percent of high school girls (compared to 4 percent of high school boys) reported doing so daily or a few times a week. According to the "1995 Youth Risk Behavior Surveillance," one in three girls (34 percent) considered herself overweight, and 60 percent of high school girls (compared to 24 percent of boys) reported that they were trying to lose weight—49 percent said that they were dieting, 8 percent said that they took laxatives or vomited to lose weight, and 9 percent said that they took diet pills to control their weight (Kann, et al., 1996).

I never feel happy with who I am, or should I say with my body. Every day I try to start a new diet. I try not to eat anything until the end of the day, and by then I'm so starving, I overeat, and then I feel bad about myself. Then I start over the next day and try to do better, but it never seems to work. A lot of times I feel out of control, so I try to diet so I can feel like I can try to control myself better.

– Beth, age 16
SELF-DESCRIPTION: "white American female"

Although eating disorders occur in girls across race and ethnic groups, white girls most often develop anorexia and bulimia, followed most closely by Hispanic girls (National Institute of Mental Health, 1993). This is consistent with research findings that black girls report more positive body images than both white and Hispanic girls. In a 1996 survey of more than 150 girls aged 11 to 17, the Melpomene Institute, in collaboration with YWCA of the U.S.A., found that 40 percent of the black girls studied considered themselves attractive or very attractive, compared to only 9.1 percent of the white girls. Thirty-six percent of the black girls in the study responded that they felt competent and capable about their bodies, in contrast to 7.6 percent of the white girls. Thus it is not surprising that anorexia and bulimia more often strike white girls. Interestingly, only binge eating disorder (binging without purging) is found equally among white and African American individuals (National Institute of Mental Health, 1993). And, unlike anorexia and bulimia, one-quarter to one-third of people with binge eating disorder are men (National Institute of Mental Health, 1993). This may be due, in part, to the relatively less strict societal emphasis placed on thinness for men as opposed to women.

Studies of the causes of eating disorders have found several related factors which may predispose individuals to anorexia or bulimia. Anorexia, in particular, is often associated with young women who have low self-esteem; who are perfectionists, obedient, and private about their feelings; and who live in families that tend to be strict and to place strong emphasis on physical attractiveness and weight control (National Institute of Mental Health, 1993). Some researchers have explored possible biochemical links to eating disorders, including the impact of neurotransmitter and hormone levels in the body. Still others speculate that eating disorders may be linked to genetics, since eating disorders often occur in both mothers and daughters (National Institute of Mental Health, 1993).

While these factors may certainly play a role in the development of eating disorders, the study of biochemical, genetic, and personality differences tends to emphasize individual characteristics while obscuring the role of cultural influences. Often approached from a medical or psychiatric model, much mainstream research on eating disorders fails to consider the societal messages and practices in which girls are immersed, and that many girls internalize. Indeed, in a 1995 Harris poll commissioned by Girls Incorporated, more girls (15 percent) than boys (8 percent) said they dieted or exercised to look like a character they had seen on television (Girls Incorporated, 1995). As psychologist and researcher Steiner-Adair (1990) has demon-

towards mastery and even perfectionism find destructive outlets, however, when turned against their own bodies.

According to *The Commonwealth Fund Survey of the Health of Adolescent Girls* (1997), girls' experience of abuse is strongly associated with eating disorders. In the Commonwealth Fund's nationally representative sample of 3,586 girls across 265 schools, girls who reported having been abused were almost three times as likely to report bingeing and purging as those who did not report being abused. Thirty-two percent of the girls who had been abused said they binged and purged (compared to 12 percent of non-abused girls), and 13 percent reported bingeing and purging at least daily. These findings suggest that concerned adults should broaden their thinking about eating disorders; they need to understand and address the multiple, interconnected factors impacting on girls' physical and psychological health.

Despite the prevalence of extreme weight concern and excessive dieting among adolescent girls, parents and clinicians may miss opportunities to help girls before they develop severe cases of eating disorders. Adults need to be proactive in addressing the negative body images and cultural messages which encourage so many girls to harm their bodies through strict dieting, bingeing, and/or purging.

Further, although eating disorders are associated with myriad other health issues, including smoking and drug abuse (French, et al., 1995; National Center on Addiction and Substance Abuse, 1996), they are too often treated separately. Girls may be best served when eating disorders are viewed holistically as part of young women's overall physical and psychological health. As Rutgers University health educator and psychologist Donna Schoenfeld

---

I'm proud of my body, and I like how it looks, how it moves, and how I feel. I don't know why people starve themselves and take to diets instead of being happy with yourself the way you are. I feel like God gave me this body, and my mother gave me this body, and it's mine to feel good about.

– Charlene, age 16

SELF-DESCRIPTION: "strong, African American young woman who feels good about herself"

---

strated, girls who accept traditional images of femininity or the "superwoman" are more likely to have anorexia than girls who are able to critique those images. And clinician Susie Orbach (1982) observed over 15 years ago that bulimia is linked to the mixed messages women receive about food and their own entitlement. Whereas women are encouraged to provide food for others as a sign of love and nurturance, they are encouraged to deprive themselves of the pleasures of eating. Finally, some girls may approach body weight as an area of their lives in which they can exert control (Thompson, 1992). Their positive impulses

points out, prevention efforts have only recently begun to address the complex social and cultural issues involved in the development and experience of eating disorders. Shoenfeld calls for health educators and others to ground both their prevention and treatment approaches in a multidisciplinary understanding of the different cultural influences on girls of various race, ethnic, and class backgrounds.[8]

In addition to watching for signs of negative body image or eating disorders, adults can help girls to think critically about the narrow images of beauty and "perfection" they may encounter. One helpful strategy for encouraging girls to critique media images has been developed by Girls Incorporated. In their "Girls Re-Cast TV Action Kit," Girls Incorporated invites girls to reflect on the characters and messages they see and hear on television, and to compare those to what they know from real life. The Action Kit includes guiding questions for girls to ask themselves when watching television, a fun quiz to see how realistic television characters and families are, and suggestions for how girls can speak out against negative images they see portrayed in the programs they watch. The Action Kit, which is available on the Internet, encourages girls to take action by writing to producers to tell them what they like and do not like about the shows' themes or characters, inviting teachers and classmates to create a school project about these issues, and developing their own positive shows with friends to act out at school or in their communities.[9]

HIV/AIDS PREVENTION

Although many adolescents still discount the relevance of HIV and AIDS to their own lives, an estimated 25 percent of all new HIV infections in the United States occur in people between 13 and 20 years old (Office of National AIDS Policy, 1996). And since diagnosed AIDS cases result from HIV infection occurring an average of 10 years earlier, many of the AIDS cases diagnosed among adults in their twenties are likely to stem from HIV infection in adolescence (Centers for Disease Control and Prevention, 1993b). While the increasing incidence of HIV/AIDS should be of concern to everyone, recent trends have particular relevance for adolescent girls who, along with adult women, are now the fastest growing group of new HIV cases worldwide (World Health Organization, 1995).

Moreover, black women and girls represent a disproportionately high percentage of newly reported AIDS cases in the United States: 54.5 percent of new female cases reported in 1994 were non-Hispanic black women over age 13, a group that comprises only 11.7 percent of the overall U.S. female population. Among other HIV-infected women, 24.2 percent were non-Hispanic white; 20.4 percent were Hispanic; and less than 1 percent were Native American, Asian, and Pacific Islander women (Costello and Krimgold, 1997). The overrepresentation of black women and girls among new HIV cases occurs in nearly every age category, from under 5 through age 64, with black women and girls presenting infection at two and often three times the rate of white and Hispanic women of the same ages (Centers for Disease Control and Prevention, 1996).

According to the Centers for Disease Control and Prevention (CDC) (1997), of teens aged 13-19 who were diagnosed with AIDS as of December 1996, 55 percent of females (compared with 3 percent of males), contracted HIV through heterosexual contact. Fifteen percent of 13- to 19-year-old women diagnosed with AIDS by December 1996 became infected through sharing needles with other drug users (Centers for Disease Control and Prevention, 1997, cited in Girls Incorporated, 1997a). These findings underscore the need for culturally-sensitive educational programs, greater access to condoms and information about their use for HIV/AIDS prevention, needle exchange programs, and enhanced outreach to girls in groups where the risk of infection is particularly high.

Despite increased public awareness of the dangers of unprotected sex and intravenous drug use, many girls continue to engage in behaviors that increase their risk of HIV infection. In a 1995 CDC survey of male and female students in the ninth through twelfth grades who had had intercourse within the preceding three months, only 54 percent reported using a condom at the last sexual encounter (Kann, et al., 1996). While that number leaves almost half the population of teens having intercourse potentially exposed to STDs, it nevertheless reflects an improvement since 1991, when a similar CDC survey found that only 46 percent of those who had had intercourse within the preceding three months reported using a condom during last intercourse (Centers for Disease Control and Prevention, 1993).

Alcohol use may also increase risk of infection, as girls who drink more than five times per month have been found to be one-third less likely to use condoms during sex than girls who do not drink (National Center on Addiction and Substance Abuse, 1996). These findings suggest that alcohol and drug awareness programs need to address not only the direct health dangers associated with substance abuse, but also the indirect risks. Conversely, programs aimed at promoting safer sex practices need to discuss the connections between alcohol and drug use, and condom use.

Although HIV prevention programs for adolescents are critical to preventing the spread of the virus, only 37 states currently require HIV education in schools (NARAL Foundation, 1997). Further, many state-approved HIV curricula restrict discussion of topics which might be construed as promoting sexual activity, including safer sex practices (Silin, 1992). Ignoring the sexual realities of their students, many programs stress abstinence-only approaches and do not offer condoms, discuss their proper use, or explore the sexual dynamics that can make safer sex practices difficult for girls to enforce with their partners (NARAL Foundation, 1997). Some parents and community groups have fought against condom distribution in and around schools, as well as against needle exchange programs,

itive and holistic approach by nurturing girls' sense of entitlement to healthy bodies and respect from others. All youth should have access to the information, skills, resources, and confidence they need to make conscious, life-affirming decisions and to enforce their own choices. (Sexuality education is discussed further in chapter on Education.)

A lot of kids my age don't worry about STDs, but they should. That's why I do peer educating. These kids think if they get HIV they can just get a shot or something and they'll be cured. It's really hard to convince them that they could die, and so they have to protect themselves. Kids need more information they can relate to.

— Rosa, age 17

SELF-DESCRIPTION: "a Latin educator trying to make a difference"

---

which remain controversial and difficult to fund despite their potential for reducing the spread of HIV among intravenous (IV) drug users and their partners. Among 13- to 19-year-old girls diagnosed with AIDS through 1996, 40 percent of those whose HIV infections were attributed to heterosexual contact reported having had contact with a male IV-drug user (Centers for Disease Control and Prevention, 1997, cited in Girls Incorporated 1997a). Without needle exchange programs, the health risks are increased for anyone who injects drugs themselves, as well as anyone who has unprotected sex with IV-drug users.

Clearly, prevention is critical. HIV/AIDS prevention programs may save adolescents' lives, but to do so, they must reach their intended audience effectively. Thus, programs must be culturally sensitive and developmentally appropriate while offering adolescents complete and accurate information. Programs should be developed in collaboration with young people and their families; they can also incorporate peer educators, who may be particularly effective in encouraging teens to discuss sensitive issues.

While programs should discuss abstinence as a viable and respectable choice, girls and boys also have a right to clear and accessible information about how to obtain and use latex condoms, spermicide, and dental dams, all of which can decrease the spread of HIV. Teens need nonjudgmental contexts where they can examine social and psychological barriers to choosing abstinence or practicing safer sex. They also need opportunities to develop their own empowered responses to potential pressure from partners to have unprotected sex. While prevention programs must include skill-building and concrete information about HIV/AIDS and other STDs, fear-based approaches are not helpful. Educators and advocates should take a pos-

DEPRESSION AND RELATED CONCERNS

Adults often associate adolescence with a time of mood swings, melancholia, and withdrawal from previously enjoyed activities. Yet these tendencies can also signal clinical depression, a painful and sometimes debilitating condition which afflicts millions of adolescents. Adolescent depression, disturbing in its own right, is also linked to a number of other physical and mental health problems, including low self-confidence; poor body image and eating disorders; and increased rates of smoking, drinking, and use of illegal drugs (The Commonwealth Fund, 1997). While depression can affect both boys and girls during childhood and adolescence, girls are twice as likely as boys to be depressed (Nolen-Hoeksema, 1990). The Commonwealth Fund survey (1997) also found variations in frequency of depressive symptoms among girls of different races: Asian girls were most likely to report symptoms of depression (30 percent), followed by Hispanic girls (27 percent), white girls (22 percent), and black girls (17 percent).

Depression among girls is often linked to a negative body image, with severely depressed girls reporting more overall dissatisfaction with their bodies than either non-depressed or mildly depressed girls (Koff, Rierdan, and Stubbs, 1990; Rierdan and Koff, 1991). Depression is also more often found in adolescent girls with a history of abuse than in their non-abused peers (Cole and Putnam, 1992; The Commonwealth Fund, 1997). Depression in girls often occurs in conjunction with substance abuse and the development of eating disorders, and depressed girls are three times more likely to become pregnant than non-depressed girls (Ms. Foundation, 1994, citing The Commonwealth Fund, 1993). Girls with moderate to severe depressive symptoms have also been found to be more than twice as likely to smoke (23 percent versus 11 percent), drink (25 percent versus 11 percent), and use drugs (30 percent versus 14 percent) than girls with low or no depressive symptoms (The Commonwealth Fund, 1997).[10]

Suicide, suicide attempts, and suicidal thoughts are also strongly associated with depression. Girls are considerably more likely than boys to consider seriously and attempt suicide. According to the "1995 Youth Risk Behavior Surveillance," 30 percent of high school girls reported seriously considering suicide, compared to 18 percent of boys. The representation of Hispanic girls was particularly high, with 34 percent reporting seriously considering suicide. Black girls were the least likely of U.S. girls to contemplate suicide, although the percentage remains high at 22 percent (Kann, et al., 1996). Thirteen percent of girls reported attempting suicide in 1995, compared with five percent of boys (Kann, et al., 1996). However, in 1992, adolescent boys were five to seven times more likely than girls to die from their suicide attempts (National Center for Health Statistics, 1996). And although only recently receiving attention in the literature, information on girls' self-mutilation (such as cutting or burning oneself) is slowly emerging, and has begun to reach girls through articles in teen magazines such as *Sassy* (Pedersen, 1996) and *Seventeen* (Todd, 1996), and the issue has been highlighted in such popular adult media as the *New York Times* (Egan, 1997).

Since symptoms of depression (including profound sadness, feelings of loss or hopelessness, withdrawal, loss of appetite, and changes in sleeping patterns) may be perceived by adults as similar to behaviors stereotypically associated with adolescent "moodiness," and particularly those associated with adolescent girls' behavior (i.e., withdrawing rather than acting out), clinical depression in girls may go unnoticed. However, given the correlation between depression and serious eating disorders, suicide, early pregnancy, and substance abuse, it is most important that depression be detected and treated as early as possible. Hotline workers, crisis counselors, and other advocates must also be sensitive to gender and cultural issues, and alert to manifestations of depression or suicidal fantasies that are particular to girls.

Unfortunately, many girls who experience depression feel unable to get help. The Commonwealth Fund's study of girls' health found that 44 percent of girls with symptoms of depression reported going without needed care (1997). Only 28 percent of girls with severe symptoms of depression and 18 percent of girls with moderate symptoms said they had seen a mental health professional in the previous year.[11] Of the adolescent girls with depressive symptoms, 46 percent cited concerns about confidentiality— or not wanting their parents to know that they were having problems—as their reason for not getting help. Twenty-seven percent of girls with symptoms of depression reported that they had no one to turn to, compared to only eight percent of girls with few or no depressive symptoms. These findings underscore the need to reach out to adolescents who show symptoms of depression or related concerns, to ensure that they have access to confidential advocacy and mental health care, and to stress to them that these services are, indeed, confidential.

TOBACCO, ALCOHOL, AND OTHER DRUG USE

Although first-time tobacco use among adults has decreased significantly in the last decade, cigarette smoking among adolescent girls has become a cause for serious concern. Since 1975, girls have been at least as likely as boys to smoke cigarettes, and smoking is on the rise for both sexes (Girls Incorporated, 1997b). A recent series of annual studies of approximately 50,000 students across the nation in eighth, tenth, and twelfth grades found that while more than one in eight (13 percent) eighth grade girls reported smoking in 1991, that number increased to more than one in five (21 percent) in 1996 (Johnston, O'Malley, and Bachman, 1997). Girls who smoke put themselves at higher risk for heart disease, lung cancer, and

Smoking's stupid. People be thinking it looks really cool, but me and my friends just think it's stupid. I play basketball and I sing in the chorus, and so I need to be in good shape, and I need to have a clear voice. That's more important to me than looking so-called cool. Nothing cool about killing yourself.

– Edwena, age 15
SELF-DESCRIPTION: "a together black woman"

bladder cancer than non-smokers. Since 1986, in fact, more women have died each year from lung cancer than from breast cancer (National Center on Addiction and Substance Abuse, 1996). Overall, the Centers for Disease Control and Prevention (1993a) estimates that tobacco use is responsible for one in five deaths in the United States. Yet it is the single most preventable cause of death in this country.

Nearly all first use of tobacco occurs before high school graduation, and more than one in three smokers begin before age 14 (Office on Smoking and Health, 1994). According to a 1995 survey by the CDC, 34 percent of high school girls nationwide smoked in 1995 (defined as smoking cigarettes at least once in the 30 days prior to the survey), with 16 percent indicating that they smoked frequently (defined as smoking on 20 or more of the thirty days prior to the survey) (Kann, et al., 1996).

There's lots of drinking at this school, and most of the kids are into it, even us "good kids." A lot of adults are in denial about it, because they think it couldn't happen to their kids. But it does. Girls drink as bad as the boys, except it's worse for girls because then boys think they can take advantage of them. Boys have to worry about drinking and driving, but girls have to worry about that plus getting pregnant, getting raped, getting a bad reputation, and all sorts of things that boys don't. It's a double standard. Drinking makes you feel invincible and helps you fit in and forget your inhibitions, but it also makes you vulnerable as a girl.

— Judy, age 15
SELF-DESCRIPTION: "white girl"

However, smoking rates among girls vary considerably by race, with black girls reporting significantly less cigarette use than either black boys or girls of other races (Kann, et al., 1996). Among the girls surveyed by the CDC, the rate of current cigarette use was highest among white, non-Hispanic girls (40 percent), followed by Hispanic girls (33 percent), with black, non-Hispanic girls reporting the lowest rate (12.2 percent). Rates of frequent cigarette use showed similar discrepancies, with only 1.3 percent of black girls reporting frequent use, compared to 20.8 percent of white, non-Hispanic girls and 9.3 percent of Hispanic girls (Kann, et al., 1996). Other studies have found that Native American girls' rate of smoking is comparable to that of white girls, and that Asian American and African American girls are less likely to smoke than girls in other race groups (French and Perry, 1996). While girls' overall use of cigarettes is high, their use of smokeless tobacco (chewing tobacco and snuff) is significantly lower than that of boys.

While a great deal of research has been devoted to determining predictors of adolescent smoking in general, fewer studies have dealt with gender-specific factors that contribute to girls, in particular, initiating cigarette use (French and Perry, 1996). However, French and Perry's 1996 review of research on adolescent women and smoking in the *Journal of the American Medical Women's Association* points to several psychosocial factors which may underlie girls' high rate of smoking. One of the most common reasons that

girls initiate smoking is to control weight (National Center on Addiction and Substance Abuse, 1996). A recent survey of 877 girls found that those who expressed concerns about their weight or who had dieted recently were twice as likely to be current smokers as those who were neither concerned about their weight nor recent dieters (French, et al., 1994). Further, girls who were concerned about weight but did not smoke at the beginning of the study were more likely than either boys or girls who were not weight-conscious to initiate smoking within the next year. In other words, weight concern may serve as a fair predictor of girls' tendency to start, and continue, smoking.

In a more recent survey of more than 33,000 male and female adolescents, frequent dieting was found to increase the likelihood of smoking among girls in grades 7-12, although this relationship was not found among boys (French, et al., 1995). Such findings are disturbing, since nearly half (49 percent) of a nationally representative sample of ninth grade girls in 1995 reported dieting (Kann, et al., 1996), and chronic dieting is found among 12 percent of white girls, 15 percent of Hispanic girls, 10 percent of Native American and Asian girls, and 8 percent of African American girls (Story, et al., 1995). These findings suggest the need to approach smoking as an important aspect of the body image pressures that confront adolescent girls.

Many girls apparently smoke to relieve stress. In fact, *The Commonwealth Fund Survey of the Health of Adolescent Girls* (1997) found that among girls who smoked "several or more" cigarettes per week, stress relief was the most frequently cited reason for smoking (66 percent), followed by being around others who smoke (53 percent), wanting to try it (15 percent), and considering it fun (5 percent). Smoking was also found to be related to depression: girls with depressive symptoms were more than twice as likely to report smoking (23 percent) as were girls with low or no depressive symptoms (11 percent).

Girls also may initiate smoking to satisfy a desire to feel more mature or autonomous and to fit in with peers (French and Perry, 1996). Interestingly, girls who are self-confident and outgoing are also more likely to begin smoking, perhaps because they identify with the images of health, slenderness, sexuality, and popularity offered in cigarette advertisements. A 10 year study of 6000 children found that while girls who are active in sports or individual leisure pursuits are less likely to begin smoking, those who participate in organized social activities and opposite-sex friendships have an increased likelihood of starting to smoke (Swan, Creeser, and Murray, 1990). These data provide yet another reason to advance sports as a positive choice for girls.

Although information exists on overall adolescent drug use, less information is available on the use of drugs by girls of various race or class backgrounds. However, social psychologists Johnston, O'Malley, and Bachman (1997) offer one compelling source of data on drug use trends in their "Monitoring the Future" study. The researchers have polled U.S. high school seniors annually since 1975 on their use of illicit drugs—including marijuana, amphetamine stimulants, heroin, LSD, and cocaine—adding samples of eighth- and tenth-graders to the study in 1991. In 1996, the survey of approximately 50,000 students from 424 public and private secondary schools revealed a rise in the use of illicit drugs among students, continuing a steady increase in drug use which began in 1991 among eighth-graders and in 1992 among 10th and 12th graders. The percentage of eighth-graders who used any illicit drug in the 12 months preceding the study more than doubled between 1991 and 1996 (from 11 percent to 24 percent). Between 1992 and 1996, the proportion of tenth-graders using any illicit drugs in the previous 12 months almost doubled (from 20 percent to 38 percent), and the proportion of twelfth-graders using illicit drugs during that time period rose by approximately one-half (from 27 percent to 40 percent). Eighth grade girls, in particular, were three times more likely in 1996 to have smoked marijuana than in 1991 (from 5.1 percent to 16.9 percent) (Johnston, O'Malley, and Bachman, 1997). According to the National Center on Addiction and Substance Abuse (1996) at Columbia University, virtually all girls who use illicit drugs begin by smoking cigarettes.

In 1996, the National Center on Addiction and Substance Abuse at Columbia University published the results of a two-year literature review, entitled *Substance Abuse and the American Woman,* which provides disturbing informa-tion on girls' use of alcohol and illegal drugs. Based on analysis of data from over 1,700 scientific articles, surveys, and government documents, the review found that girls between 12-18 years old are now just as likely as boys in that age group to drink alcohol and use illegal drugs. Girls, on average, begin drinking alcohol when they are 15 years old, the same age as boys. Among women aged 19-44, the average age for beginning marijuana use was 17.2 years old, only slightly older than men in the same age group, whose average age of first marijuana use was 16.7 years.

Like cigarette smoking, girls' use of drugs such as cocaine and heroin was found to be tied to their desire to be thin, and alcohol use was linked to a desire for greater popularity. While alcohol, marijuana, and other drug abuse has serious consequences for adolescents of both sexes, the Columbia review found that substance abuse has some particularly dangerous implications for girls and women, including increased risk of sexual assault, unintended pregnancies, and domestic violence. As noted previously, the review also found that girls who reported drinking more than five times a month were one-third less likely to use condoms than girls who did not drink, putting them at increased risk for unplanned pregnancy, HIV/AIDS, and other STDs.

Alcohol and drug misuse is dangerous in and of itself; but it is also associated with other important risks to girls' health and safety. Thus, efforts to prevent unplanned pregnancies, violence against women and girls, and HIV/AIDS and other STDs should emphasize the role of alcohol and other drugs in heightening risks. Alcohol and drug prevention programs should also highlight the connections between substance abuse and related health and safety concerns.

I don't have a regular doctor yet. I'd like one for me and my baby, but I don't have the health plan. Especially teen mothers need to have a regular doctor that's near their house, because what if something happens to the baby?

– Tamika, age 16
SELF-DESCRIPTION: "understanding, outspoken, quiet at times"

GIRLS' ACCESS TO HEALTH CARE

In order for girls to experience optimum health, they must have access to quality, affordable, and confidential health care. Beyond discouraging unhealthy practices and encouraging girls to engage in behaviors and activities that support their health, adults need to ensure that girls can see health care providers and mental health professionals for both preventive care and treatment of health problems. Unfortunately, many girls (and boys) have difficulty obtaining such health care. Indeed, a national survey by Louis Harris and Associates for the Commonwealth Fund (1997) found that 29 percent of high school girls and 23 percent of high school boys surveyed reported at least one instance when they were unable to get needed care. Among the girls surveyed, Asian American girls were most likely to lack a regular source of health care (26 percent), followed by black girls (21 percent), Hispanic girls (20 percent), and white girls (13 percent).

The Commonwealth Fund survey (1997) found that among girls who reported not getting needed care, the most frequently cited reason (41 percent) involved fears that they would have to tell parents that they had a prob-

that most adolescent girls felt their doctors should discuss such issues with them: 66 percent felt their doctors should talk about eating disorders; 65 percent said they should talk about sexually transmitted diseases; 65 percent said they should talk about taking drugs; 56 percent said they should talk about drinking alcohol; and 50 percent said they should talk about physical or sexual abuse. Unfortunately, a far smaller percentage of girls surveyed said their doctor had actually spoken with them about these issues: 24 percent reported that their doctor had discussed eating disorders; 28 percent had discussed sexually transmitted diseases; 28 percent had discussed taking drugs; 23 percent had discussed drinking alcohol; and only 10 percent had talked about abuse (The Commonwealth Fund, 1997). These findings speak loudly to the need for health care professionals to open up discussion of important issues with adolescents, rather than waiting for girls to mention these topics. Given girls' desire to talk about such issues, along with their fre-

---

What I don't like is that doctors always think they know more than you about what you're feeling. They don't really listen, not at all. I know my body really well, and I know when there's something wrong and where there's something wrong, and what it feels like, but he don't want to listen. I think girls, especially teen girls, need somebody who will listen to us and take us seriously, because, you know, it's kind of hard enough to talk about your body's private things, without having somebody be like, condescending or cutting you off, too.

– Latisha, age 18
SELF-DESCRIPTION: "African American teen mother, educated person"

---

lem. Concerns about confidentiality appear to be more pressing for girls than for boys. Whereas 41 percent of high school girls reported fearing telling their parents about a health problem, only 27 percent of high school boys gave this reason for not getting needed care. Further, 35 percent of girls reported an instance when they felt too embarrassed to discuss a health problem with a health care professional, compared to 21 percent of boys. Girls who reported experiencing abuse or symptoms of depression were more even more likely to report a situation where they were too embarrassed to discuss a health problem with a doctor (52 percent of abused girls, and 51 percent of girls with symptoms of depression).

Interestingly, despite their potential embarrassment, girls do express an interest in talking with doctors about "sensitive topics." The Commonwealth Fund survey found

quent embarrassment about doing so, physicians and other health care providers must take the lead by creating safe and respectful contexts for discussion, and by bringing up these issues in their interactions with adolescents.

Economic issues are central to adolescents' likelihood of receiving health care. Among high school students in the Commonwealth Fund survey who did not receive needed health care, 36 percent of girls and 30 percent of boys pointed to lack of insurance as the reason for not receiving care (1997). Of those girls who knew whether or not they had insurance, 44 percent of uninsured girls (compared with 25 percent of insured girls) said they had experienced a time when they did not get care they needed. Girls without insurance were more than two times as likely as girls who had insurance (29 percent versus 12 percent) to report that they did not have a regular source of health care. Lack of transportation was cited as a reason for not obtaining needed care by 11 percent of high school girls and 6 percent of high school boys.

Through organizations such as Planned Parenthood, as well as through local clinics, adolescents can receive quality, confidential, and affordable health care. According to *The Commonwealth Fund Survey of the Health of Adolescent Girls*, girls were especially embarrassed about discussing sexuality, menstruation, body changes, contraception and pregnancy, physical and sexual abuse, and STDs with their doctors (1997). In addition to more generalized health care, girls are in particular need of health care professionals and agencies who bring a sensitive and respectful approach to adolescents' gynecological needs. These organizations and health care providers can help girls to develop positive feelings about their bodies, to foster a sense of entitlement to their own well-being, and to become active, informed participants in their health care.

CONCLUSION

Although health educators and advocates appropriately point out that health issues involve more than an understanding of risks and disease, the findings discussed above reveal many disturbing trends in girls' health and health behaviors. Overall, rates of smoking, alcohol and drug abuse, and use of diet pills and laxatives for weight loss are high among adolescent girls. Girls are far more likely to experience eating disorders and depression than are boys. They report contemplating and attempting suicide more frequently than their male peers—although boys are more likely to die from their suicide attempts. While condom use is increasing among adolescents, only 54 percent of high school seniors reported using a condom during their last sexual encounter in 1995. And while girls' participation in sports and exercise has increased since the passage of Title IX in 1972, it still lags behind that of boys.

At the same time, important variations exist in the health behaviors of girls across different ethnic backgrounds. For instance, while girls' overall rate of smoking is high, African American girls are much less likely to smoke than are girls of other races or their African American male peers. African American adolescents are also less likely to experience eating disorders than other girls, and they are much more likely to report positive feelings about their bodies' appearance and capabilities than are white girls. However, they are as likely as their white peers to experience binge eating disorder (bingeing without purging). And non-Hispanic white girls were more likely than Hispanic girls or black, non-Hispanic girls to have exercised regularly in 1995.

Access to quality health care is a serious issue among adolescent girls. In a 1997 study, girls who reported an instance when they were unable to obtain needed health care attributed their lack of care to concerns about confidentiality, embarrassment over talking about "sensitive topics," and lack of health insurance. Girls cited embarrassment about talking with doctors more frequently than did boys as a reason for not obtaining needed care, and girls who experienced abuse or depressive symptoms were more likely to have had an instance of not receiving needed care. Girls who lacked health insurance were more than twice as likely as insured girls to lack a regular health care provider. Asian American girls were most likely to be without a regular source of health care, followed by black girls, Hispanic girls, and white girls.

While adolescence is a potentially healthy time for girls, adults need to help girls critique and resist societal pressures that promote excessive thinness; alcohol, tobacco, and other drug abuse; and unsafe sex practices. Girls need to learn to respect their bodies; develop healthy self-concepts; find quality, affordable, and confidential health care; create safe places to discuss depression and related issues (as well as things that are going well); and incorporate regular physical activity into their lives. Many of the current statistics are, indeed, discouraging. But such findings should compel concerned adults to redouble their efforts to enable girls to envision and strive for optimum health for both body and mind.

• The leading causes of premature death among women–including cancer, heart disease, and AIDS–are associated with behaviors begun during adolescence. (Ms. Foundation, 1994; Costello and Krimgold, 1997).

• Girls and women account for 90 percent of all cases of eating disorders (National Institute of Mental Health, 1993). Eating disorders have the highest mortality rate (10 percent) among all types of psychiatric disorders (National Institute of Mental Health, 1993). Girls 7-17 years old are now the heaviest users of diet pills (Schupak-Nauberg and Nemeroff, 1993).

• Overall, smoking is on the rise for girls. However, black girls are much less likely to smoke than girls of other races; white girls are more likely to use cigarettes than girls of any other racial group (Johnston, O'Malley, and Bachman, 1996). In 1991, 13 percent of eighth grade girls reported smoking, or more than one in eight. In 1996, the number jumped to 21 percent, or more than one in five (University of Michigan 1996, cited in Girls Incorporated, 1997b). Smoking initiation among girls is strongly associated with weight concerns and dieting (French, et al., 1994; 1995).

• Fifty-five percent of 13- to 19-year-old young women diagnosed with AIDS as of 1996 contracted HIV through heterosexual contact (compared to only 3 percent of diagnosed young men in that age group); 40 percent of those young women became infected by partners who reported using IV drugs (Centers for Disease Control and Prevention, 1997). Fifteen percent of young women aged 13-19 who were diagnosed with AIDS through 1996 were infected through use of shared needles with other drug users (Centers for Disease Control and Prevention, 1997).

• Girls who drink more than five times per month have been found to be one-third less likely to use condoms during sex than girls who do not drink (National Center on Addiction and Substance Abuse, 1996).

• Girls are twice as likely as boys to experience depression during adolescence. Girls are also more likely than boys to consider and attempt suicide. Thirty percent of adolescent girls report having thought seriously about suicide (compared to 18 percent of male youth) and 12 percent of girls attempted suicide in 1995 (Kann, et al., 1996). Boys, however, are more likely to die from their suicide attempts.

• Participation in sports is linked with decreased incidence of depression, pregnancy, and smoking initiation among teenage girls (President's Council, 1997; Girls Incorporated, 1997c). However, the percentage of high school sophomore girls who participated on sports teams fell from 46 percent in 1980 to 41 percent in 1990, while the percentage of sophomore boys participating remained constant at 63 percent (National Center for Education Statistics, 1993).

• Many girls lack access to health care when they need it. One study found that uninsured girls were more than twice as likely as girls with insurance to report not getting needed health care. Girls were more likely than boys to attribute lack of needed care to fears about telling parents of a problem and to embarrassment about talking to a doctor about sensitive subjects. Asian American girls were least likely to have a regular source of health care, followed by black girls, Hispanic girls, and white girls (The Commonwealth Fund, 1997).

HOLISTIC APPROACH TO HEALTH. Following the lead of progressive health educators around the country, research, policy discussions, and programs promoting health should embrace the psychological and sociopolitical needs of young women, as well as the needs of their bodies. While specific health concerns such as smoking, sexually transmitted diseases, substance abuse, and eating disorders certainly require individual attention, these should be understood as interrelated parts of an integrated whole, rather than as discrete symptoms of risk or illness.

EMPOWERING PROGRAMS. Health education programs should help empower girls and young women to make choices which they deem healthy and appropriate for their own lives. Scare tactics and punitive approaches are neither effective nor conducive to developing girls' healthy sense of entitlement, and positive feelings about their bodies. These approaches should be replaced with encouragement for girls to probe the dangers and benefits of various practices, and to explore the personal, social, and political realities which hinder healthy behaviors. To make this positive approach work, health educators and girls themselves need full information, as well as resources and options to make healthy decisions.

OPPORTUNITIES AND TOOLS FOR CRITIQUE. Girls need to have contexts and opportunities to critique the cultural images and practices that hurt them. Girls who see constant images that equate female attractiveness and maturity with extreme slenderness, dieting, smoking, and unsafe sex practices will benefit from finding their own critical voices. Adults can also help both boys and girls to question sexist ideologies which encourage young women to defer to boys and men in their sexual encounters, and which may discourage them from insisting on condom use and other safer sex practices. Programs such as the media literacy program sponsored by the Henry J. Kaiser Family Foundation may help girls to critique such potentially harmful cultural images and messages.[12]

EXPANDED ATHLETIC OPPORTUNITIES. Since exercise and participation in sports have been associated with a healthier body image; decreased incidence of depression, pregnancy, and smoking in girls; and decreased chances of heart disease and cancer in later life; it is important that girls' athletic programs be provided in all schools and communities across the country. Just as important is the provision of avenues for girls who are not traditionally considered athletes to become involved in regular exercise, sports activities, and health-oriented leisure pursuits. Particular attention should be given to providing full access to girls who may not have the financial means to join health facilities or purchase sporting equipment. Institutions can help by hiring more female coaches for all-boys, all-girls, and mixed-sex teams; increasing funding, equipment, and playing time for girls; insisting that coaches of both sexes model respectful behavior towards females; and enthusiastically publicizing girls' sports activities.

SUPPORTIVE PUBLIC POLICY. The increase in girls' sports participation immediately following the 1972 passage of Title IX suggests that supportive public policy can break down barriers, and bring about changes that may enhance girls' health. Concerned adults should support programs that educate youth about the risks associated with the use of alcohol, tobacco, and other drugs, and that ensure that youth have access to information on HIV/AIDS prevention in the context of comprehensive sexuality education. Policymakers should work to ensure that all adolescents (and adults) receive needed health care and insurance by supporting agencies that provide quality, affordable, accessible, and confidential care.

INCREASED FUNDING AND ACTIVISM. Increased funding and activism are needed to challenge the tobacco and weight-loss industries' targeting of young girls, the restriction of adolescents' access to safer sex information, and the lack of opportunities for, and attention to, girls in sports and physical education programs. Continued funding is also needed for clinics and advocacy programs so that girls (and boys) have access to affordable mental health services, pregnancy and STD prevention services and materials, health information, and routine preventive health care.

CHAPTER THREE

Sexuality

A DOLESCENCE IS A TIME not only of physical and cognitive changes, but also of awakening desires, intimate relationships, exploration of sexual identities, and changes in girls' understanding of themselves as sexualized individuals. Girls may be thinking about and experiencing their bodies and relationships in new ways. Often, these changes are exciting and empowering, representing an emergence into new realms of maturity and intense emotions. Yet these changes may also be accompanied by confusion, anxiety, and a need to deal with unwanted or unintended consequences of girls' own and/or others' behavior. Whether girls experience their sexuality as healthy and welcome or as dangerous, shameful, and alienating may depend upon the messages they receive about female sexuality and their own entitlement to pleasure and intimacy. Girls' understandings and feelings about their sexuality are shaped not only by gender, but also by diverse cultural norms, their families' and communities' values, and societal attitudes toward sexuality and sexual identity.

Adolescent girls' sexuality encompasses a wide range of topics. Among the issues informing girls' overall sexual well-being are pregnancy and reproductive rights; sexual identity; HIV/AIDS and other STDs; sexual abuse; sexuality education; and access to information and resources. While this report addresses each of these topics individually, this chapter focuses on sexual identities and portrayals of girls' sexual activity, pregnancy and reproductive decisions, and girls' access to information and resources. Readers will note that sexual abuse, sexuality education, and HIV/AIDS and other STDs are elaborated in other chapters (violence, schooling and health, respectively).

SEXUAL IDENTITY AND PORTRAYALS OF GIRLS' SEXUAL ACTIVITY

In discussions of adolescents "at risk," attention often turns quickly to questions of girls' sexuality. For two decades, national data indicated a steady increase in the percentage of girls aged 15 to 19 who have had intercourse, from 29 percent in 1970 to 36 percent in 1975, 47 percent in 1982, 53 percent in 1988, and 55 percent in 1990. However, the percentage of females aged 15-19 who reported having ever had intercourse recently took its first downturn— from 55 percent in 1990 to 50 percent in 1995 (Abma, et al., 1997). A 1995 survey indicated that 49 percent of non-Hispanic white girls, 53 percent of Hispanic girls, and 67 percent of black girls aged 15-19 reported ever having had sexual intercourse (Centers for Disease Control and Prevention, 1996). Those reporting having had intercourse before age 15 in 1992 were 26 percent of non-Hispanic white girls, 25 percent of Hispanic girls, and 39 percent black girls (Centers for Disease Control and Prevention, 1995). In 1995, five percent of female students and 13 percent of male students in the U.S. reported initiating sexual intercourse before age 13 (Centers for Disease Control and Prevention, 1996). These numbers are cause for concern, because research has shown that girls who have earlier sexual intercourse face greater risk: earlier sexual intercourse tends to mean more sex partners, which has been associated with increased risk for sexual victimization, unplanned and/or unwanted pregnancies, HIV/AIDS, and other STDs (Mosher and Aral, 1991).

While debates about adolescent girls' sexuality raise legitimate concerns about the health risks associated with adolescent sexual intercourse, they have been laden with many problematic assumptions. Considerable data has been collected on girls' "sexual activity"—including age of first intercourse, numbers and ages of partners, use or non-use of contraception—and correlation between these activities and incidence of STDs and unplanned pregnancies. However, the very notion of "sexual activity" has been left virtually unchallenged in the mainstream literature. In both government

---

Girls who are sexually active, especially if they don't hide it, they're seen as cheap or easy. Guys be like, you know, "I'm gonna see what I can get. You done her? Yeah, I done her, too." And adults look down on you when you're a sexually active teen, like they never did it when they were young too, right?

– Natasha, age 16

SELF-DESCRIPTION: "Jamaican American, heterosexual, young girl"

---

and academic research, sexual activity is typically defined as heterosexual intercourse. Largely absent are data on the wide range of girls' sexual experiences with self or other girls, or non-coital experiences with males. For instance, while the 1996 annual report of the U.S. Department of Health and Human Services offers extensive statistics on the incidence of girls' heterosexual intercourse at various ages, it makes no mention of sex with other girls or women, masturbation, or sexual activity other than intercourse with males.

The absence of such information, and the uncritical use of such terms as "sexually active," are problematic in several, interrelated ways, because they:

- marginalize lesbian and bisexual girls and overlook autoeroticism by equating sexuality with heterosexuality and sexual activity with male/female intercourse;
- frame sexuality as an event, rather than as a fluid and multidimensional part of girls' identities;
- dichotomize "sexual activity" and "virginity," suggesting that girls not engaged in heterosexual intercourse are asexual;
- reproduce sexist and heterosexist notions that girls' and women's sexual lives do not begin until the moment of vaginal/penile penetration; and
- may discourage adolescents from practicing safer sex through masturbation and non-intercourse sexuality with partners because these are not thought to count as "real sex."

A related problem involves the judgment often placed

on the sexuality of adolescent girls (Tolman, 1996; Tolman and Higgins, 1996). Although correlation between early sexual intercourse and experiences of unintended pregnancy, STDs, and sexual abuse are certainly cause for concern, research and popular discussions too often assume that adolescent girls' sexual expression itself is necessarily problematic. Debates about girls' sexuality typically focus on danger, disease, and pregnancy, giving little or no consideration to potentially healthy aspects of girls' sexual experiences and ignoring adolescent girls' desire and entitlement to sexual pleasure (Fine, 1988).

It is important, then, for concerned adults to examine critically the popular assumption that girls' sexual expression is inherently negative. Rather than simply trying to curtail adolescent girls' sexual activity, the discussion should turn to the question of how lack of access to condoms, other contraceptives, information, and abortion services; sexist ideologies; and cultural tolerance of male sexual violence and exploitation collude to put girls at risk for unwanted outcomes of their sexual behavior. Individual girls and/or their families may have moral objections to various expressions of girls' sexuality. But researchers, educators, activists, and advocates who want to support girls' sexual health cannot afford to base their work on unquestioned, moralistic assumptions.

Popular discussions of girls' sexuality often reveal a pervasive "good girl/bad girl" or "victim/villain" dichotomy, not unlike the "madonna/whore" dichotomy long underlying portrayals of adult women's sexuality. Within this framework, "good girls" are often cast as those who resist the advances of boys and men, acting as gatekeepers for male sexual behavior, controlling not only themselves but the males around them (Phillips, forthcoming; Tolman and Higgins, 1996). Girls who have heterosexual intercourse are typically treated in one of two ways: portrayed as passive recipients of male sexual behavior, victims of boys or men, who are presumed to be the only sexual initiators; or vilified in media, popular discussion, and sex education classrooms as "wild," "loose," or "lacking self-respect" (Phillips, 1997). Girls who express their sexuality and are later sexually victimized are, like adult women, often held responsible for their own abuse, with suggestions that they somehow "asked for it" simply because they are sexual.

Important recent work counters oversimplified images

of girls' sexuality in mainstream research and public debates. Several books and studies explore the complexities of girls' sexual decision-making, desire, and sense of entitlement to sexual pleasure. Beginning with the assumption that the sexuality of girls is fluid and multidimensional, research by Tolman (1996), Tolman and Higgins (1996), Phillips (1996), Thompson (1995), and Fine and McPherson (1995) finds that girls' sexuality is indeed far more complex than statistics on age of first intercourse or number of partners reveal. One five-year study launched in 1995 under the direction of Deborah Tolman at the Wellesley Center for Research on Women explores whether and how internalized beliefs about the value of traditional "femininity" relate to female adolescents' risk of unintended pregnancy.

In another study, Postrado, Weiss, and Nicholson (1996) have found several compelling predictors of early adolescent girls' initiation of sexual intercourse. As part of the Girls Incorporated Preventing Adolescent Pregnancy Program, the researchers administered a series of annual surveys to 267 girls aged 12-14 who participated over a three year period. Designed to predict factors influencing girls' initiation of sexual intercourse as young teens, the surveys included questions about girls' racial identification, age, attitudes toward pregnancy, educational expectations, participation in a pregnancy prevention program, "sexual bravado," involvement with a steady boyfriend, and mothers' educational levels. The researchers found that having a steady boyfriend was a strong predictor of initiating sexual intercourse; that "sexual bravado" was a weaker, but still significant predictor; and that positive feelings about pregnancy were correlated with having a steady boyfriend, which was, in turn, related to an increased likelihood of initiating intercourse. Factors associated with a lower likelihood of initiating sexual intercourse included higher educational aspirations and longer participation in one of the programs ("Will Power/Won't Power") offered by Girls Incorporated's Preventing Adolescent Pregnancy Program.

Sharon Thompson's 1995 book, *Going All the Way: Teenage Girls' Tales of Sex, Romance, and Pregnancy,* describes girls' thoughts and feelings about pregnancy, their relationships, and their sexual experiences. Based on inter-

views with 400 racially and socially diverse girls, Thompson places girls' narratives in a broader sociopolitical and historical context. In her interviews with girls with heterosexual experience, she finds, "[i]n general, the more a teenage girl viewed the elements of sex, reproduction, and love as fused and expected them to generate the central meaning of her life, the less likely she was to use protection or contraception and the greater likelihood of...a loss of strength, possibility, and confidence" (1995: 284). In contrast, girls who anticipated pleasure but were also able to balance their desire for love with other concerns were more likely to see the importance of protection and contraception and to develop "social and erotic insight." Ironically, given adults' encouragement for adolescents to delay sexual intercourse until they are in love (if not married), being in love was the most powerful force influencing girls to endanger themselves both sexually and emotionally.

Thompson's interviews with lesbian youth elicited their reflections on both the personal pleasures of sexual desire and relationships with other girls, and the difficulties that often arise when "coming out" to others. Many participants reported knowing that they were lesbians from a young age and feeling that "[i]t wasn't a problem. It was an identity, a source of pleasure and love, fantasy, and hope" (1995: 179). Yet others struggled with the realization of their desires for other girls, and many experienced the pains

---

I am an 18-year-old lesbian. I do not hide what I am. In fact, I am very open about my sexuality. A lot of people put me down— basically men— and when they find out that I am gay, it just gets worse. I wish that the gay community would have more support from society. Things are hard enough out in the world. The last thing we need is people putting people down just because they happen to like the same sex. Life is hard, and it is especially hard when you are a young woman and gay.

– Laura, age 18
SELF-DESCRIPTION: "Latina lesbian"

---

of homophobic reactions from friends, families, and schools. Thompson's work reveals a range of outcomes, from happily-ever-after relationships to isolation and personal difficulty, depending largely on the extent to which others offered support for the feelings and relationships of these young lesbians.

Margaret Schneider's (1997) interviews with 25 lesbian adolescents reveal similar variations in the coming out process. In their interviews, girls spoke of the intertwined processes of developing their identities as lesbians and as adolescents. Schneider found that the evolution of a "positive lesbian identity" depends on finding both external support systems and personal resources. While some girls were able to resist the homophobic attitudes that surrounded them and to maintain positive feelings about themselves and their relationships throughout their adolescence, others reported painful experiences of rejection or isolation. Many described a sense of strength cultivated through their struggles to come out and through their identification with other girls and women. Echoed throughout the interviews was a strong desire to find ways to interact with other young lesbians, rather than having to rely on adult spaces (such as adult lesbian sports teams or "the bar scene"), so that they could develop peer friendships and form intimate relationships with other lesbians their age.

PREGNANCY AND REPRODUCTIVE DECISIONS

Adults who debate adolescent girls' health and sexuality frequently cite pregnancy and teen parenting as primary concerns. Indeed, while recent statistics on rates of teen pregnancy, birth, and contraceptive use indicate some positive trends, overall teen pregnancy and birth rates remain cause for serious concern. Although public health campaigns have helped encourage the use of condoms and spread awareness of the causes of both STDs and pregnancy, an alarmingly high number of teens who have heterosexual intercourse still fail to use any form contraception (U.S. Department of Health and Human Services, 1997; Kaiser, 1996). And although teen pregnancy rates and teen birth rates have shown declines since 1992 (Child Trends, Inc., 1997), the U.S. teen birth rate still ranges from two to seven times higher than that of most comparable industrialized nations (Alan Guttmacher Institute, 1994).

Studies of rates of teen pregnancy, teen births, and adolescents' contraception use has illuminated the following findings and trends:

- Approximately 10 percent of all U.S. girls aged 15-19 became pregnant in 1990 (Centers for Disease Control and Prevention, 1995a).
- Recent research suggests that between 65 percent (U.S. Department of Health and Human Services, 1997) and 86 percent (Alan Guttmacher Institute, 1994) of births to teenagers were unintended when they were conceived.
- Only 24 percent of teens having intercourse report using birth control "most of the time" when they have sex, 15 percent say "only sometimes," and 11 percent say

"never" (Henry J. Kaiser Family Foundation, 1996).
- In 1995, only 54 percent of high school students having intercourse reported using a condom at last sexual intercourse. Seventeen percent reported that they or their partners used birth control pills (Centers for Disease Control and Prevention, 1996).

Concern with the high rates of teen pregnancy and birth is warranted for several reasons. According to data provided by Child Trends, Inc. (1996), among young women who gave birth during high school, the majority (62 percent) dropped out at some point, either before pregnancy (25 percent) or after giving birth (37 percent). The data show that Hispanic teenagers who are pregnant or who give birth are more likely to drop out (71 percent) than white teens (64 percent) or black teens (54 percent). Teen mothers are also less likely to go on to college than are women who delay pregnancy past adolescence (Alan Guttmacher Institute, 1994). Further, despite public concern about "out-of-wedlock" births, Michelle Fine finds in her 1991 book, *Framing Dropouts,* that pregnant girls who marry are more likely to drop out of school, to live in poverty, and to have a second child within two years than are their peers who do not respond to pregnancy or parenthood by getting married.

Early pregnancy raises economic challenges for many adolescent girls. Twenty-eight percent of teen mothers live in poverty during their 20s and 30s, compared to seven percent who give birth after adolescence; however, some of this difference is attributable to teen mothers' greater likelihood of coming from "disadvantaged backgrounds" (Alan Guttmacher Institute, 1994). In addition to the economic difficulties pregnant and parenting teens already face, the new welfare reform law (discussed further in Chapter 6) directly affects adolescent mothers, restricting the conditions under which they may receive welfare benefits, and denying increased aid to provide for teen mothers' subsequent children. Based on unsubstantiated claims that cutting benefits will decrease "incentives" for adolescent girls to become pregnant, this law endangers the health and economic well-being of girls and their families (Seavey, 1996).

The high rates of teen pregnancy and births raise concerns not only for adolescent girls, but also for their children. Babies born to adolescent mothers face significant challenges, according to several research studies initiated by the Robin Hood Foundation and reported by Child Trends, Inc. (1996). According to Child Trends, compared with children born to mothers who are 20 to 21, children born to mothers who are 17 or younger tend to have lower cognitive scores and greater difficulty in school; to have more health problems (yet to receive less health care); to receive less stimulation and support in their home environments; to have higher incarceration rates; and to have higher rates of teen births themselves. These patterns remain consistent even when researchers compensate for background differences that distinguish teen girls who become parents (Child Trends, Inc. 1996).

Each year, approximately half of all teen pregnancies end in birth. Fourteen percent end in miscarriage, and approximately 35 percent end in abortion (Alan Guttmacher Institute, 1994). In the late 1980s and early 1990s, the number of abortions, the abortion rate, and the proportion of pregnancies ending in abortion all declined among teens. Comparable declines in abortion did not occur among older women (Child Trends, Inc., 1996). Fluctuations in abortion rates may reflect the changing legislation and funding climate over the last decade, as well as the importance of economic issues in the decision or ability to have an abortion.

The following findings demonstrate both the rates of abortions among adolescents and the limited availability of abortion services:

- Abortion service providers were available in only 16 percent of U.S. counties as of 1992, and 94 percent of counties in nonmetropolitan areas offered no abortion services (Henshaw and Van Vort, 1994).
- Approximately twenty-five percent of all abortions in the United States are performed on adolescent girls (Alan Guttmacher Institute, 1994).
- The abortion rate among 15- to 19-year-old girls having intercourse decreased by 24 percent between 1980 and 1990, due in part to restricted access and funding of abortion services for adolescents (Males, 1993).
- Approximately 75 percent of girls from higher income families terminate their unintended pregnancies in abortion (Alan Guttmacher Institute, 1994).
- Fewer than half of girls from poor or low-income families terminate unintended pregnancies in abortion (Alan Guttmacher Institute, 1994).

Changes in the availability of federal funding for abortion services predictably increase the discrepancy in abortion rates among girls from different class backgrounds. Differing access to health care, often a function of econom-

ics, may also impact on how early pregnancies are detected. Thus, girls who can afford abortion services and who have access to early pregnancy testing may be more likely to terminate their unintended pregnancies in abortion. These trends, as with other factors concerning adolescent sexuality and self-reported behavior, are difficult to track since many teens and women are reluctant to divulge information concerning their sexual histories, especially relating to abortion.

According to Sharon Thompson (1995), changes in the teen birth and pregnancy rates are not simply attributable

---

Someday I'd like to have kids. But not yet, not now. I've got too much I want to do with my life, and from what I see, having kids as a teenager weighs you down. There's a lot of pressure though, to have sex with your boyfriend, and girls who have babies, everybody's like, "oh that's so cute, oh, she's so lucky." It is like a status symbol for a lot of people, but my cousin has a baby and she can't go anywhere, she can't do anything. I want to wait, but it is hard, you know? It is hard.

— Cecilia, age 16
SELF-DESCRIPTION: "black, urban female"

---

to the increasing rate and decreasing age at which teen girls have intercourse. Rather, Thompson argues that the rise in teen pregnancies and births in the late 1980s reflects complex social and historical changes in legislation, economics, and gender and family expectations. Based on a detailed review of policy and social changes, and pregnancy rates and birth rates, she concludes that factors that tend to increase the teen pregnancy rate include restricted availability and economic barriers to contraception and abortion services; inadequate sexuality education; anti-abortion rhetoric; and a valorizing of maternity. Not only may these factors help to increase the rate of pregnancies; they may also increase the number of those pregnancies resulting in births.

In recent years, considerable debate has centered on the extent to which teen births are the result of adolescent girls' sexual relationships with older men. Some researchers have concluded that the majority of children born to teen girls are fathered by adults. For instance, in their analysis of California birth records, Males and Chew (1996) conclude that 65.5 percent of those children born to "school-age mothers" (age 18 and younger) in 1993 were fathered by "post-school-age" men, averaging four years older than their teen partners.[13] Similarly, according to Landry and

Forrest's (1995) analysis of National Maternal and Infant Health Survey (NMIHS) data on 9,953 15- to 49-year-old mothers who had a live birth in 1988, half of the infants born to girls aged 15-17 were fathered by men who were at least twenty years old. Fathers of children born to 15- to 17-year-old girls were, on average, four years older than their partners. Both the Males and Chew study and the Landry and Forrest study found that the younger the age of the mother, the larger the gap between her age and that of her partner.

However, other researchers suggest that these studies overstate the extent of the phenomenon. For instance, Ooms (1997) notes that the majority of teen births involve 18- to 19-year-old girls, whose adult partners are just a year or two older. Lindberg and her colleagues at the Population Studies Center of the Urban Institute re-analyzed the same data set used by Landry and Forrest (1995), but dropped from their analysis girls who were aged 18-19, those who were married, and those whose partners were less than five years older, since the researchers considered these relationships to fit "squarely within societal norms" (1997: 61). Using these adjusted criteria, they found that only eight percent of these births involved older partners. Yet Males critiques this re-calculation, noting that by the criteria of Lindberg et al., even relationships between 15-year-old girls and 20-year-old men are considered unproblematic. Males also points out that by excluding 18- and 19-year-olds from their analysis, Lindberg and her colleagues apply a double standard to teen mothers and adult fathers, holding

collaboration with Planned Parenthood of Greater Northern New Jersey (PPGNNJ) to explore the dynamics and implications of adult-teen relationships for those involved, and for their families and communities. Based on open-ended interviews and focus groups with 127 racially and socially diverse male and female teens and adults, the study found that female participants with experience in adult-teen relationships often considered themselves less likely to suggest or insist on contraception use with adults than with teen partners.[15] They reported that they were more reluctant to risk compromising an adult partner's (as opposed to a peer's) sexual pleasure by using condoms; that they felt less need for contraception because they trusted that their partners would stand by them if they became pregnant; and/or that they felt too intimidated by an older partner to insist on contraceptive use. Some girls also reported being pressured by an adult partner to reverse a previous decision to terminate an unwanted pregnancy. In each of these cases, however, the adult male left during the pregnancy or shortly after the birth of a child. In many cases, girls reported cutting ties to school, families, or peers in order to please a jealous older partner, leaving themselves and their children particularly vulnerable when their partners left. Throughout the study, girls and women with experience in adult-teen relationships noted problems due to power differences involving age, gender, and access to resources.

In a recent study of 150 black and Hispanic girls aged 14-17, Miller, Clark, and Moore (1997) found that, on average, girls whose first partners were at least three years older reported significantly younger ages of first intercourse (13.8 years versus 14.6 years) than girls with peer-age first partners (partners ranging from one year younger to less than three years older). They also learned that girls with older first partners were significantly less likely than girls with peer-age first partners to have used a condom at first intercourse (63 percent versus 82 percent), at last intercourse (29 percent versus 44 percent), or in the six months prior to the study (44 percent versus 66 percent).

My boyfriend is a lot older than me, like he's 24 and I'm 15. He really makes all the decisions, and like, he says where we're going to go, what I can do and can't do, and stuff like that. I want to do things, like live life and have fun, but he doesn't want me to. He says he needs to protect me, and maybe he's right, because he's good to me, but it also keeps me from being with my friends.

– Debra, age 15
SELF-DESCRIPTION: "white, heterosexual teen"

---

teen girls responsible for 100 percent of the "behavior problem" of "teen pregnancy" but holding adult men responsible for only 8 percent of that total.[14]

In the midst of continued debate about the prevalence of teen pregnancies and births involving adult men, Phillips (1997) has recently completed a year-long study in

prior to the study (44 percent versus 66 percent).

Further, they discovered that girls with older first partners were over three times more likely ever to have been pregnant (38 percent versus 12 percent). The researchers suggest that first experiences of intercourse may be one important means by which older male partners influence or reinforce adolescent girls' later sexual risk-taking behavior. Therefore, they advocate intervention efforts that help adolescents to develop negotiation and communications skills geared toward interactions with older partners, since girls may have difficulty engaging in self-protecting behaviors in sexual encounters with more experienced partners.

In light of such findings, it is important to take seriously the potential negative consequences of adult-teen relationships, regardless of the percentage of teen births attributable to them. However, as Peggy Brick of PPGNNJ points out, public response must not focus solely on punishing men involved with adolescent girls.[16] Rather, concerned adults should focus on educational approaches that incorporate understandings of the complex meanings and power dynamics of relationships between adult men and teen girls. Toward that end, PPGNNJ is currently developing Unequal Partners, a pregnancy prevention curriculum designed to help teens explore the consequences of, and consider alternatives to, adult-teen relationships.

There are some promising trends today. Evidence suggests that teens are increasingly likely to use contraception, to practice "safer sex," and to delay pregnancy. For instance:

- Despite the rise in the teen birth rate that occurred in the late 1980s, the teen birth rate is now lower than it was in the 1950s and 1960s. (Child Trends, Inc., 1997).
- The teen birth rate, which increased by one-quarter between 1986 and 1991, began a slow but steady decline in 1992. Whereas 62.1 births occurred per thousand females aged 15-19 in 1991, that number decreased to 59.6 in 1993, and to 54.7 in 1996 (Child Trends, Inc., 1997).
- In 1993, the teen birth rate dropped slightly among non-Hispanic white and black teens, but stayed the same among Hispanic teens. The birth rate for Hispanic teens and black teens were similar: 107 births per 1000 Hispanic females aged 15-19, and 99 births per 1000 non-Hispanic black females. For non-Hispanic white females aged 15-19, the 1995 rate was 39 births per 1000 (Child Trends, Inc., 1997).
- The teen pregnancy rate also declined, after peaking in 1990 and 1991 at 115 pregnancies per 1000 females aged 15-19, to 111 per 1000 in 1992 (Child Trends, Inc., 1996).
- Although condom use among teens is still low, condom use at first intercourse has tripled in two decades, from 18 percent in the 1970s to 36 percent in the late 1980s and 54 percent in the 1990s (Abma, et al., 1997).
- Overall use of contraception is also increasing among teens: 76 percent of those who began having inter-course in the 1990s reported using contraception at first intercourse, up from 64 percent in the late 1980s (Abma, et al., 1997).
- Eighty-seven percent of female high school students, and 86 percent of male high school students, report being taught specifically about HIV/AIDS in school or at home (Kann, et al., 1996). Ninety percent of women aged 18 to 19 report receiving formal instruction on STDs, safer sex to prevent HIV, and how to say no to sex (Abma, et al., 1997).

Many of these numbers indicate a turnaround in the early 1990s, just as education and intervention programs on adolescent sexuality and HIV/AIDS gained momentum. In a 1995 survey sponsored by the Henry J. Kaiser Family Foundation, a majority (76 percent) of U.S. teens aged 12-18 years said the "average teen" has enough information about how girls get pregnant. However, nearly three out of five (58 percent) said that teens do not have enough information about how to use different kinds of birth control. Even among teens who had already had sexual intercourse, 36 percent said they personally needed more information about how to use birth control, and 30 percent said they needed more information about where to get it (Henry J. Kaiser Family Foundation, 1996). Thus, it seems that while most adolescents are getting some information on contraception, they may need that information to be clearer, more practical, and more personally relevant in order for it to be useful to them.

Campaigns to encourage the use of contraception have had some positive effect. But more efforts are clearly needed to reach younger girls, girls of color, and those who may lack financial and material resources to prevent unwanted pregnancies. All adolescents need to grasp the importance of using contraception correctly and consistently. Sullivan's (1990) study of the male role in teen pregnancy and parenting has found that adolescents' failure to use birth control stems from lack of knowledge, poor access to contraceptives, and a desire to avoid planning for sex. Sharon Thompson (1995) found that girls who confound sex, love, and reproduction are less likely than other girls to use contraception. These findings suggest a need not only for greater access to information and resources, but also increased education to help girls understand the importance of protecting themselves from unwanted/unplanned consequences.

ACCESS TO INFORMATION AND RESOURCES

At the same time that the incidence of HIV/AIDS is increasing among adolescents, and girls are condemned for their pregnancies, some parents, legislators, and policymakers are trying, often successfully, to restrict or deny access to information and resources that could help prevent STDs and unwanted/unplanned pregnancies. Further, adults who advocate for girls' sexual entitlement and safer sex are often attacked for their efforts on behalf of adolescents. Such backlash was seen in the misrepresentation and public outcry following former Surgeon General Joycelyn Elders' endorsement of responsible discussion between adults and teenagers about masturbation.

Although the passage of Title IX in 1972 ensured that pregnant and parenting girls could continue their educa-

---

My mother put me on the pill when she knew I was being sexually active, which was like a year ago. Every morning, I just take my little pill, and that way I know I won't get pregnant. Me and my boyfriend love each other, but we're both too young to be thinking about having a kid. Condoms is a different story. They're such a pain, and my boyfriend doesn't like them, and I don't really either. We try to use them, because there's other things besides just pregnancy. But it's hard to be consistent, because, well, it's just kind of hard.

– Kianna, age 16
SELF-DESCRIPTION: "a Latina girl who's sweet and kind"

---

tion in federally-funded schools, and the Adolescent Health Services and Pregnancy Prevention Act of 1978 made family planning and abortion counseling and referral available to adolescents, several other laws have seriously threatened girls' access to pregnancy prevention and abortion services (Thompson, 1995). For instance, the 1977 Hyde Amendment restricted federal abortion funding, and the 1981 Adolescent Family Life Act essentially prohibited funded institutions from offering contraceptive services and abortion referral. As a result, girls with low incomes are often unable to afford the rising cost of contraceptives or abortions. Further, as of 1994, 28 states had mandatory parental involvement laws requiring parental notification or consent for minors seeking abortions (Alan Guttmacher Institute, 1994), endangering the health of those who are unable to turn to parents for support in preventing or terminating pregnancies. Several states have implemented or are considering implementing mandatory 24-hour waiting periods before women of any age can have an abortion. Although abortion remains legal, the availability of abortion services is severely limited and has decreased by 31 percent between 1978 and 1992. Five states restrict or prohibit discussion of abortion in schools;

only Vermont and the District of Columbia require that sex education include the topic of abortion (NARAL Foundation, 1995).

Inadequate access to comprehensive sex education further limits the information and resources available to both teenage girls and boys. Only 23 states and the District of Columbia currently require schools to provide sexuality education, although 37 states and the District of Columbia do require that schools provide HIV/AIDS and other STD education (NARAL Foundation, 1997). In many schools, educators are prohibited from discussing sex, let alone abortion or contraception, further decreasing the likelihood that adolescents will find the support they need to prevent unwanted outcomes of their sexual encounters. Twenty-six states require abstinence instruction; only 14 of those states require that schools also provide information about contraception, pregnancy, and disease prevention (NARAL Foundation, 1997). Although President Clinton devoted 37 million dollars to pregnancy prevention programs in his 1997 budget, these programs must stress abstinence, rather than delving broadly and thoroughly into the various sexual decisions and realities of adolescents. (See Chapter 5 for further discussion of sexuality education.)

In addition to difficulties in obtaining information and resources to prevent unwanted outcomes from sexual encounters, girls face barriers to health care once they become pregnant. Although the percentage of young adolescent mothers receiving prenatal care in their first trimester rose from 31 percent in 1975 to 43 percent in 1992, far fewer girls under age 15 receive early prenatal health care than do adult women (Monthly Vital Statistics Report, 1976; 1994).

CONCLUSION

Although the sexuality of girls is diverse and multilayered, research on girls' "sexual activity" tends to focus narrowly on heterosexual intercourse. Further, studies and public debate about girls' sexuality often emphasize risks—such as unintended pregnancy, STDs, and victimization—overshadowing the positive aspects of girls' sexual feelings and experiences. Research on teen pregnancy rates, teen birth rates, and contraception use show some promising trends: adolescent pregnancy and birth rates have been declining since 1992, and condom use is increasing among adolescents. However, both pregnancy rates and birth rates remain two to seven times higher than in most comparable industrialized nations, and nearly half the adolescents who report having heterosexual intercourse do not use condoms regularly.

In addition, studies estimate that 65 percent to 86 percent of all teen pregnancies are unintended. Research on the percentage of teen births attributable to relationships with adult men has yielded widely discrepant findings, depending on how data from birth records are analyzed. Nonetheless, studies have found that girls who are involved with adult men may feel less able to practice safer sex, are more likely to have ever been pregnant, and are more likely to have first intercourse at younger ages than girls who are involved with peers.

Restrictions on sexuality education, policies preventing educators from discussing reproductive options or distributing condoms, laws requiring 24-hour waiting periods and parental notification/consent for girls seeking abortions, and laws limiting funding for abortions all restrain adolescents' access to abortion services, comprehensive sexuality education, and condoms and other forms of contraception. Although public discussion of safer sex practices has increased, and although 36 percent of adolescents who have had intercourse say they need more information about how to use contraception, and 30 percent say they need more information about where to obtain it, 26 states require abstinence-only instruction in sex education.

While many discussions of girls' sexuality focus on danger and disease, some recent research has highlighted the positive aspects and addressed the complexities of girls' diverse sexual experiences. Studies, for example, suggest that while homophobic attitudes and practices can make lesbian adolescents' coming out processes painful and difficult, lesbian girls can also develop strength and pride in their sexuality. A recent study of girls' thoughts about sex, romance, and pregnancy has found that those who fuse notions of love and sexuality are more likely to become pregnant as teenagers. Another study has found that girls' likelihood of pregnancy is related to a complex interaction of educational aspirations, attitudes about pregnancy and teen motherhood, steady relationships with males, "sexual bravado," and duration of participation in a pregnancy prevention program.

Such studies move past narrow portrayals of girls' sexual activity, and open up critical discussions of the nuances of girls' sexuality. Adults who wish to nurture girls' healthy sexual development need to understand that the sexuality of girls is complex, fluid, and diverse; research studies also need to reflect these understandings.

● While national data exist on age of first intercourse, little data are available on prevalence of other types of girls' sexual activities, including sexual experiences with other girls, experiences of pleasure with self, or non-intercourse-related sexual experiences with males.

● Of girls aged 15-19 in 1995, 53 percent of Hispanic girls, 49 percent of non-Hispanic white girls, and 67 percent of non-Hispanic black girls report having had sexual intercourse. Five percent of female students and 13 percent of male students reported having had intercourse before age 13 (Centers for Disease Control and Prevention, 1996).

● The teen birth rate has been declining slowly but steadily since 1992, after rising by one-quarter between 1986 and 1991 and peaking at 62.1 births per 1000 females aged 15-19. In 1995, there were 56.9 births in that category (Child Trends, Inc., 1996). However, the U.S. teen birth rate remains high, ranging from two to seven times higher than that of comparable industrialized Western nations (Moore, et al., 1996).

● Teens' use of contraception is increasing: 76 percent of those who began having intercourse in the 1990s reported using contraception at first intercourse, up from 64 percent in the late 1980s (U.S. Department of Health and Human Services, 1997). However, among teens who have already had sex, 36 percent say they need to know more about how to use birth control, and 30 percent say they need information about where to get it. Less than half (49 percent) say they "always" use contraception when they have intercourse (Henry J. Kaiser Family Foundation, 1996).

● An estimated 65 percent (U.S. Department of Health and Human Services, 1997) to 86 percent (Alan Guttmacher Institute, 1994) of all teen pregnancies are unintended.

● In 1991, the most recent year for which abortion data are available, U.S. teens had 858,000 pregnancies (not counting miscarriages), of which 326,000 ended in an abortion and 532,000 ended in a live birth. In the late 1980s and early 1990s, the number of abortions, the abortion rate, and the proportion of pregnancies ending in abortion all declined among teens, but not among older women (Child Trends, Inc., 1996).

● Approximately 25 percent of abortions in the United States are performed on adolescent girls. Girls of higher income are more likely to terminate their unintended pregnancies in abortion (75 percent) than are girls who are from poor or low-income families (less than 50 percent). Eighty-three percent of 15- to 19-year-old adolescents who gave birth in 1988 were from poor or low-income families (Alan Guttmacher Institute, 1994). Restrictions in funding and services may make abortion particularly inaccessible to teens from low-income families.

● As of 1992, abortion service providers were available in only 16 percent of counties in the U.S. In nonmetropolitan areas, only six percent of counties had abortion services. Between 1978 and 1992, the number of U.S. counties with an abortion service provider decreased by 31 percent (Henshaw and Van Vort, 1994).

● As of 1994, 28 states had mandatory parental involvement laws affecting minors who seek abortions. Of those minors who had abortions, 61 percent did so with the knowledge of at least one parent; 45 percent of parents are told of girls' abortions by their daughters. The vast majority of parents support their daughter's decision to terminate her pregnancy. (Alan Guttmacher Institute, 1994).

● According to analysis of California birth records, nearly two-thirds (65.5 percent) of children born to girls 18 and younger in 1993 were fathered by "post-school-age men," who averaged four years older than their teen partners (Males and Chew, 1996). But of births to 15- to 19-year-olds in 1988, only 8 percent were to unmarried minors with a partner five or more years older (Lindberg et al., 1997).[17] In one qualitative study, girls reported feeling less able to insist on contraceptive use with older partners than with peers. Girls in adult-teen relationships also often cut ties with peers, families, or school, leaving them with less support for themselves and their children when older partners left (Phillips, 1997).

MORE RESEARCH. In addition to quantitative information about frequency of sexual behaviors among adolescents, more qualitative research is needed to move beyond one-dimensional portrayals of girls' sexual experiences, and to provide deeper understandings of the complexities of lesbian, bisexual, and heterosexual girls. Researchers should focus on positive aspects of girls' sexual experiences, rather than emphasizing only the potential risks associated with adolescent sexual behavior. More studies are needed to understand conditions that foster girls' healthy sense of entitlement to their own bodies and diverse forms of sexual expression, as well as conditions that promote girls' abilities and/or willingness to protect themselves from negative consequences of sexual behaviors.

ATTENTION TO DIVERSITY. National surveys on incidence of "sexual activity" need to include information about more diverse groups of adolescents, including in particular Asian American and Native American teens, lesbian and bisexual girls, and teens with disabilities. These studies should also include information about the wide range of sexual practices beyond heterosexual intercourse. More information is also needed to understand how socioeconomic factors may impact on girls' sexual and reproductive options and decisions.

ACCESS TO REPRODUCTIVE INFORMATION, PRODUCTS, AND SERVICES. Both girls and boys need greater information, and confidential access to condoms and reliable forms of contraception. Girls need access to affordable, routine gynecological care, and information on all of their legal options for dealing with a pregnancy. Concerned adults should lobby against any laws or proposed legislation that threaten adolescents' access to confidential family planning, abortion, prenatal care, STD prevention/treatment services, and sexuality education programs.

ACCESS TO HEALTH CARE. Better access to quality medical care is needed to ensure the health of pregnant girls, teen mothers, and their children, regardless of income. Adolescents who carry their pregnancies to term must receive better prenatal and postnatal care. This means that all individuals must have quality, comprehensive health insurance, and that agencies that provide free or reduced-cost health services must be supported, well-funded, and well-advertised to adolescents.

CHANGES IN THE WELFARE REFORM LAW. Monitor the impact of provisions in the new welfare reform law that deny benefits to unmarried adolescent mothers who do not live at home, and that restrict teenage mothers already receiving aid from receiving increased benefits to care for another child. Monitor on the state level the impact of provisions where the safety of women and children is compromised. Although supporters of these provisions speak of reducing "incentives" for teen parenthood, no reliable evidence supports claims that reduced benefits decrease teen pregnancy rates (Seavey, 1996). Without such benefits, many adolescent mothers lack adequate resources to care for themselves and their children.

CHAPTER FOUR

Violence

EVEN AS GIRLS strive to maintain their hope and resilience, they face a staggering amount of violence in a variety of forms. Yet research and policy debates about violence and victimization often fail to consider girls' particular experiences, perspectives, and needs. While many girls endure sexual violence, battering, and harassment, violence against women is typically cast as a problem facing adults. And although three out of every four child victims/survivors of violence are girls (U.S. Bureau of Justice Statistics, 1996), violence against children is typically cast in gender-neutral terms.

Girls may experience victimization and survival differently than boys or adult women, and girls across diverse groups may have experiences that differ in important ways from one another. Further, girls' understandings of and responses to violence may be shaped by the interpretations and actions (or lack of action) of adults in their lives, as well as by messages offered in their surrounding cultures. This chapter considers the incidence of various forms of violence against girls and presents research findings on girls' experiences of victimization and survival. To broaden the picture, this section also considers recent findings regarding girls who are perpetrators of violence and other crimes.

GIRLS' EXPERIENCES OF VICTIMIZATION

At a time when an antifeminist backlash has fueled attacks on researchers' and activists' concerns with violence against women, it is perhaps more important than ever to sift through the controversies surrounding girls' and women's experiences of victimization. In the last decade, not only have the efforts of the feminist antiviolence movement frequently been misrepresented, but so have the voices of survivors themselves. Asserting that young women have been seduced by second-wave feminists into adopting a "victim mentality," several writers have suggested that women falsely accuse men of rape, harassment, and other forms of violence and that feminist claims of the incidence of these crimes have been grossly exaggerated.[18] However, in her critical examination of this backlash, anthropologist Peggy Sanday exposes how the "the

crusade against anti-rape feminism" (1996: 239) tends to condone, and thus perpetuate, male sexual aggression; ignore or belittle young women's experiences of victimization; and silence young women's critiques.

In contrast to claims that young women claim victimization where none exists, there is good reason to believe that girls and women dramatically underreport violence. In light of the victim-blaming attitudes that permeate the criminal justice system, the media, and popular discussion, it makes sense that many hesitate to report abuse to the police. Yet a staggering number of women are raped, battered, and harassed each year. For example, battering is currently the single largest cause of injury to women in the United States, accounting for more injuries to women than muggings, rapes, and automobile accidents combined (United Nations Human Development Report, 1995).

Recent findings suggest that girls and women not only underreport violence, but also resist naming their experiences of victimization, even to themselves. In an in-depth, qualitative study with adolescent and young women aged 18-22, Phillips (forthcoming) found that although 27 of the 30 participants interviewed had experienced encounters that fit legal definitions of rape, harassment, and/or battering, only one described her own experience as "victimization." While young women were quite willing to label other women's experiences as rape, harassment, or battering, they resisted such terms when reflecting upon their own adolescent experiences. Persuaded that "real" victimization must be much more severe than their own violent or coercive encounters, and struggling to preserve a sense of independent self in a culture that polarizes victimization and autonomy, these young women were willing to describe the pain of their experiences, but unwilling to use victim labels or to excuse themselves from responsibility for their own abuse. These findings suggest that, far from inventing or exaggerating claims of victimization, girls and young women appear very unlikely to claim victimization, even when, according to the law, it has occurred.

My uncle lives in the house next door, and he's like a child molester, I guess you could say. He used to make me do things when I was like, twelve and thirteen. I never felt like I could tell anybody, 'cause he's family and all. But then when he started going after my little sister, that's when I told my mom. She just said we should stay away from him and this and that, but we never told anybody else because we were afraid the whole family would get in trouble.

– Sara-Maria, age 17
SELF-DESCRIPTION: "Hispanic teen woman"

In her 1996 book, *A Woman Scorned: Acquaintance Rape on Trial*, Peggy Sanday takes on backlash writers who claim that women and girls are ambivalent about their sexual desires or that they accuse men of acquaintance rape when they have actually consented to sex. Sanday offers an extensive and critical examination of rape cases on college campuses, violence statistics, existing laws, and antifeminist rhetoric. Based on her research, she rejects the myth that acquaintance rape is overreported and supports an incorporation of the notion "no means no" into rape laws. Sanday stresses the high incidence of incest and rape among girls and its impact on their development, asking, "[w]hat kind of people might we be, what kind of society might we become if violence against women were reduced to a minimum and women found their own way into adulthood? Might not women be more confident, more self-assured, less frightened and lost; men more sensitive and compassionate?" (1996: 259).

The assertion that "no means no" has been helpful in feminist efforts to stress that nonconsensual sex, with or without physical violence, is rape. However, some feminists have questioned whether, despite its importance in raising public awareness of sexual violence, this slogan may unwittingly obscure the complexities of young women's decision-

making. Recent research with adolescent girls and young women has found that many have internalized society's confounding of female sexual expression and negative repercussions (Fine, et al., 1994; Phillips, forthcoming). Consequently, many girls report feeling an internalized pressure to say "no" when they actually do wish to express themselves sexually. Given the fear of escalated violence if they refuse to give in to male pressure, some girls report saying "yes" or falling silent when they want to say "no" (Phillips, 1996; Tolman and Higgins, 1996). These findings suggest that while "no means no" is useful as a legal guide, society must also look beyond such straightforward notions in order to understand this issue more fully.

SEXUAL AND PHYSICAL ABUSE

Girls face an alarming amount of violence, both inside and outside of their homes. In the Commonwealth Fund's recent survey of a nationally representative sample of 3,586 girls in fifth through twelfth grades, 21 percent of high school girls said they had been physically or sexually abused (1997).[19] Of those who said they had been abused, 53 percent said the abuse took place in their homes, 65 percent said the abuse had happened more than once, 57 percent said they had been abused by a family member, and 13 percent said the abuser was a family friend. Half of the girls surveyed who said they had been sexually abused said they had also experienced physical abuse. In addition, eight percent of high school girls said they had been forced by a boyfriend or a date to have sex against their will.

Sexual abuse, whether involving physical violence or coercion, is a widespread problem for girls. In far too many cases, girls' first sexual experience takes the form of victimization by adults or peers. Since sexual violence is typically underreported, it is difficult to know precisely how many girls are actually sexually victimized. However, even the numbers of reported cases are alarming: ·

- Current estimates suggest that between one in three and one in four girls are sexually victimized by the time they are 18 years old or in the twelfth grade (Finkelhor and Dziuba-Leatherman, 1994; Benson, 1990).
- According to a 1992 survey, 62 percent of all forcible rape cases occurred to victims/survivors who were under 17 years of age; 32 percent of victims of rape

were between 11 and 17 years old; 29 percent of victims were younger than 11 years old (National Victim Center, 1992).[20][21]

- In 1996, convicted rape and sexual assault offenders serving time in state prisons reported that two-thirds of their victims were under the age of 18. Fifty-eight percent said their victims were 12 and younger (U.S. Bureau of Justice Statistics, 1997).

In the vast majority of cases, girls are raped by someone they know. In a 1991 study, data from three states show that of female rape victims under 12 years old, 96 percent knew their attackers. While only 4 percent of assailants were strangers, 46 percent were family members (20 percent were the girls' fathers) and one-half were acquaintances or friends. Among 12- to 17-year-olds, 15 percent were raped by strangers, 20 percent by family members, and 65 percent by acquaintances or friends. Of those 18 and older, one-third were raped by a stranger, 12 percent by a family member, and 55 percent by an acquaintance or friend (U.S. Bureau of Justice Statistics, 1992). In other words, the younger the victim, the more likely she was assaulted by a family member. But for all age groups, rape results most frequently from assaults by friends or acquaintances.

The high incidence of girls who are raped by family members and acquaintances speaks to a need to reconceptualize commonly held notions of rape as an act committed by a stranger, and involving extreme physical violence. Whereas many parents and prevention programs focus on "stranger danger," the statistics cited above indicate that most girls are not helped by such an approach. In addition to encouraging girls to fear those who are least likely to victimize them (strangers), and to trust those who may pose the most potential for danger (family and acquaintances), the emphasis on "stranger danger" may have important repercussions later in life. For instance, in a 1994 study of 205 undergraduate women, Arnold Kahn, Virginia Mathie, and Cyndee Torgler found that acquaintance rape survivors whose preconceived notions about the circumstances of a typical or "real" rape involved violent force by a stranger were less likely to acknowledge their experiences as rape than those who understood that rape could involve acquaintances and/or little force. Clearly, both adolescents and adults must develop better understandings of the realities of rape in order to promote prevention, reporting, and recovery.

While sexual abuse of girls has been more thoroughly studied, physical violence in girls' dating relationships has only recently come to public attention. Although battering has traditionally been thought of as an adult women's problem, researchers have begun to investigate battering among teens. However, like adult women, girls often do not reveal the victimization they experience, whether out of love, shame, fear of retaliation, or fear of not being heard (Phillips, 1993). As a result, relatively little is known about their experiences, and estimates about the prevalence of girls' abuse in relationships are likely to be underestimated.

In addition, many girls and boys witness male violence against their mothers. Activists in the battered women's movement have made a persuasive case that witnessing abuse of mothers is, itself, a form of child abuse. Witnessing male violence may set the tone for boys to accept violence as normal, and for girls to see it as inevitable in their own relationships. The U.S. Department of Justice (1994) indicates that an average of 572,032 women in the United States experience violence by an intimate each year, and the number of reported domestic violence cases increased by approximately 117 percent between 1983 and 1991. It is not possible to tell whether the increase in reported cases represents an increase in the incidence of violence against women, an increase in women's tendency to report their victimization, or both. However, since violence against women so often goes unreported, estimates based on reported cases are likely to be quite conservative.

Girls' experiences of abuse may have other important health implications. For instance, the Commonwealth Fund's recent survey found that girls who reported that they had been sexually or physically abused were more than twice as likely as non-abused girls to report smoking (26 percent versus 10 percent), drinking (22 percent versus 12 percent), and using illegal drugs (30 percent versus 13 percent).[22] In addition, 32 percent of girls who had been abused reported bingeing and purging, compared to 12 percent of girls who had not been abused.

Even more disturbing, abused girls were less likely than their peers who had not been abused to receive health care when they needed it. Among high school girls who reported having been sexually or physically abused, 45 percent reported an instance when they did not receive needed health care, compared to 21 percent of the girls who said they had not been abused (The Commonwealth Fund, 1997). Although 50 percent of all high school girls in the Commonwealth Fund study felt that physicians should discuss physical or sexual abuse with them, only 10 percent reported that their doctor had ever actually discussed these topics. Further, 18 percent of abused girls said they had no one to turn to for support.

In light of this correlation between abuse and other high-risk behaviors, as well as abused girls' increased likelihood of not receiving needed care, adults should be particularly attentive to signs of abuse and reach out to girls (and boys) in need of support. Adults need to empower girls to come forward with reports of abuse. Health care providers cannot wait for girls to approach the issue of abuse with them; rather, they should initiate conversations in safe and respectful ways with the youth in their care. It is important for all youth to have access to sensitive, respectful, and confidential, and affordable physical and mental health care.

I didn't want to tell anybody what happened to me, because I was too ashamed and embarrassed that I let it happen. I figured everybody would be like, 'we told you so,' because nobody liked my boyfriend. But I loved him, and I never expected him to hit me or force things during, like, sex. I don't say I was a victim, because I want to think on some level that he did love me.

– Karan, age 18
SELF-DESCRIPTION: "white, heterosexual woman"

In addition to experiencing violence in their families and relationships, many girls report that they both witness and experience general forms of violence in their communities and schools. As Heather Johnston Nicholson, Research Director at Girls Incorporated, points out, studies conducted by 13 Girls Incorporated affiliates suggest that many girls are frustrated by peer violence and danger in their neighborhoods. In addition to violence resulting from sexism, girls are frequently exposed to violence fueled by other power imbalances—including cases where larger, older, and/or nondisabled youth bully smaller, younger children and/or children with disabilities. Such cases occur both within and across gender.[23] Many youth also experience verbal or physical abuse based on race, class, or sexual identity aside from, or in addition to, gender.

SEXUAL HARASSMENT

The realities of sexual harassment against girls are only recently coming to light in the popular literature. Like battering and rape, sexual harassment is often presumed to affect only adult women. Media treatment of sensationalized cases further blurs the realities of sexual harassment of girls. In fact, research in schools indicates that sexual harassment is widespread among adolescents and children (Linn, et al., 1992; Lee, et al., 1996; Stein, 1992; 1995;

Stein, Marshall, and Tropp, 1993). Adolescents are disproportionately the targets of sexual harassment, with more young women aged 16-19 reporting harassment than any other group (U.S. Merit Systems Protection Board, 1988). Results of the AAUW Educational Foundation's recent survey of sexual harassment, *Hostile Hallways,* indicate that 83 to 85 percent of girls experience sexual harassment in their schools (AAUW, 1993).

According to Stein (1992; 1995), harassment occurs while other people watch; it is indeed a public performance conducted primarily by boys toward girls (Stein, Marshall, and Tropp, 1993; Lee, et al., 1996). Peggy Orenstein picks up this point in her popular book, *SchoolGirls,* when she writes, "the behavior is less a statement about sexuality than an assertion of dominance" (1994: 116). Linn and her colleagues concur, stating, "[s]exual harassment is essentially about the abuse of power in relationships" (1992: 106). Indeed, as Orenstein notes, while boys' harassment of girls and same-sex peer harassment among boys are common, girls harass boys much less frequently; if harassment were simply a matter of sexual flirting or teasing, rather than power, such gender discrepancies would not exist.

Incorporating cultural power imbalances, sexual harassment by adolescents involves not only gendered power, but often includes racist, homophobic, and ableist dimensions, as well (Linn, et al., 1992). For instance, boys' harassment of other boys often involves sexist or homophobic insults to their manhood or sexuality, referring to targets with such terms as "girl," "sissy," "faggot," or "queer." Such behavior harms not only the boys who are targeted, but also the girls and gay males around them, as their identities are presumed inherent insults to "real" manhood. Further, as Harilyn Rousso notes, girls with disabilities may be particularly vulnerable to sexual harassment from peers, as well as to unwanted touching from school aides, van drivers, and other adults. Yet Rousso notes that girls and women with disabilities are often absent from discussions of sexual harassment, despite the fact that negative stereotypes make women and girls with disabilities frequent targets of verbal and physical abuse.[24]

While sexual harassment against adult women often (but not always) goes on behind closed doors, peer-to-peer harassment often occurs very openly in schools, despite the fact that it is illegal (Linn, et al., 1992; Stein, 1992; 1995). Although reports of peer-to-peer sexual harassment among middle school and high school students are increasing (Siegel, 1995), still few cases are filed, and even fewer are pursued (Linn, et al., 1992). Teachers and school officials often downplay the significance of sexual harassment among students, not only looking the other way, but standing by as girls are harassed in front of them in classrooms and school corridors (Stein, 1995). Often dismissed as adolescent pranks, rites of passage, or awkward attempts at sexual teasing, sexual harassment is seldom interrupted by the very adults who are in a position to advocate for respectful treatment of all students (Stein, 1992; 1995; AAUW, 1993; Orenstein, 1994; Pastor, McCormick, and Fine, 1996). Even when sexual harassment is addressed, intervention seldom occurs at an institutional level. As Jennifer Pastor, Jennifer McCormick, and Michelle Fine (1996) point out, even the most concerned teachers often deal with harassment, even by chronic offenders, privately and on a case-by-case basis. The result is that both girls and boys witness sexist, racist, and homophobic behavior being displayed publicly, in front of adults and peers, without repercussion.

By allowing harassment to thrive publicly and failing to address the problem on an institutional level, schools essentially collude in its expression, promoting a hostile environment which condones the wielding of gendered, racist, and heterosexist power. Boys are thus taught, by the silence of adults, that male domination is acceptable, perhaps even humorous, and not subject to consequences. Left to fend for themselves, girls (and boys) who are victims and witnesses of sexual harassment are more likely to lose trust, confidence, and enthusiasm for school (Stein, 1992).

Students and adults working to develop or improve school harassment policies can find helpful guidelines provided by the NCRW in the premier issue of its journal *IQ*, entitled, *Sexual Harassment. A Look at a Disturbing Trend Among Teens*. In that issue, NCRW suggested key elements of a good sexual harassment policy, adapted from the NOW Legal Defense and Education Fund Legal Resource Kit. Their recommendations include soliciting input from all school constituencies, including teachers, students, and staff; obtaining clear written statements from top district administrators that harassment will not be tolerated; defining clearly what behaviors are prohibited; explaining in detail how to file a complaint and what sanctions will be imposed for engaging in harassment; ensuring confidentiality for all involved; protecting students and teachers who file complaints from retaliation; providing neutral and well-trained investigators who will pursue complaints; dis-

tributing the policy to all members of the community; providing education and training for all teachers, students, and staff; offering information about people and services who can help students deal with the impact of sexual harassment; and developing mechanisms to review and evaluate the effectiveness of the policy. These guidelines can be used by any school wishing to take a strong and proactive stand on this critical issue, so that all students are able to learn in a supportive and gender-fair environment.

GIRLS' PARTICIPATION IN VIOLENCE AND CRIME

It is important to note that in addition to being victims of violence, girls are sometimes perpetrators of violence and other crimes. According to FBI data, approximately one-quarter (25.6 percent) of all juvenile (under age 18) arrests in the United States in 1995 involved females (Federal Bureau of Investigation, 1996). However, only four percent of all adolescent girls become involved with the juvenile justice system each year (Girls Incorporated, 1996). Although the majority of girls' arrests are for non-violent crimes, a recent study indicates that both girls' and boys' arrest rates for violent crimes (murder, rape, robbery, and aggravated assault) increased between 1986 and 1995 (Federal Bureau of Investigation, 1996). While girls are still much less likely to be arrested for crimes involving violence than are boys, girls' arrest rates for violent crimes increased much more dramatically than the rates for boys during that same period (Federal Bureau of Investigation, 1996).

Arrest records analyzed by the Federal Bureau of Investigation (FBI) reveal that the percentage of offenders who are girls varies considerably with different types of crime. Among juvenile arrests in 1995, girls were arrested in 5.8 percent of murder cases, 19.6 percent of aggravated assault cases, 9.2 percent of robbery cases, 32.5 percent of larceny-theft cases, 8 percent of weapons cases, 12.5 percent of drug cases, 14.8 percent of motor vehicle theft cases, 15.6 percent of cases of driving while intoxicated, 29.8 percent of curfew violations, 28.8 percent of liquor law violations, 47.7 percent of prostitution cases, and 57.6 percent of runaway cases (FBI, 1996). Although the FBI reports these statistics by race as well as gender, they do not offer a breakdown by race within each gender, nor do they offer analyses by social class; therefore, these percentages represent girls' involvement in arrests across race and class groups. As these statistics demonstrate, girls represent only a small percentage of juveniles who commit violent crimes. Yet they account for nearly half of those arrested for prostitution and more than half of runaway cases. Since many runaways and youth involved in prostitution also may have histories of abuse, it is important to consider the relationship between victimization and participation in these types of crimes.

Concerned by the increasing incidence of aggressive acts by girls, and the dearth of research and policy addressing girls' participation in violence, the Center for Women Policy Studies has recently introduced a *National Program on Girls and Violence*. In 1995, the Center published preliminary findings from its national survey on girls' experiences of violence. The survey, responded to by nearly 500 readers of two adolescent girls' magazines (*New Moon: The Magazine for Girls and Their Dreams and Teen Voices: A Magazine By, For, and About Teenage and Young Adult Women*), asked girls about their understandings and experiences of violence, their participation in physical fights, and their efforts to protect themselves and to find help when they are abused. Because these responses come from girls who read these two magazines and have chosen to complete and return a survey on violence, they may not represent other girls' experiences or views. But their responses are nonetheless compelling. Among its findings, the survey revealed that:

- Eighty-four percent of respondents had witnessed physical violence.
- The most frequently-cited place for witnessing violence was in school, followed by television and movies, their homes, and their neighborhoods.
- Forty-two percent of respondents consider girls as violent as boys.

I think victimization is a big problem in my neighborhood, for girls, especially. Almost always girls. Things like you get groped and felt up, and other, worse things too. And it's worse that they always blame the girl, like what she was wearing, or she's sexually active, so she must be a whore, or she's making it up just to get a guy in trouble. People watch it going on, but nobody wants to stop it.

— Tia
SELF-DESCRIPTION: "friendly, nice, teen mom"

- Thirty-six percent had been in physical fights during the last year.

Asked for the top five reasons that girls commit violence, 54 percent attributed girls' violent acts to being victims of violence; 50 percent responded that "they want to look tough;" 43 percent attributed girls' violence to lack of a good family life; 41 percent said they want "to get

even with someone;" and 38 percent responded that they "need to protect themselves" (Center for Women Policy Studies, 1995).

When girls do enter the criminal justice system, they may face differential treatment compared with boys. Girls Incorporated and the Office of Juvenile Justice and Delinquency Prevention recently collaborated in creating a forum and publication, *Prevention and Parity: Girls in Juvenile Justice* (1996a), to examine girls' interactions with the juvenile justice system. They found that the juvenile justice system typically fails to attend to the needs of pregnant or abused teens and often places girls in programs and facilities designed for boys. The report reveals that girls' offenses, far more than boys', are punished more severely than their infractions merit. Girls of color in particular are often judged and treated with undue harshness.

Girls Incorporated and the Office of Juvenile Justice and Delinquency Prevention recommend increasing home- and community-based prevention and early intervention efforts; designing research on young women which aims to challenge stereotypes and guide programming; and ending practices which result in unequal treatment for girls in the juvenile justice system. Job training programs, programs for pregnant and parenting teens, and programs that address the needs of girls who have been sexually abused or who have a history of substance abuse are all important in enabling girls to leave the juvenile justice system better able to live healthy, productive lives.

CONCLUSION

Although discussions of violence against women typically focus on the experiences of adults, and discussions of child abuse often treat the issue as though it is gender-neutral, girls are frequently the victims/survivors of violence against women and children. Indeed, one-in-three to one-in-four girls are sexually victimized by the time they are 18; three out of every four child abuse survivors are girls; and 62 percent of all reported cases of forcible rape cases in 1992 involved girls under 17. In contrast to recent backlash claims that young women overreport violence, recent studies have found that girls and young women often resist naming their violent or coercive experiences as victimization, rape, or abuse, even to themselves. Among adolescent girls in one large-scale survey who said they were abused, 29 percent had told no one about their experience.

Girls are most likely to be raped by someone they know. For all age groups, girls' assailants are most frequently friends and acquaintances; the younger the victim, the more likely it is that rape is committed by a family member. According to the Commonwealth Fund's study of adolescent girls' health, girls cited their homes as the most frequent place where sexual or physical abuse occurred (53 percent), and 65 percent said that they experienced abuse more than once. That study also found that girls who reported being abused were more likely to smoke, drink, use illegal drugs, and report symptoms of depression than girls who had not been abused. They were also more likely to report at least one instance when they did not get needed health care. Only 10 percent of the girls surveyed (abused and non-abused) said their physician had discussed abuse with them, although 50 percent said their doctors should discuss this issue.

In addition to experiencing victimization in their homes and relationships, many girls (and boys) face violence and harassment in their neighborhoods and schools. Although sexual harassment is often portrayed as a phenomenon affecting adult women, peer-to-peer harassment among adolescents is widespread. Very often, sexual harassment happens in public spaces in schools, in front of both adults and peers. Yet adults often fail to interrupt the harassment in their midst, thus silently condoning the behavior. While both girls and boys are harassed, boys are overwhelmingly the perpetrators of sexual harassment. Sexual harassment involves an abuse of power, rather than an expression of sexuality. Peer-to-peer harassment often involves homophobia, racism, and ableism, as well as sexism. In addition to harming the target(s) of harassment, sexual harassment creates a hostile climate for those who witness such behaviors, particularly if adults look on without intervening.

Finally, some girls are involved in perpetrating violence and other crimes. Although one-quarter of juvenile arrests involved girls in 1995, most girls were arrested for nonviolent crimes. However, girls' arrest rate for violent crimes is increasing much more rapidly than that of boys. Girls involved in the juvenile justice system often face differential treatment: girls are more likely than boys to be punished more harshly than their infractions merit, and girls of color are particularly likely to be punished severely. In addition, the juvenile justice system often fails to attend to the needs of pregnant and abused girls.

Adults must take seriously girls' (and boys') claims of physical and sexual abuse, and sexual harassment. Adolescents need safe and confidential contexts to talk about these painful experiences, and for adults to help them address the gender-based and biased attitudes that often underlie victimization. Since many adolescents express concerns about confidentiality and embarrassment about discussing abuse with health care professionals, adults should take a proactive stance regarding these issues, rather than waiting for adolescents to bring them up. Schools can create an environment free of sexist hostility by developing and implementing clear, enforceable sexual harassment policies. Concerned adults can advocate for the rights of girls who are involved with the juvenile justice system; particular attention is needed to meet the needs of pregnant girls, girls who have abused, and girls of color.

● Current estimates are that between one in three and one in four girls are sexually victimized by the time they are 18 years old or seniors in high school (Finkelhor and Dziuba-Leatherman, 1994; Benson, 1990).

● Adolescent girls are disproportionately the reported victims of rape. The National Victim Center (1992) found that 62 percent of all reported forcible rape cases in 1992 involved victims/survivors who were younger than 17 years old.[25]

● Despite some claims that young women have embraced a "victim mentality" and falsely accuse men of sexual violence, recent research suggests that adolescent girls and young women who have been raped, harassed, or battered tend to refuse to label their own experiences as victimization, rape, or abuse (Kahn, Mathie, and Torgler, 1994; Phillips, 1996).

● Although adults may be more likely to warn girls about sexual danger posed by strangers, 96 percent of survivors under 12 years old, 85 percent of those 12 to 17 years old, and 67 percent of those 18 or older were raped by family members, friends, or acquaintances (U.S. Bureau of Justice Statistics, 1992).

● High school girls who say they have experienced sexual or physical abuse are more likely to report smoking, drinking, and using illegal drugs than are high school girls who say they had not been abused. Further, adolescent girls who have been abused are more likely than non-abused girls to report having gone without health care when they needed it (The Commonwealth Fund, 1997).

● Reports of peer-to-peer sexual harassment among middle school and high school students are increasing (Siegel, 1995); yet, few cases are filed and even fewer cases are pursued, despite the fact that sexual harassment is illegal (NCRW, 1993). Peer-to-peer sexual harassment often occurs very openly in schools, in front of adults and other students (Linn, et al., 1992; Stein, 1992; 1995). Sexual harassment in schools primarily involves boys harassing girls (Stein, Marshall, and Tropp, 1993; Lee, et al., 1996).

● Sexual harassment represents an abuse of power, not harmless adolescent teasing, and often includes hateful stereotypes. When allowed to go on uninterrupted, sexual harassment harms not only the particular target(s), but also those who witness the harassment (Lee, et al., 1996; Stein, 1992; 1995).

● Approximately one-quarter (25.6 percent) of all 1995 juvenile arrests in the United States involved girls (FBI, 1996).

● Although both girls' and boys' arrest rates for violent crimes (murder, rape, robbery, and aggravated assault) increased between 1986 and 1995, girls are still much less likely than boys to be arrested for violent crimes (FBI, 1996).[26]

● A 1995 survey of readers of girls' magazines conducted by the Center for Women Policy Studies found that 36 percent of girls reported being in a physical fight in the last year; that 84 percent of girls reported witnessing physical violence; and that the most frequently-named place for witnessing violence was school (Center for Women Policy Studies, 1995).

● Girls often face differential treatment in the juvenile justice system. The system tends to overlook the needs of pregnant or abused girls, and frequently places girls in programs and facilities intended for boys (Girls Incorporated, 1996).

INFORMATION AND ACTIVISM. Increased research can shed light on girls' experiences as both victims and perpetrators of violence. Activists should continue their efforts to counter misrepresentations of girls' and women's experiences by providing accurate, persuasive information about the prevalence of violence against women and girls. They should also stress that abuse does not always involve physical violence, but may include verbal harassment, coercion, and manipulation.

ATTENTION TO YOUTH. The anti-rape and battered women's movements have increasingly highlighted the prevalence of violence against girls. These efforts must continue to ensure that the needs and realities of female adolescents are included in advocacy work on these issues. Research on girls' victimization should address variations in girls' experiences and responses to violence and coercion across races, cultures, social classes, and sexual identities.

ADULT SUPPORT. Girls need support from adults and institutions to name, report, and pursue cases of violence against them. Counselors, educators, and health care professionals need to explore issues of violence with girls and boys, and offer support to those who have witnessed and/or experienced abuse or harassment. Adults also need to interrupt and address harassment in their midst, rather than ignoring it or handling it in private.

ENCOURAGEMENT OF GIRLS' ENTITLEMENT. From a young age, girls should develop their sense of entitlement to be treated with respect, and to refuse unwanted touching or sexual contact by both strangers and acquaintances. Adults can also help both girls and boys to challenge cultural ideologies and practices which condone and promote male aggression.

CLEAR LAWS AND CULTURAL AWARENESS. Rape laws should be guided by the understanding that "no means no" in order to recognize that sex without consent is rape, even in the absence of physical violence. At the same time, researchers and advocates should not allow the statement that "no means no" to obscure the complex relationships between consent and coercion in girls' sexual experiences.

INSTITUTIONAL SUPPORT. Schools should take far greater responsibility in ensuring that harassment of students is not tolerated, and in protecting the rights of students who make claims of sexual harassment. All schools need to have clear, enforceable harassment policies, which should be expanded to better reflect the realities of adolescents and young girls. Harassment laws and policies should be more consistently enforced.

JUDICIAL REFORM. In an effort to better meet the needs of girls, researchers and policy makers should give increased attention to girls' experiences as both victims and perpetrators of violence, increase prevention and early intervention efforts, and end practices that treat female offenders differently.

MORE CRITICAL RESEARCH. More research is needed to understand teen girls' experiences of violence and victimization. Studies should emphasize how girls define, make sense of, resist, and try to prevent victimization in their lives, and the forms of support that can help them to cope. Particular attention should be paid to girls' experiences of battering in their relationships, as little of the domestic violence research has focused on teens. Researchers should also work with boys and men to learn the conditions that support their respect for girls and women, and those conditions that promote or condone harassment, rape, and battering. Research is also needed to understand the perspectives of girls who are perpetrators of violence and other crimes. Further research that examines girls' interactions with the juvenile justice system can identify the skills and resources needed to stay out of the criminal justice system.

CONTINUED AND INCREASED FUNDING. Advocacy organizations need funding to help girls deal with the impacts of violence in their lives. Health care agencies providing affordable and confidential services to adolescents should receive greater funding, so that girls can seek help in dealing with abuse and related health concerns. Funding is needed to increase home- and community-based prevention and intervention programs for girls in the juvenile justice system. Funding is also needed for job training, so that teen girls can thrive after they leave the juvenile justice system.

CHAPTER FIVE

Schooling

OTHER THAN FAMILIES, schools provide perhaps the most critical context in which girls can develop a sense of intellectual competence or failure, personal worth or marginalization, and optimism or despair about their futures. Further, girls' achievement and participation in schools can have profound and lasting consequences for their options and well-being in adulthood. Since most girls spend a great deal of their time in and around schools, educational issues are among the most important to understand, not only for teachers and school administrators, but also for girls' advocates, clinicians, researchers, policy makers, and parents and other caregivers. Research has shown that educational reforms that are good for girls also tend to benefit boys (AAUW, 1996a).

This chapter addresses issues pertaining to representation of girls in educational research; girls' academic achievement; curricular issues and academic programs for girls; single-sex versus mixed-sex learning environments; sexuality education; college attendance and dropping out; and conditions that support positive academic experiences. Throughout these sections are discussions of gender equity, as well as other issues (such as findings on self-esteem, pregnancy, drug and alcohol abuse, and economic factors) which may be associated with girls' experiences of schooling.

REPRESENTATION OF GIRLS IN EDUCATIONAL RESEARCH

The relationship between education and gender is both complex and important. Gender issues (as well as race, class, and cultural issues) infuse and help shape educational environments. Issues such as gender inequity, sexual harassment, discrimination, and gender differences in student feedback often create an academic environment which marginalizes girls. Girls' educational experiences may impact on their sense of self, degree of risk for teenage pregnancies, future wages, and opportunities for leadership. Schools can pose barriers to girls' achievement and well-being, but they can also make a powerful difference in supporting girls' aspirations and preparing them for bright futures. Yet, until fairly recently, little attention has been paid to girls' particular needs and experiences of schooling.

Addressing the near invisibility of girls in research on education, the AAUW's Educational Foundation funded Susan McGee Bailey and her colleagues at the Wellesley Center for Research on Women to research and write a comprehensive review of girls' achievement, participation, and treatment in public K-12 schools. They reviewed 35 reports on education issued by special task forces and commissions between 1983 and 1991. Their analysis, discussed in *The AAUW Report: How Schools Shortchange Girls* (1992)—a compelling and critical synthesis of over 1,300 studies on gender and schooling—found that few of the reports considered gender in their recommendations. Only four of the reports included background information or analysis by sex or framed educational issues in terms of gender. Further, the research team found that, to the extent that gender was considered, most reports suggested that becoming pregnant, dropping out, and adding to the number of poor, female-headed households were the only significant problems affecting girls.

In addition to a shortage of data on girls and schooling in general, little clear information exists about diversity across girls' educational experiences. For instance, as noted in *The AAUW Report: How Schools Shortchange Girls* (1992), when government studies do include information analyzed by sex, these data are typically presented separately from data on race, ethnicity, age or grade level, and family or school background. Thus, while it is not difficult to find national educational statistics on adolescents as a whole, and it is possible to find statistics on female versus male students or on students in certain race groups, these studies rarely provide information about age/grade, race, class, and school background combined with sex when discussing differences among students' educational realities.

Although researchers in general have been slow to attend to girls' experiences in schools, several recent AAUW reports have highlighted important educational trends involving girls. In 1991, the AAUW Educational Foundation published *Shortchanging Girls, Shortchanging America,* the first national survey to address the connection between girls' decline in self-esteem and their experiences in schools. This report was followed by the abovementioned *The AAUW Report: How Schools Shortchange Girls* (1992). Since then, the AAUW Educational Foundation has published *Growing Smart: What's Working for Girls in School* (1995), a comprehensive review of literature on various educational approaches and their impact on girls' achievement and development; *The Influence of School Climate on Gender Differences in the Achievement and Engagement of Young Adolescents* (1996b), based on a study of more than 9000 middle-grade students in nearly 400 schools; and *Girls in*

Teachers treat the guys differently than the girls. It's almost like they like the girls better, but they respect the guys more. I think maybe because we don't give them as many problems, they're glad we're there, but they seem to expect the guys to think better and be better at things like physics and computers. I don't know if they think guys are more intelligent, but they seem more interested in them when they say things, and they take the girls for granted.

– Holly, age 17
SELF-DESCRIPTION: "white, senior, female"

---

the Middle: Working to Succeed in School (1996a), an in-depth, qualitative study of how racially, ethnically, and socially diverse girls navigate their way through middle school, and how the context of schooling can either support or hinder their learning experiences.

Together, these reports have unearthed problematic educational practices and trends which overlook girls' needs,

impede their academic achievement, and threaten their psychological well-being. They also point to girls' successes, the ways they negotiate the barriers they face, and the conditions that can help them grow into skilled, confident young women. Many of these issues are discussed in the sections below.

GIRLS' ACADEMIC ACHIEVEMENT

Although recent reports on gender issues in schooling suggest some areas of struggle for girls, in terms of overall academic achievement, girls appear to be doing considerably better than popular discussions would suggest. School achievement is a complex phenomenon which may vary across subject areas and which may be assessed in a variety of ways. The most typical forms of measurement include grades and performance on standardized tests. By these measures, girls' overall achievement rivals and, in some cases, exceeds that of boys (National Center for Education Statistics, 1997a; 1997c; Cole, 1997).

A closer examination, however, reveals at least four manifestations of gender discrepancies:

- While girls and boys show similar achievement in some subject areas, they show relatively greater or lesser strengths in other areas.
- In some subjects, girls' and boys' average scores are similar, but one group outperforms the other at advanced levels of those subjects.
- Although girls or boys may demonstrate greater overall performance in a particular subject area, their performance in various sub-skills (i.e. math computation versus math concepts) may vary within that subject.
- Whereas girls' and boys' overall performance is often similar at lower grade levels, boys' and girls' performance in particular subjects may diverge at later grade levels (Cole, 1997).

Looking across these aspects of academic performance, it is possible to identify areas where girls' achievement has consistently been strong, where girls have shown recent progress, and where girls need particular attention to enhance their achievement.

Overall, girls achieve consistently higher grades in all school subjects than do boys—this difference is largest in English, followed by social studies, science, and math

(Cole, 1997). On standardized tests, however, boys' and girls' scores vary across different subjects. The National Center for Education Statistics periodically considers achievement in various subject areas for students in fourth, eighth, and twelfth grades and reports their findings in the National Assessment of Educational Progress (NAEP).[27] Their findings show that, in general (i.e., not differentiating among boys and girls from different race or class backgrounds), girls outperform boys on standardized tests of reading achievement (National Center for Education Statistics, 1997a). Although both twelfth grade girls' and boys' reading scores showed a decline between 1992 and 1994, girls had higher average reading scores at all three of the grade levels tested in 1994 (National Center for Education Statistics, 1997a).

In the subject of U.S. history, on the other hand, the NAEP showed no significant differences in performance of girls and boys in fourth or eighth grades. However, in twelfth grade, male students showed higher overall levels of performance than did female students. Yet within this subject area, gender differences were inconsistent across different themes of U.S. history. For instance, girls in eighth and twelfth grades performed better than their male peers on the theme, "Gathering and Interaction of Peoples, Cultures, and Ideas," while boys at all three grade levels performed better than their female peers on the theme, "The Changing Role of America in the World" (National Center for Education Statistics, 1997a).

Whereas girls have long outperformed boys in reading, their achievement in math and science has recently been a source of considerable concern among educators, researchers, and advocates. However, both government data and studies reviewed for the AAUW Educational Foundation by Wellesley's Center for Research on Women suggest that the gap between girls' and boys' proficiency in these areas has narrowed considerably. Indeed, both Wellesley's review (AAUW, 1992) and the U.S. Department of Education's National Center for Education Statistics (1997a) indicate that overall gender differences in math and science achievement are actually quite small.

While girls' average SAT math scores continue to lag behind those of boys (College Board, 1997), other indicators suggest that girls' achievement in math and science has improved. For instance, according to the NAEP 1996 Mathematics Report Card for the Nation and the States, for math, the "average scale scores for eighth- and twelfth-grade males and females showed no significant differences in 1996" (National Center for Education Statistics, 1997b).

That study did note higher math scores for fourth grade males than fourth grade females—but this difference was not found in the later grades. NAEP statistics indicate that girls' overall math proficiency improved at all three grade levels between 1992 and 1996, and that the percentage of girls and boys scoring at or above basic proficiency was roughly comparable.

While the long-time gender gap in mathematics proficiency between girls and boys appears to have largely disappeared by the 1996 assessment, the gap between percentages of boys and girls who achieved at high levels in science remained more notable (National Science Board, 1996). On the one hand, in 1996, the NAEP data showed little difference between *average* scores for males versus females in science (National Center for Education Statistics, 1997). In grades 4 and 8, the difference in boys' and girls' scores was not statistically significant. On the other hand, in grade 12, boys, on average, outperformed girls, and the percentage of boys *excelling* in science exceeded the percentage of girls who excelled (the top ten percent of boys in twelfth grade scored 196 or better, while the top ten percent of girls scored 187 or better). As discussed later in this section, the fact that fewer girls excel in science than boys—measured by how many score in the highest percentiles of a national assessment test—suggests that adults may be more apt to nurture older boys' achievement and interest in science. It is important to note that these data include boys and girls across race/ethnicity groups and social class backgrounds; therefore, they reveal only overall sex differences in proficiency.

More subtle gender differences are seen through the results of *The ETS Gender Study: How Females and Males Perform in Educational Settings* (Cole, 1997), a four-year study of similarities and differences in male and female academic performance. The study analyzed information from over 400 different tests and more than 1500 data sets. It looked at nationally representative samples from fourth grade through graduate school (including large-scale testing programs, large federal studies, and tests such as the SAT and ACT used for college and graduate school admission). The study considered not only general subject areas, but also 15 different types of skills within those subject areas. For instance, math skills were broken down into areas of computation and concepts, and verbal skills were broken down into areas of reading, vocabulary reasoning, and language use. An examination of these subskills reveals that while boys or girls may show stronger performance in a general subject area, their skill levels may vary across different categories within that subject (Cole, 1997).

The ETS study found only very small gender differences in nine of the 15 categories (Cole, 1997). Very small differences favored females in study skills, verbal-reading, math-computation, abstract reasoning, verbal-vocabulary, and social studies. Very small differences favored males in math-concepts, spatial skills, and natural sciences. In areas with larger differences, females outperformed males on verbal-writing, verbal-language use, and perceptual skills, while males outperformed females on geopolitical and mechanical/electronic skills.

The data examined for the ETS study show that while twelfth grade boys do generally perform at higher levels than girls in math, girls actually perform better than boys in some aspects of mathematics. Females showed somewhat stronger scores for math computation, while males showed slightly stronger scores in the area of math concepts. Yet, at more advanced levels of math and science, boys in twelfth grade continue to outperform girls. As Cole notes, "in national twelfth grade samples, males outnumber females in the top 10 percent on math tests by 1.5 to 1 and in science by 2 to 1" (1997: 18). Based on the overall performance of boys and girls in math, Coles concludes, "our results indicate that females still have some distance to go to achieve equal representation in the top ranks, but that does not alter the quite favorable picture of female achievement overall" (1997: 18).

In examining the research on girls' achievement, several caveats must be considered. First, it is important to note that although gender discrepancies appear in some areas of school achievement, these differences do not mean that males or females are inherently more skilled in some subjects and less skilled in others. Indeed, the discrepancies between fourth grade boys' and girls' performance are quite small, if they are present at all (Cole, 1997). As Cole notes, "larger differences do not occur until later, and then at different times for different subjects" (1997: 13). Such findings suggest that it is important to consider how girls and boys might be encouraged more in different subject areas, perhaps leading to better performance in some subjects in the later grades. Concerned adults must therefore continue to support students in the areas where they already show strength, while also providing additional opportunity and encouragement for students in areas where they demonstrate lower achievement.

Similarly, it is important to understand that while boys and girls show different achievement levels in some subject areas and sub-skills, discrepancies in student achievement involve more than gender differences. For instance, in reading, students' higher achievement is associated with having a greater array of reading materials at home; reading for leisure; having more frequent discussions of studies at home; watching less television; reading more in the classroom and for homework; being asked more frequently by teachers to explain what has been read; and being asked more frequently by teachers to offer various interpretations of what has been read (National Center for Education Statistics, 1997a). In short, contextual factors play an important role in students' proficiency, both in reading and in other subject areas. While gender differences in achievement levels have, understandably, been cause for concern, educators, families, and community members must also focus on promoting home, community, and school conditions and practices that are associated with higher levels of achievement for both boys and girls.

It must be noted that gaps in achievement levels appear not only between genders in some subjects, but also within gender. For instance, an examination of 1997 SAT math scores shows that males' average math score (530) is higher than females' average math score (494), and that within each race group, males have higher average math scores than their female counterparts (College Board, 1997).[28] But within gender, discrepancies in average math SAT scores also appear across race groups. For example, according to the College Board (1997), among females who took the SAT math exam in 1997, Asian American females had the highest average score (545), followed by white females (510), American Indian females (460), Hispanic/Latina females (449), and black females (416). Thus, one can see that while Asian American females' average math score was lower than Asian American males' average score (578), their scores were also higher than males' overall average math score (530) and higher than the average math scores of females from other race groups.

When interpreting findings on achievement levels, it is also important to consider that most studies of academic achievement are based on analysis of scores on standardized tests. Instruments such as the SAT and achievement tests tend to be good general predictors of future school performance, although the SAT has been found to overpredict men's first-year college grades while underpredicting women's (Bridgeman and Wendler, 1989). However, the ability of standardized tests to predict school success may be due, in part, to the fact that the language forms, skills, and knowledge required to score well on these exams mirror those required to perform well in school. Standardized tests generally presume not only particular skills, but also knowledge of the dominant culture—the very knowledge typically underlying both the content and form of schools. Therefore, it is important to recognize that these tests are not necessarily good indicators of academic or intellectual capabilities, as they may disadvantage those students whose knowledge, skills, and language are not well represented either on tests or in schools. Given the eurocentric, androcentric, and social class biases woven through the traditional canon, students who are poor, of color, immigrant, and/or female may be falsely perceived as less capable when judged by test scores alone. Such judgments confuse standardized performance with intellectual ability.

As more researchers, educators, and policymakers stress the importance of math and science in the lives of girls, it is important to consider how public discussion about these issues has taken shape in recent years. Much of the discussion about girls' achievement in math and science has stressed that it is important to prepare girls for an increasingly technological workforce if the United States is to compete effectively in the global economy into the next century. While this may make a compelling argument for gaining public support and funding for programs promoting girls' math and science achievement, it is important not to frame girls' achievement in these areas as simply an economic issue. Girls are not simply a means to an end, valued only to the extent that they promote larger social and economic goals. Rather, girls' achievement is significant in its own right. The promotion of girls' achievement in math and science should stem primarily from an understanding of girls' experiences in these subjects, and from a conviction that they are fundamentally entitled to develop as competent, intellectual individuals who are encouraged and well-prepared to pursue any areas of study and work they choose. Further, the emphasis on math and science should not overshadow the strong verbal skills girls have long demonstrated, as these skills are also essential to girls' ability to achieve across subject areas, to think critically, and to make their voices heard.

Finally, it is important to note that statistics on math and science achievement do not tell the whole story. Studies of boys' and girls' career aspirations, types of science and math experiences, and confidence in their abilities in these subjects suggest more substantial gender discrepancies. For instance, in the 1991 AAUW Educational Foundation study, *Shortchanging Girls, Shortchanging America,* researchers from the Greenberg-Lake Analysis Group report that the percentage of girls who say they like math is lower for high school girls than for girls in elementary school, and this percentage difference is larger for girls than for boys. Whereas 81 percent of elementary school girls and 84 percent of elementary school boys like math, 72 percent of high school boys like math, compared to only 61 percent of girls. At the same time, boys are much more confident of their abilities in math across grade levels, and the gap between elementary school and high school girls' confidence in this area is greater than that between elementary and high school boys. Only one third of elementary school girls studied said they are good at math, compared to one half of the elementary school boys. More disturbingly, only one in seven high school girls said they are good at math, compared to one-quarter of high school boys.

The percentage of both girls and boys who dislike math is lower for elementary school students than for high school students (AAUW, 1991), although more girls than boys describe math as their least favorite subject in elementary school (15 percent of girls compared with 9 percent of boys) and in high school (28 percent of girls, compared with 21 percent of boys). Echoing Carol Dweck and her colleagues' (1978; 1980), earlier findings of gender differ-

School's the place where I feel safe. Not that it's always the greatest, but at school, I can forget about my worries for awhile and just think about what I'm trying to learn and trying to be with my life. Sometimes it's hard to concentrate with everything going on at home and all, but I like to just get into my mind and learn about new things. It kind of gives me hope.

– Donyelle, age 13
SELF-DESCRIPTION: "African American teen"

ences in attribution for academic difficulties, the girls in this study were more likely to interpret their difficulties in math as personal failures while boys interpreted their difficulties as stemming from the nature of the subject itself.

Interestingly, girls' enjoyment of math and science is associated with (although not necessarily a cause of) other important factors, including higher self-esteem, more positive overall feelings about schoolwork, stronger commitment to career aspirations, and greater confidence in physical appearance (AAUW, 1992). In the AAUW Educational Foundation's 1991 poll, girls who reported liking math and science were more likely to describe themselves as "happy the way I am" (48 percent) compared to girls who did not like these subjects (35 percent). Girls who like math were also more likely to believe that they could realize their career aspirations than girls who dislike math (AAUW, 1991).

Girls today do generally show an interest in current technology. In fact, many say they would like increased exposure to technology and computers. According to a 1997 poll, *Teens and Technology*, conducted by the Gallup Organization (1997):

- About two out of three (62 percent) girls in the seventh and eighth grades feel that they need more computer education from their schools.
- Nearly equal proportions (40 percent) of seventh- and eighth-grade boys and girls have high confidence in their computer skills.
- More than one-third (35 percent) of girls said they spend between three and nine hours a week on computers. More than half (56 percent) said they would like to spend more time on computers; only three percent said they would like to spend less.

CURRICULAR ISSUES AND ACADEMIC PROGRAMS FOR GIRLS

Of critical importance are the classroom materials with which students and teachers are engaged. Too often, school curricula focus on the accomplishments of white European and American men, failing to address important contributions of women, men of color, and those working from nonwestern perspectives. To the extent that these con-

give all students a skewed sense of both the fields they are studying and the people who have shaped their history.

In light of the gender bias woven into most textbooks and other learning materials, the National Women's History Project (1997) recommends that teachers invite students to critique their own textbooks by examining the images presented, and filling in the accomplishments of women who are missing. They also suggest that teachers encourage students to write letters to the editors of their textbooks to recommend that they incorporate the names and activities of women the students have identified. Such activities (which should also include critiques of race, culture, and class bias in curricular materials) not only focus attention on the accomplishments of men and women of color, nonwestern men and women, and white women, but also encourage students to think critically about the "facts" they are learning and to take action to transform the quality of their own and others' educational experiences.

Kate Winter of SUNY/Albany has recommended that teachers involve students in discussions of gender equity in textbooks, films, and so forth by evaluating materials on the basis of four criteria:

- invisibility of women and women's accomplishments;
- "unreality" (i.e., false representations of "the traditional family" that pose women as nurturers and men as workers;
- stereotyping of women's roles and contributions; and
- fragmentation by adding women or women's accomplishments as afterthoughts (as in highlighted add-on text boxes in otherwise gender-biased chapters).

Other helpful strategies may include assigning more novels with women and men of color as protagonists; encouraging students to write essays on women's contributions to history, math, science, literature, and the arts; developing hands-on science and math activities that require students to work cooperatively, and that

---

I want to be a veterinarian, so I have to try really hard at school. It doesn't always come naturally to me, but I work really hard to keep my grades up. I have always known I wanted to work with animals, and my parents really supported me to aim high. My teachers know this is my plan, and they encourage me and tell me what I need, like biology, chemistry, and math, to prepare myself for college. I know I will succeed at my plans.

– Karayah, age 16
SELF-DESCRIPTION: "mixed Black-Hispanic student who loves animals and loves life"

---

tributions are considered, they are often singled out as notable exceptions in such fields as science, mathematics, history, literature, and the arts, rather than incorporated fully into the curriculum. Typically presented as gender- and race-neutral portrayals of "the facts," such male-centered and eurocentric curricula may marginalize girls and

place girls in critical roles for completion of the projects; asking students to interview women in their communities, and to write essays or create an artistic project based on what they learned; and developing social studies projects in which students research gender, race, economic, and global trends in various fields, following up by inviting women from non-traditional occupations to speak with the class.

Although curricula designed specifically to promote young women's achievement are more common at the college level, a growing number of educators, researchers, and advocates are developing such curricula for middle school and high school students. Particularly innovative are curricula which have been initiated and developed in close collaboration with girls themselves. For instance, based on their own experiences at the 1995 United Nations Fourth World Conference on Women held in Beijing, a group of girls working with *New Moon* (an international magazine edited by girls) and the University of Minnesota at Duluth have created a curriculum for girls and boys from kindergarten through twelfth grade. The curriculum includes lesson plans that focus on global issues and that stress participation and action, both locally and internationally. Incorporating a wide variety of learning materials, including slide presentations, videos from the Beijing conference, and girls' articles from *New Moon,* the secondary school curriculum encourages students to conduct their own research on national and international policy issues concerning girls and women, and to understand how data on girls and women are used in policy decisions. At both elementary and secondary school levels, the curriculum invites students to engage in critical discussions of such issues as educational opportunities, health, safety, and families (for more information, see NCRW's *IQ* issue entitled, *Beyond Beijing: Who's Doing What to Turn Words into Action*).

Another creative curriculum highlighting girls' and women's issues comes from the Women of Color Resource Center.[29] A team of advocates, teachers, teacher educators, and high school girls is currently completing work on a high school curriculum for both girls and boys that builds on the momentum and insights from the Beijing conference. Initiated by young women from Berkeley High School in California, and developed in collaboration with educators, advocates, and teacher trainers from the Women of Color Resource Center, the University of California at Berkeley, Mills College, Berkeley High School, and JFK University, the curriculum uses the Beijing conference's Platform for Action as a springboard for ideas about materials and activities.

The curriculum is built around issues of concern to girls and women—both in the U.S. and internationally—and is carefully designed to be of interest to boys as well as to girls. Curricular units include girls' access to education; nutrition; sexual trafficking of girls; body image and self-esteem; gender division of labor in the home; sexual harassment; girls with disabilities; girls and sports; sexual and reproductive rights; girls and labor issues; and images of girls in the media. Each unit focuses on the theme of human rights, and stresses women's and girls' rights as integral to any analysis of human rights. Students use literature to explore the issues they are studying, and discuss them in global contexts. The curriculum has been tested through workshops and teach-ins with high school students, in community youth programs, and with teachers and teacher trainers, and is currently in its final stages of development.

At the middle school level, Susan McGee Bailey, Executive Director, and Janet Kahn, Senior Research Scientist, from the Wellesley Center for Research on Women, are currently co-directing the development of a new curriculum designed to connect girls and boys to global issues, and to help them think critically and expansively about human rights.[30] Prompted by the focus on the girl-child at the Beijing conference, the curriculum is being field-tested and piloted in several public and private schools across the country; it incorporates feedback from both teachers and students. Its emphasis on issues of global citizenship dovetails with middle school students' thoughts and priorities, including their particularly keen focus on issues of identity and fairness. It also encourages girls, as well as boys, to think about taking action to make a difference, at precisely the time in their development when many believe that girls begin to doubt their capabilities and entitlement to speak out.

The curriculum uses personal narratives, case studies, videos, policy information, and news coverage to expose students to the life experiences of people from a wide range of cultures. It also prompts students to see how they, themselves, fit into the global issues they are studying. The focus on human rights and the interconnectedness of the world's populations comes through in each of the four curricular units being developed. In addition to this overarching emphasis, each curricular unit has a particular substantive focus, such as education, war, the environment, and the international garment trade. Through the lens of the different units, students examine such dilemmas as how international discussions can honor people's unique cultures, and yet also determine what rights people should be guaranteed across cultures.

Students are asked to think about the roles that youth can play, and have played, in changing policies, and to consider what they can do to make a difference—both as consumers and as activists. They are also prompted to think broadly about the impacts of the issues they are studying on people's lives. For example, using the notion of a "ripple effect," students talk and write about the impacts of war in terms of education and economics. They explore the experiences of those who are fighting, those who become separated from families in transit, those who are witnesses of war, and those who are refugees in other countries. Throughout the entire curriculum, emphasis is placed on global citizenship, and on women's and youth's perspectives across different cultures. The curriculum also helps students to reflect on their own responsibilities as global citizens, and the roles they can play in defining how their own and others' lives unfold.

As these curricular programs demonstrate, educators can help to promote girls' achievement and involvement by helping students to think critically about the societies and cultures in which they live, and to expand their understanding of global power issues. Educators can introduce students to a wide range of learning materials—including films, novels, poetry, biographies, and nonfiction books and articles that highlight perspectives and contributions of women, and men of color—to supplement or replace traditional textbooks. They can encourage students to search for and study reports by government agencies, policymakers, and researchers to scrutinize both their findings and underlying assumptions about gender, race, class, disability, and sexuality. Using these materials, educators can encourage students to reflect on their own experiences through writing and discussion, and to use these reflections to make connections to how and what they are learning.

Particular attention should be paid to curricula and classroom practices in areas where girls and women have traditionally been underrepresented, such as math, science, and technology. By connecting these subjects to girls' experiences and emphasizing the work of women and men of color and global perspectives throughout the curriculum, all students may be helped to develop their competence across a wide range of fields. Since traditional curricular materials provide students with powerful (and often negative) messages, it is vital that educators work to transform these messages by promoting gender-fair, comprehensive curricula that encourage all students to become engaged and critical learners.

In addition to transforming curricula, several groups have also developed programs designed to involve girls in areas in which they may be marginalized in traditional classrooms. Understanding girls' potential to enjoy and excel in math and science, and yet mindful of the traditional underrepresentation of girls in advanced math and science courses and careers, concerned educators and advocates have developed programs for girls that encourage

them to pursue and succeed in these subjects.[31] One such program is *Operation SMART* (Science, Math, and Related Technology), developed by Girls Incorporated to foster early interest in math and science. Through both in-school and afterschool activities, students in first through twelfth grades explore math and science by conducting hands-on experiments, taking field trips, and participating in discussions with women in math and science careers.

Rather than a pre-set curriculum, *Operation SMART* is a philosophy that enables program participants to choose the activities that interest them, and to integrate them into other subject areas. The program encourages innovative approaches to help girls take risks and explore new areas, fostering full and meaningful participation for both girls and boys. Building on the success of *Operation SMART*, Girls Incorporated of Rapid City, Iowa began offering *Teaching SMART* in 1997. *Teaching SMART* is a program designed for elementary and high school teachers to increase awareness of gender issues and help develop gender-equitable classrooms.

Whereas some programs focus on developing girls' early interest in math and science, others work to fuel that interest at the high school level. For instance, the Northwest Center for Research on Women has developed *Rural Girls in Science*, a program designed to encourage girls from rural high schools to become involved in science. The program includes mentoring, community activities, computer networks, science clubs, and a summer camp for girls, as well as training institutes for their teachers and counselors. The results of a 1997 survey of former participants suggest that the program is very successful. In fact, all 40 of the rural ninth grade girls who attended the science summer camp five years ago are currently attending college, and half of them are majoring in science.

Still other programs help girls and young women explore science careers both in high school and throughout their college years. *The Douglass Project for Rutgers Women in Math, Science, and Engineering,* for example, offers summer and weekend programs for high school girls, as well as ongoing support for undergraduate women in math and science fields. Its program for high school students gives girls the opportunity to explore a range of science specializations by participating in hands-on activities, touring laboratories, attending career fairs, and/or undertaking month-long internships. During the program, girls live for one or two weeks with undergraduate women who are majoring in math, science, or engineering. Girls work cooperatively, they need not be advanced-level students, and they do not receive grades for their participation.

Founded in 1986, the program appears to have a strong, positive impact on girls' educational and career aspirations, self-confidence, and attitudes toward science.

Programs such as these make clear that girls can and do enjoy and excel in math and science, particularly when curricular materials are stimulating, classroom practices are gender-equitable, and mentors/role models are available to help them explore possibilities, and envision themselves in math and science careers. The once significant gender gap in math and science test scores and course-taking is closing (National Center for Education Statistics 1997b; Cole, 1997), but concerned adults should continue efforts to ensure that all girls, as well as boys, are offered every opportunity to participate fully across subject areas, especially those where girls have not traditionally flourished.

SINGLE-SEX VS. MIXED-SEX LEARNING ENVIRONMENTS

In light of the sometimes disturbing findings of recent reports such as the AAUW Educational Foundation's *How Schools Shortchange Girls* (1992) and *Growing Smart: What's Working for Girls in School* (1995), some educators and families have explored all-girls schools or groups as a possible remedy to the gender inequities often found in traditional schooling. Much debate has focused on the merits and limitations, as well as the legality, of single-sex learning environments. Current federal law prohibits any sex segregation in public schools, other than for sex education, remedial classes, singing groups, and contact sports. However, some schools and districts have begun experimenting with ways to provide single-sex experiences while conforming to federal regulations.

All-girls schools and classrooms are receiving increasing attention from teachers, researchers, and advocates. Proponents of single-sex schooling assert that all-girls environments promote higher achievement levels for girls, foster their self-esteem, and offer opportunities for leadership and participation that are often usurped by boys in mixed-sex schools and classrooms (Shakeshaft and Libresco, 1992). Since girls-only schools and programs are more likely to focus on women in positions of strength, leadership, and scholarship, and may be more likely to have a higher proportion of women teachers and administrators (espe-

cially at the secondary school level), girls in such environments may have more access to women role models who can help them envision wider possibilities for their futures.

Monaco and Gaier's (1992) research on achievement in single-sex versus mixed-sex environments suggests that in either type of school environment, girls profit from time spent in settings free of distractions and competition from boys, where they can develop confidence through achievement, assume leadership roles, and explore career possibilities. Since all-girls schools and classrooms tend to provide such a setting, many believe that girls should have access to single-sex environments in public education. Experiences of many educators and students seem to support these claims (Lee and Marks, 1990).

Opponents of single-sex public schooling, on the other hand, argue that such learning environments are discriminatory. Drawing parallels to prohibitions against race segregation in federally-funded schools, critics such as the American Civil Liberties Union maintain that rather than encouraging gender parity, sex segregation in public schooling illegally promotes gender bias by excluding students on the basis of sex. Further, at a time when girls have

There is definitely a double standard that the teachers have. The boys are more encouraged to go into technical training and science, but even though there's girls who are good at math, they're not really encouraged. It's not like they exactly try to discourage them, but it's like they're not given any encouragement either. And some teachers, they get all enthusiastic when a boy gives the right answer, but when a girl gives a right answer, they just be like, "um, um." And when a boy does something bad, he maybe gets yelled at, but when a girl does it, it's more like they're disappointed in you.

– Zakiyyah, age 17
SELF-DESCRIPTION: "African American, a student and mother"

successfully pursued sex-discrimination lawsuits and gained admission to traditionally all-male academies such as the Citadel, Virginia Military Academy, and Philadelphia's Central High School, many feminists are concerned that an endorsement of single-sex schooling will erode progress made toward gender equity.[32] Many educational researchers and reformers charge that the move toward single-sex learning environments detracts from efforts to improve mixed-sex schools by promoting simplistic responses to the complex problems of public education (Bailey, 1996).

Despite laws banning sex segregation in federally-funded schools, some districts have found ways around these regulations to create or preserve all-girl classes, programs, or schools. In most cases, single-sex courses or extra-curricular clubs are incorporated into mixed-sex schools. For instance, in a recent legal challenge, a middle school in Ventura, CA, was able to retain its all-female math class by renaming it *Power Learning for Underrepresented Students* (PLUS). Although theoretically open to all underrepresented students, no boys enrolled in the course. In New York City, however, a new public school for girls opened in the fall of 1996. The first girls-only public school in the city in a decade, the Young Women's Leadership School in East Harlem took in 50 seventh grade girls for the 1996-1997 school year, and enrolled 165 students in seventh, eighth, and ninth grades for the 1997-1998 school year. The school has thus far been able to proceed despite federal and city laws prohibiting school segregation, in part by claim-

---

Nobody wants to talk about sex with kids. My health class, they just talk about the body parts and how they operate. But that's not talking about sex. Kids need more information. Everybody's doing it, so people should just wake up and understand and give us some advice and some information that's useful.

— Jacqui, age 14
SELF-DESCRIPTION: "white, straight female"

---

ing that it is a "program" which is part of a larger co-educational school (although it is housed in a separate building), rather than a free-standing school. As such, it does not require the consent of the New York City Schools Chancellor or the Board of Education. Although the New York Civil Liberties Union and the New York Civil Rights Coalition have challenged the legality of the school, claiming that it has failed to conduct affirmative outreach to boys, the Young Women's Leadership School has the support of the New York City Schools Chancellor and is currently planning to expand.

The New York City Chapter of the National Organization for Women (NOW-NYC) opposes the Young Women's Leadership School, calling it "a giant step backward for girls, women, and the feminist movement."[33] The Board of NOW-NYC claims that single-sex schools promote gender stereotypes, and reward teachers and boys for

sexist attitudes. While they acknowledge that the Young Women's Leadership School may enhance self-confidence and opportunities for the small number of girls who actually attend, they stress that such schools divert public attention from the need to improve schooling for all girls. They contend that sex-segregated schools do not promote tolerance or sex equity, and they warn that removing boys from the classroom does not automatically end sexism in school.

In a roundtable discussion of research on single-sex education convened by the AAUW Educational Foundation in November 1997, educational scholars considered the potential role of single-sex education in broader educational reform. Drawing on over twenty years of research on single-sex elementary and secondary education, the roundtable participants noted that long-term impacts of single-sex education remain unknown, due largely to a lack of longitudinal data. In their publication, *Separated by Sex: A Critical Look at Single-Sex Education for Girls,* which is based on the roundtable, the AAUW Educational Foundation (1998) reports that while some single-sex programs have benefits for some students, it is not possible to determine whether those benefits are attributable to the single-sex nature of those programs, or to some other elements that could be created in mixed-sex settings as well. Indeed, they note that single sex educational approaches are so varied— from all-girl schools to single-sex after-school programs—that no broad generalizations can be made regarding the effectiveness or ineffectiveness of single-sex education.

Among other essays, the AAUW report includes a review of the literature by Pamela Haag (1998) entitled, "Single-Sex Education in Grades K-12: What Does the Research Tell Us?" On the one hand, Haag's review reveals that girls in single-sex schools may be more likely than girls in mixed-sex schools to prefer subjects like math and physics, and are less likely to see such subjects as "masculine." On the other hand, Haag finds that research has not identified any consistent evidence that single-sex schools are related to decreases in sex stereotyping. Interestingly, Haag's review of the research literature indicates that while girls in single-sex math and science classes tend to perceive those classes as superior to mixed-sex classes, those in all-girl classes do not demonstrate higher achievement in these areas. Overall, the AAUW Educational Foundation's report concludes that single-sex learning environments do not necessarily eliminate sexism or lead to increases in achievement, although they may foster some girls' confidence. The report calls for more detailed research in this area, as well as more multi-faceted approaches, stating that several round-table participants "agreed that simply creating single-sex classes, without providing for teacher training or other support, would probably not be enough to create meaningful change" (1998: 9).

In her 1996 essay, "Shortchanging Girls and Boys," Susan McGee Bailey suggests that educators and others learn from the successes of girls-only learning environments, and incorporate these insights into the development of more equitable and supportive educational strategies in mixed-sex schooling. Bailey stresses that too often, the focus on single-sex schooling results in simplistic strategies that fail to address complex social realities in schools and society. Thus, she recommends working toward gender-equitable schooling for both boys and girls by exploring gender, race, and social class issues explicitly with students; engaging in critical examinations of classroom practices and assumptions; and developing curricular materials and teaching strategies that foster learning for both sexes.

SEXUALITY EDUCATION

In an era of increasing social conservatism, as well as increasing rates of HIV/AIDS and other STDs, and still-high (though recently declining) pregnancy and birth rates among adolescents, sexuality education continues to be a hotly debated topic, often fraught with problematic assumptions and misunderstandings.

Despite findings that the vast majority of Americans favor sexuality education, beginning as early as elementary school (Sears, 1992), sexuality curricula have come under increasing attack in recent years. Some parent associations, school boards, religious groups, and school officials have argued that open discussion (and in some cases any discussion) of sexuality in schools will promote "promiscuity" and a corruption of "family values." Yet in a nationwide evaluation study of sex education programs for the U.S. Department of Health and Human Services, Moore, et al., (1995b) found that exposure to sex education does not increase the likelihood that adolescents will engage in sex, nor do abstinence-only programs reduce adolescents' sexual activity. Nonetheless, some groups have fought, in some cases successfully, to restrict the topics addressed and language used, or to eliminate sex education from the curriculum entirely. In Utah, for instance, it is a Class B misdemeanor for educators to discuss condoms with their students without prior parental consent (Sears, 1992). In some districts, educators must teach abstinence as the only

viable form of birth control or disease prevention. And five states (Connecticut, Illinois, Louisiana, Michigan, and South Carolina) specifically restrict or prohibit discussion of abortion in schools (NARAL Foundation, 1995).

Overall, the availability of sex education has increased dramatically over the last 15 years. Whereas only three states mandated sexuality education in 1980 (Haffner, 1990), 23 states and the District of Columbia did so in 1997 (NARAL Foundation, 1997). Approximately 80 percent of the nation's largest school districts currently offer some form of AIDS education to their students. Despite its increased availability, however, the types of sexuality education offered vary widely across districts, particularly when comparing public and private schools. Twenty-six states currently require abstinence instruction, but only 14 of those also require schools to provide students with instruction about contraception, pregnancy, and disease prevention (NARAL Foundation, 1997). Many schools offer sexuality education as just one unit in health, physical education, or biology classes. Most remain very limited in scope, focusing on biology, hygiene, and abstinence, and normalizing heterosexuality and married, procreative sex. Eight states recommend or require schools to teach that homosexuality is an unacceptable lifestyle and/or to teach students that homosexual behavior is a crime by state law (NARAL Foundation, 1995). Indeed, at a 1996 Planned Parenthood conference, human sexuality educator Deborah Roffman noted that in one school, she was not allowed to utter the word "sex" in her sexuality education class. With new restrictions placed on funding, programs must now stress abstinence in order to share in the 37 million dollars President Clinton has devoted to pregnancy prevention programs in his 1997 budget.

The availability of a course or unit called "sex education" is not enough. Even where such courses are technically available, students are often denied an opportunity to raise their own questions and concerns, and to gain access to the full range of information and resources they need to support personal decision-making. In an exhaustive evaluation of sex education and pregnancy prevention programs prepared for the U.S. Department of Health and Human Services, Moore, et al., (1995b) found that few such programs are theory-based. And as James Sears observes in his book, *Sexuality and the Curriculum* (1992), the conventional sex education curriculum tends to be content-based, to stress rationality and promote linear thinking, and to avoid acknowledgment of pleasure, pain, and intimacy. Based on a cognitive approach, sex education typically emphasizes information and sexual decisionmaking at the expense of discussions of social and emotional concerns. Yet the information that is conveyed is often partial, and only certain sexual decisions may be taught as appropriate.

In a 1995 qualitative study by Phillips, a diverse group of women, aged 18-22, were asked to describe the lasting messages they took away from their sex education classes in middle school and high school. The participants reported learning primarily about the reproductive system, menstru-

---

I'm a lesbian teenager who would like to know about sex and relationships too, only with other women instead of with guys. I have to sit through the discussion of the stuff related to intercourse and birth control and everything, but they don't have to sit through a discussion of things that apply to me. Nobody talks about the things I want to know about, which is relationships and loving other women and how to deal with people's obnoxious attitudes.

– Carla, age 17
SELF-DESCRIPTION: "a spiritual, white, beautiful lesbian"

---

ation, the importance of abstinence (although several of the students were already involved in sexual relationships), and, in some cases, contraception. Consistent with Michelle Fine's (1988) discovery of a "missing discourse of desire" in public schools, none of these women recalled any discussion of pleasure or desire in their sex education. Also absent was a consideration of sexuality outside the realm of heterosexual intercourse.

Perhaps most disturbing, however, were the "unofficial" messages that these women received about their bodies, their sexualities, and their roles as girls and young women. Echoing Fine's 1988 description of the hidden curriculum in public schools, as well as a missing "discourse of male accountability" (Fine, et al., 1994), the participants reported that their teachers often communicated disdain for girls (but not boys) who did not choose abstinence; discomfort with students' questions about pleasure, birth control, homosexuality or bisexuality; and an assumption that girls needed to protect themselves from "naturally" aggressive males. Several women also noted teachers' racist assumptions that the Latina and African American girls in their classes were "promiscuous," while the Caucasian and Asian American girls were presumed to be virgins. Overall, these young women learned that the educators in their lives viewed sex as dangerous, masturbation and same-sex partners as abnormal, and "good girls" (but not boys) as virgins. Interestingly, the participants reported that these attitudes did not affect

their sexual behaviors, but did promote feelings of shame, alienation, anger, and disillusionment with teachers.

These findings are echoed by educators, activists, counselors, health care professionals, and adolescents themselves. At Planned Parenthood of Central Pennsylvania's Sixth Annual Sexuality Conference, "Unveiling Reality: Teen Sexuality in Today's World" (March, 1996), participants engaged with a panel of adolescents who spoke of the importance of clear, open, and respectful sex education for themselves and their peers. The panel was composed of African American, Latino/a, and Caucasian males and females and included self-described "sexually active," "virgin," and parenting adolescents ranging in age from 13-20. These adolescents painted an unfortunately bleak picture of their own sex education, noting that the adults in their lives were often hesitant to discuss sexuality openly with them. However, the panelists stressed that adolescents need clear information and discussion about the issues actually confronting teenagers, rather than the often watered-down information (such as biology and hygiene) that adults typically offer them. Furthermore, several panelists countered the argument that sex education should be confined to the home. These adolescents stated that they did not feel comfortable discussing sexuality with their parents, and instead wished for more opportunity to address their questions and concerns explicitly with teachers or other concerned adults.

Teens in one survey (Kaiser, 1996) said that they received information on pregnancy and birth control from many different sources, relying most heavily on teachers, school nurses, and sex education classes (40 percent said they got "a lot" of information from this source; 29 percent said "some") and their parents (36 percent "a lot"; 36 percent "some"). Most teens (55 percent) said they considered their parents the most "reliable and complete" source when it came to information about sex and birth control. Yet, while three-quarters of teens (74 percent) said that at least one parent had talked to them about sex, less than half (46 percent) said they had discussed birth control, and only 55 percent said they had discussed STDs. The survey directors concluded that teens need more complete information about sexuality, including more practical information about where to acquire birth control and how to use it effectively, and that such information comes "too late" for too many teens.

In order better to meet the needs of adolescents, Deborah Roffman of the Park School in Baltimore calls for educators and other concerned adults to expand their notions of sexuality to include all aspects of body, sensuality, and pleasure experienced both with self and others. In her presentation at Planned Parenthood of Central Pennsylvania's teen sexuality conference, Roffman (1996) encouraged schools and families to work together to help children and adolescents develop clearer understandings by providing them the opportunity to think and talk about sexuality explicitly with each other and with adults. Roffman advocated developmentally-appropriate discussions of bodies, sexuality, and pregnancy from an early age, helping children to understand sexuality as a healthy part of their own identities.

Such an approach informs *The New Positive Images: Teaching Abstinence, Contraception, and Sexual Health,* a 1996 contraceptive education manual developed by Peggy Brick and her colleagues at The Center for Family Life Education of Planned Parenthood of Greater Northern New Jersey. *The New Positive Images* stresses that young people have not only a need, but also a right, to understand their sexuality, and to explore their decisions within broader social, historical, and ethical contexts. While the curriculum considers abstinence from intercourse as a viable option "for anyone at anytime," it also promotes positive images of contraception, and offers clear information on how to obtain and use various methods. The approach engages young people in discussions of social attitudes about sexuality; personal values regarding relationships, sexuality, and contraception; informed decisionmaking; and attitudes and practices that promote or discourage contraception use. Used by sexuality educators in the United States, Canada, Australia, and England, the curriculum provides a positive example of respectful, youth-centered, explicit, and culturally-sensitive approaches to sexuality education and pregnancy prevention.

According to Susan Cote, director of counseling and health education at Kent Place School (a private, all-girls, K-12 school in Summit, New Jersey), sexuality education must offer girls knowledge that is not fear-based, and that validates a wide range of feelings and relationships.[34] Along with health education consultant Donna Fonte, and in consultation with girls and their parents, Cote recently developed the school's *Women's Life Studies* curriculum, a comprehensive, theory-driven, and developmentally guided curriculum which emphasizes young women's sense of self-worth and ownership of their bodies.

Beginning in kindergarten and continuing through twelfth grade, girls are introduced in developmentally appropriate ways to issues ranging from relationships, personal safety, body changes, and eating disorders, to drug use, HIV/AIDS, abortion, and sexual abuse. Unlike most sexuality education programs, topics are not postponed until girls have already confronted difficult issues on their own. For instance, by grade four, girls discuss menstruation (including experimenting with pads and tampons), cigarette smoking, and alcohol; by grade five, they discuss AIDS; by grade six, they discuss pregnancy, sexual abuse, and communicating with health care professionals; and by grade ten, they discuss sexual orientation, abortion, and gynecological care. Perhaps most impressive, the curriculum places these issues in a framework of cultural power and gender dynamics, stresses girls' healthy entitlement and critique, and explores ways for girls to communicate and advocate for their own needs.

While these curricula offer impressive models of comprehensive sexuality education, such approaches are all too rare, and are particularly difficult to introduce in public schools. This was demonstrated in the early 1990s when a group of parents, educators, and politicians in New York City barred introduction of the "rainbow curriculum," a curriculum which would have stressed respect for people from all family backgrounds, including those in which parents or other caregivers are gay, lesbian, or bisexual. As such a response reveals, educators and youth advocates continue to face strong opposition to programs that embrace a diversity of sexual choices and perspectives, and that encourage students to think critically about dominant sexual ideologies and power arrangements.

LEAVING SCHOOL: COLLEGE ATTENDANCE AND DROPPING OUT

Girls and boys, young women and men, drop out of school for a variety of reasons. But as Bailey, et al., warn in *How Schools Shortchange Girls* (AAUW, 1992), variations in definitions and data collection make reliable statistics on dropout rates difficult to obtain and interpret. For instance, since it is mandatory for students to attend school until age 16, younger teens who stop going to school may be considered "truant" (rather than "dropouts") in some school districts. Further, the distinction between dropping out and taking time away from school is only borne out by time, since a "dropout" can return to finish high school or to get a Graduate Equivalency Diploma (GED) at any point.[35] High school graduation rates often vary drastically across districts and are not revealed within broad national statistics. Available government data indicate that nationally, 87 percent of 25- to 29-year-olds had received a high school diploma or GED in 1996. Ninety-three percent of white students, 86 percent of black students, and 61 percent of Hispanic students had completed high school in 1996 (National Center for Education Statistics, 1997). Whereas 95 percent of U.S. students in the highest income quartile graduated from high school in 1997, only 65 percent of students in the lowest income quartile did so (Educational Testing Service, 1997).

Girls, in general, drop out less frequently than boys (National Center for Education Statistics, 1997a). Dropout rates for girls vary considerably both across and within race/ethnic groups. Government data on national dropout rates for girls in grades 10 through 12 show that in 1993, 8 percent of Hispanic girls dropped out of school, compared to 5.3 percent of black girls and 3.7 percent of white girls. Hispanic girls were the only female students to have higher dropout rates than boys in their same race/ethnic group, with 8 percent of Hispanic girls dropping out compared to 5.1 percent of Hispanic boys (McMillen, Kaufman, and Whitener, 1994). However, Hispanic girls' dropout rates vary considerably when analyzed by national origin. For instance, McKenna and Ortiz (1988) examined Hispanic dropout rates using data from a national probability sample, and found that Cuban American and Puerto Rican girls were

Studies suggest that while adolescents who drop out of school share certain characteristics irrespective of gender, girls and boys tend to give different reasons for dropping out of high school. For instance, Michelle Fine and Nancie Zane's (1991) interviews with students in a public New York City high school showed that of those who had been retained in a grade, 92 percent of girls cited being kept back in school as a reason for their dropping out, while only 22 percent of boys offered this as their reason for leaving school.

Although adolescents who drop out of high school are often portrayed as lazy or incompetent, urban girls (and boys) who drop out may actually be more assertive, more politically aware, less conforming, and less depressed than those who stay in school (Fine, 1991). Despite some girls' apparent resilience when leaving school, however, young women who drop out of high school are more likely to become pregnant or to give birth at young ages, and are more likely to become single parents than those who stay in school (McMillen, Kaufman, and Whitener, 1994). Female dropouts are also much more likely than male dropouts in their same race/ethnic group to live in poverty (National Center for Education Statistics, 1997a; Bureau of the Census, 1993). Overall, girls with less than a high school education earn 38 percent less than those with a high school diploma (National Center for Education Statistics, 1997a).

I want to go to college, and I would like to be a lawyer some day. I have this teacher at school, and she said I'm really argumentative, and that that's good for a lawyer. I used to just get in trouble for being too loud and opinionated, but since my teacher showed me how to speak my mind so that people will listen. She really helped me to think about where I want to go in life, so instead of just being angry all the time, now I feel like I'm putting my anger in a good direction.

– Maggie, age 13
SELF-DESCRIPTION: "black so-called inner city youth"

---

more likely to drop out than Cuban American or Puerto Rican boys, or Mexican American and other Hispanic girls.[36]

Although girls, in general, drop out less frequently than boys, black and Hispanic male dropouts are more likely than black or Hispanic girls to return to obtain a GED within two years of leaving school (Kolstad and Owings, 1986). In other words, once black and Hispanic girls leave school, they are less likely than black and Hispanic boys to make up their educational loss.

Statistics on girls' and young women's educational attainment are, in many ways, encouraging, but they also reflect continued gender discrepancies in certain fields of study. On the one hand, young women were more likely than young men to graduate high school and to enter college in 1996 (Bureau of Labor Statistics, 1997). On the other hand, overall, more males than females receive doctoral degrees (National Center for Education Statistics, 1997a). At the masters degree level, trends appear to reflect more traditional gender-related career aspirations. In 1994, substantially more women than men received graduate degrees in health professions and education (National Center for Education Statistics, 1997a). However, a higher percentage of men than women received graduate degrees in computer sciences, engineering, and natural sciences; indeed, men are five times more likely to receive a masters degree in computer sciences and engineering than are women (National Center for Education Statistics, 1997a).

Although the gap between the proportion of women and men receiving masters degrees in these fields narrowed each year between 1970 and 1986, this discrepancy has remained stable since 1986 (National Center for Education Statistics, 1997a). Coupled with recent data showing that many girls would like more exposure to technology and computers (Gallup Organization, 1997), these findings underscore the need to enhance opportunities for girls to explore and excel in math and science fields early on in school (NCRW, 1997).

CONDITIONS THAT SUPPORT GIRLS' EDUCATIONAL EXPERIENCES

All girls, as well as all boys, deserve educational experiences that both promote their academic success, and provide stimulating opportunities to explore their identities and the cultures in which they live. Concerned adults can make an important difference—from working to increase public school funding and forging community/ school partnerships, to developing more gender- and culturally sensitive curricula, and promoting equitable classroom practices. This section considers several possibilities for enhancing girls' experiences of schooling, and ensuring that all students learn in environments that both challenge and nurture them.

At the societal level, both girls and boys need support from funders and policymakers who can increase funding to public schools, and challenge the unequal distribution of funding across districts. The vast majority of youth in the United States attend public school; only eight percent of students were enrolled in private schools in 1995 (Bureau of the Census, 1997a). Yet students' experiences inside public schools can vary considerably, not only in terms of gender, but also according to the relative affluence or poverty of the communities in which their schools are situated. Since school funding is determined largely by the tax base of local communities, youth who live in poorer districts often attend public schools which lack the resources of those in more affluent communities.

If girls (and boys) are to have access to the resources they need to excel in both academics and extra-curricular pursuits, their schools need adequate funding, staffing, and classroom space; up-to-date textbooks; hands-on learning materials; and athletic, computer, science, and arts equipment. Particularly in urban and rural districts, public school educators often struggle to stretch their resources to meet their students' needs. Increased funding and policies that pay particular attention to the needs of poorer communities can help girls as well as boys achieve high academic standards and participate in extracurricular activities.

As McDonnell and Hill (1993) note in their report, *Newcomers in American Schools: Meeting the Educational Needs of Immigrant Youth*, schools' efforts to meet the needs of immigrant students are often thwarted by a lack of concerted policy initiatives at the federal and state levels. The researchers examined immigrant students' needs and assessed how well they were being met in their schools, based on interviews with 745 students and 38 state policymakers, as well as interviews with 240 administrators, teachers, counselors, and community representatives from 57 schools across nine districts with large immigrant populations. The researchers critique the common assumption "that public schools are adequate for the majority of students, but that disadvantaged students need 'something extra'" (1993: 106). Rather, their findings suggest that urban schools generally lack adequate funding, staffing, and curricular materials that speak to the needs of diverse groups of students.

Among McDonnell and Hill's recommendations are increasing governmental attention to and investment in immigrant students' needs and experiences; providing students sustained access to teachers and counselors who speak their languages; increasing the number of bilingual educators in schools, especially those who speak "low incidence" languages (i.e., languages other than Spanish— with a particular need for those who speak Southeast Asian languages); developing and increasing availability of curricular and student assessment materials in students' native languages; integrating cultural orientation curricula into academic courses; providing increased educational and vocational opportunities for students' parents; and coordinating educational, health, and social services, provided by adults who share the languages and cultures of the students they serve.

Instead of focusing on funding and reform strategies that target specific populations as needing "something extra" or that supplement a system that is presumed adequate, the researchers call for coordinated local, state, and national investment in public schools so that the needs of all students are met. While the researchers do not focus specifically on the needs of girls, their findings suggest that increased attention to immigrant issues in school can help support the needs of both girls and boys across a wide range of language and cultural backgrounds.

Based on their review of various educational approaches, Hansen, Walker, and Flom, the authors of *Growing Smart: What's Working for Girls in Schools* (AAUW, 1995) make several suggestions for programs, policies, and approaches to learning that are likely to enhance girls' educational experiences. Among their findings are that girls are more likely to thrive in learning environments that provide mentors and role models; opportunities for leadership and exploration of new ideas; active intellectual engagement with concerned adults and other students; cooperative learning models; and consciousness-raising about gender, race, and class issues. The authors also suggest exploring the possibilities of single-sex grouping (as opposed to single-sex schools) as a temporary strategy to provide girls with a more supportive context for learning.

Teachers who wish to transform the classroom experience for girls need to pay particular attention to the curricular materials they are using. Educators who are required to work with pre-existing curricula can help students to think critically about the topics they are studying, and the learning materials they are assigned. Teachers can use the suggestions of The National Women's History Project and others (outlined in the "Curricular Issues" section of this chapter) to help students move beyond the information and images presented in traditional textbooks by considering what issues and people are missing; by critiquing the gender, race, class, and eurocentric assumptions underlying the presentation of information; and by making connections to global issues, local and national politics, and students' own lives. Teachers who must use traditional textbooks can supplement these texts in any subject area with novels, nonfiction, and policy and research reports so that students have opportunities to work with primary sources, consider nontraditional perspectives, and personalize their learning experiences.

In addition to critiquing and expanding existing materials, educators can adopt or modify existing gender-fair curricula, or develop their own. Such undertakings require the support of administrators and the cooperation of school districts. Curricular transformation also requires transformative thinking in teacher education programs in colleges and universities. Teachers-in-training and veteran teachers who are returning to school for professional development must be encouraged to probe the subject matter they are learning/teaching. They should consider innovative ways to design their courses by incorporating materials that foster girls' engagement, and that present balanced views of their subjects.

Girls can also benefit from programs designed specifically to involve them in subject areas where they traditionally have not been encouraged. Partnerships among public schools, communities, and colleges or universities have resulted in after-school, weekend, and summer programs in which girls can explore their talents and focus on their own strengths. Often emphasizing such subjects as math, science, computer science, and engineering, programs can help girls to develop their skills, and envision themselves as professionals in a wide range of fields. Programs that connect girls with mentors, give them hands-on experiences, and introduce them to diverse career opportunities can expand girls' horizons, and enable them to experience success and leadership in areas they might otherwise have found discouraging.

Studies suggest that girls' academic achievement can benefit not only from classroom activities and afterschool or summer academic programs, but also from their participation in sports. Contrary to the notion that sports take students away from their studies, participation in high school sports is associated with higher grades for both girls and boys, as well as a higher rate of girls' high school completion and attendance at four-year colleges, according to one recent study (Feminist Majority Foundation, 1995). The difference in academic achievement between athletes and nonathletes is particularly marked among Hispanic girls. On standardized tests, 39 percent of Hispanic girl athletes scored in the top quartile, compared with 23 percent of Hispanic girls who were not athletes; 20 percent of Hispanic girl athletes reported receiving "high grades" in contrast to only 9 percent of nonathlete Hispanic girls. In addition, dropout rates have been found to be lower among rural Hispanic girls, and both suburban and rural Caucasian girls who are athletes (The Women's Sports Foundation, 1989, cited in The Feminist Majority Foundation, 1995).

For the 1996 AAUW Educational Foundation report, *Girls in the Middle: Working to Succeed in School,* Jodi Cohen, Sukey Blanc, and other researchers at Research for Action, Inc. conducted extensive observations and interviews with girls and their educators, parents, community members, and male classmates. They found that middle school girls engage in a complex process of ongoing identity formation through their experiences of and relationships with their educational environments. Girls employ a range of strategies to carve out a place for themselves, explore their identities, and make their way successfully through school.

While the researchers note that success is fragile for all girls in early adolescence, they find that the quality of girls' experiences often depends on the degree to which girls' strategies mesh with the dominant culture of their schools. For instance, in schools where adults interpret girls' "speaking out" (i.e., resisting, speaking one's mind, critiquing the norms of the school, etc.) as an indication of potential leadership, girls may be encouraged to hone their inquiry skills, develop their critiques, explore their identities, and create constructive school change. However, in schools where adults interpret the same behaviors as "troublemaking," girls may experience a lack of support, develop negative feelings about themselves and their education, and become alienated from the very adults who are trying to help them. Thus, Cohen and Blanc urge adults to challenge their own assumptions and recognize that what may appear, at first glance, to be "negative behaviors" may also be indications of girls' strength, critique, potential for leadership, and struggle to find their own voices.

Based on their findings, the researchers suggest that schools make every effort to provide caring mentors who listen to girls' experiences; create opportunities for both girls and boys to develop new skills and try out new roles; foster girls' visibility, leadership, and critique in their schools and communities; encourage open dialogue about gender and cultural issues; make gender equity a priority at all levels of school reform; incorporate curricula and other materials that depict both males and females of various cultures in a wide range of roles; and listen respectfully to girls' voices and strategies, whether or not they conform to the dominant culture of the school.

CONCLUSION

When given the space and encouragement they need to explore possibilities and expand their skills, girls can emerge with the confidence and competence to pursue whatever avenues they might choose. Adults in schools, families, and surrounding communities must make every effort to listen openly and respectfully to girls' voices, to appreciate girls' strengths and struggles, and to push for institutional and cultural change that will enable girls to define the terms of their own success.

Studies of girls' achievement show that girls tend to excel in areas of language, reading, and writing, and to perform as well as boys in most areas of history. The long-time gap between girls' and boys' math and science achievement has narrowed considerably, although fewer girls than boys score in the top percentiles on standardized tests of these sub-jects. It is important to note that while girls or boys may outperform one another in certain general subject areas (such as verbal, science, or math), when those subjects are broken down into more specific sub-skills (such as math computation versus math concepts), performance may vary. For instance, boys outperform girls on math concepts, but girls outperform boys on math computation. It is essential to remember that test scores measure students' performance, but they do not necessarily indicate students' academic or intellectual capabilities, since standardized tests and traditional school curricula may not speak to the language forms and knowledge in students' diverse cultural backgrounds.

All students need access to respectful and comprehensive sexuality education. Unfortunately, sex education programs often focus on the dangers associated with sexual behaviors, rather than discussing healthy aspects of sexuality. Further, many programs restrict or prohibit discussion of such important topics as contraception, abortion, safer sex practices, and sexual identities. Although studies have shown that students want more information about such issues, and that instruction in these areas does not increase rates of sexual activity or pregnancy rates, restrictive policies often prevent educators from engaging students in critical discussions of sexuality or offering resources and information about reproductive options.

Although single-sex schooling has recently received increased attention as a possible remedy to gender bias in mixed-sex schools, many educators, researchers, and advocates stress that the elements that work well in single-sex schools must be incorporated into mixed-sex public school settings so that all girls and boys can benefit. Girls' (and boys') achievement and enjoyment of school can be enhanced when they have opportunities to work cooperatively, as well as competitively; to work with mentors; to engage with curricular materials that highlight the work and perspectives of women, and men of color; to participate in hands-on activities; and to connect what they are learning to issues in their own lives and to global issues. Programs that involve girls in nontraditional fields can enhance girls' confidence and skills both inside and outside of schools, and open up new avenues for the future.

● Despite recent concerns about a gender gap in boys' and girls' achievement in math and sciences, girls' math proficiency increased between 1990 and 1996, and no significant differences were found between eighth and twelfth grade boys' and girls' average scale scores in 1996 (National Center for Education Statistics, 1997b). While average science scores showed no significant differences for girls and boys in fourth and eighth grade in 1996, twelfth grade boys, on average, outperformed girls. A higher percentage of boys than girls scored in the highest percentiles in science (National Center for Education Statistics, 1997).

● While overall gender differences in math and science are not pronounced, girls tend to say they like these subjects less than boys, and to have less confidence in their abilities in these areas. Girls who report enjoying math and science are more likely to have higher self-esteem, to feel better about their schoolwork, to have more faith in their career aspirations, and to have greater confidence about their appearance (AAUW, 1992).

● Girls are more likely to attribute their difficulties in math to personal inability, while boys are more likely to attribute their difficulties to the nature of the subject matter (AAUW, 1992).

● Girls who drop out are more likely than girls who graduate from high school to become pregnant or give birth as teenagers, and to become single parents (McMillen, Kaufman, and Whitener, 1994).

● A higher percentage of females (42 percent) than males (36 percent) attend four-year colleges. The percentage of females attending two-year colleges (22 percent) is equal to that of males (U.S. Department of Commerce, 1993). While more females than males receive bachelors and masters degrees, more males than females receive doctoral degrees (National Center for Education Statistics, 1997). Further, attainment of higher education degrees tends to follow traditional gender patterns, with more women earning graduate degrees in health professions and education, and five times more men than women earning masters degrees in computer sciences and engineering (National Center for Education Statistics, 1997).

● Availability of sex education classes has increased in the last 15 years (Haffner, 1990; NARAL Foundation, 1997). However, sex education programs tend to focus on hygiene and biology, rather than intimacy and relationships, and they tend to offer only biological, heterosexist images of "normal" sexuality (Sears, 1992; Moore, et al., 1996).

MORE RESEARCH ON LEARNING ENVIRONMENTS. Single-sex learning environments need to be studied in greater depth. Research should consider both the long term and short term impact of all-girl schools, classes, and programs on gender equity. Since the vast majority of girls and boys attend public mixed-sex schools, current attention to single-sex approaches should not overshadow efforts to improve gender, race, and class equity in mixed-sex schools.

FOLLOW-UP ON KEY RESEARCH FINDINGS. Following the AAUW Educational Foundation's (1996) recommendations, educational environments should provide strong female role models/mentors from socially and culturally diverse backgrounds, cooperative learning approaches, opportunities for girls to assume leadership roles and explore career possibilities, and critical discussion of the assumptions underlying traditional curricula and school practices.

ENCOURAGEMENT OF ACADEMIC ACHIEVEMENT. Increased efforts must be made to improve achievement levels of both girls and boys, and to help girls increase their sense of academic competence, particularly in the areas of math and science. Educators and others can help girls envision wider career options, and discourage girls from attributing academic difficulties to personal failure.

COMPREHENSIVE SEXUALITY EDUCATION. Developmentally appropriate sexuality education programs should be made available to all students, beginning in elementary school. Sexuality education curricula should be expanded to honor a wide range of sexual choices and perspectives, and should focus on sexual health, not just danger or disease. Programs should be comprehensive, theory-based, and interactive, and should focus on adolescents' own questions and concerns, rather than adults' preconceived perceptions of their needs. They should take a multicultural approach to help students think critically about social practices and ideologies that constrain sexual development and entitlement. Parents and other caregivers should be involved in planning sexuality education curricula, and should be made aware that sexuality education does not increase sexual behavior among adolescents (Moore, et al., 1996), but that it may offer students tools and strategies to make informed, healthy decisions.

EXPANDED RESEARCH QUESTIONS. Educational research should be broadened to examine girls' particular experiences and outcomes in classrooms and schools. Studies should also examine the complex interactions of sex, race, class, culture, and educational background in shaping girls' and boys' achievement and learning experiences. Research on academic achievement should go beyond analysis of standardized test scores to include qualitative approaches and analyses of students' subjective responses to their educational experiences.

FUNDING. Further funding is needed for the design and implementation of curricula that focus on promoting gender equity and cultural awareness in schools, as well as for professional development opportunities for educators. Funding is also needed to expand programs that offer girls opportunities to explore math, science, technology, and other fields. Greater public school funding is needed, as is more equitable distribution of those funds across districts.

CHAPTER SIX

Economic Realities

G IRLS, LIKE THE REST of the U.S. population, live in a wide variety of economic conditions. While very little information exists on economic conditions specific to girls, considerable data is available on the families in which they live. Since roughly half of the children and adolescents in the United States are female, data on economic conditions of families with children can provide important information about the economic realities of both girls and boys. Particularly important is information about girls from poor or low-income families, since economic constraints can have a strong impact on the options and resources available to them. Furthermore, information about adult women's current economic situations, and racial disparities within them, can offer some indication of adolescent girls' future economic well-being.

In many discussions of economic conditions, children from families of low income are labeled "at risk." Yet as Swadener and Lubeck (1995) point out in their book, *Children and Families "At Promise": Deconstructing the Discourse of Risk,* the uncritical use of such a term leads to a deficit model whereby the sources of poverty and related problems are assumed to be located in the inadequacies of the individual, rather than in societal inequities and the unearned privilege of others.

With Swadener and Lubeck's point in mind, this chapter intends to shed light on girls' economic realities so that concerned adults may press for social change that will nurture the promise of all girls. As this report shows, girls in lower socioeconomic categories have fewer resources available to them across the spectrum, creating additional struggles. The chapter concentrates on data outlining their families' situations, and on data that describes the economic status of women as a gauge of girls' future earning potential, with the goal of providing information that can be useful to policymakers, researchers, and practitioners.

ECONOMIC CONDITIONS IN FAMILIES

I n his 1998 State of the Union Address, President Clinton spoke repeatedly of the United States' strong and growing economy. Yet for many people living in the United States, economic realities remain extremely harsh. For instance, in 1996, although the median income for all U.S. family households was $43,082, approximately 7.7 million families (11 percent) lived in poverty that same year (Bureau of the Census, 1997). The 1996 poverty threshold was set at $7,995 for a single person, and $15,967 for a family of four (one adult with three children) (Bureau of the Census, 1997). Among individuals (as opposed to families or non-family households), the overall per capita income was $18,136. Yet 36.5 million individuals (13.7 percent) lived in poverty, and 40 percent of the poor, or 14.4 million people (5.4 percent of the population), had incomes of less than one half of their poverty threshold (Bureau of the Census, 1997). Contrary to the popular notion that those living in poverty do not work, 40.8 percent of the poor worked in 1996, and 9.6 percent had full-time, year-round employment, yet remained in poverty (Bureau of the Census, 1997).

Vast discrepancies in income levels and poverty rates appear when data are analyzed by race/ethnicity and gender. For instance, U.S. Census Bureau data (1997) reveal that in 1996, overall family poverty rates were highest for families of Hispanic origin (26.4 percent), followed by black families (26.1 percent), Asian and Pacific Islander families (12.7 percent), and white families (8.6 percent). Among female-headed families (with no spouse present), poverty rates were considerably higher: 50.9 percent for families headed by females of Hispanic origin, 43.7 percent for black female-headed families, and 27.3 percent for white female-headed families (Bureau of the Census, 1997). In 1995, white female-headed families had incomes 57 percent higher than black female-headed families, and 70 percent higher than Hispanic female-headed families (Bureau of the Census, 1997).

A substantial gap is also found between female-headed and married-couple families across race/ethnic groups: in

---

My mom got let go from her job a few months ago, and she still can't find work. It's hard because she doesn't really speak English very well. I have a job after school and on weekends, but I don't make that much, plus I have to study. My boss isn't very understanding that I'm just a student and sometimes I have tests I have to study for. Sometimes I try to study at work, but I have to be careful, because I can get in trouble.

— Julia, age 17

SELF-DESCRIPTION: "Hispanic student and good worker"

1996, median family income for all married-couple families was 2.3 times as large as that for female-headed families. For families with children under 18, the discrepancy was even greater: married-couple families with children had median incomes 2.8 times as large as the median income for female-headed families with children (Bureau of the Census, 1997). However, even among female-headed families, race/ethnic disparities still persist: black female-headed families' incomes were 63 percent of those of white female-headed families, and Hispanic female-headed families were only 52 percent of those of white female-headed families (Bureau of the Census, 1997).[37]

Children account for 40 percent of the poor, yet they comprise only 27 percent of the total U.S. population (Bureau of the Census, 1997). In 1996, the overall poverty rate for all children was 20.5 percent; this rate was not statistically different from the 1995 rate (Bureau of the Census, 1997). White children are consistently least likely to live in poverty, followed by Asian children, Hispanic children, Native American children, and black children. The Bureau of the Census (1993) found that in 1992, 17 percent of white children, 39 percent of Hispanic children under 18, and 46 percent of black children under 18 lived in poverty. These statistics reveal that black children were

more than two and a half times as likely as white children to live in poverty, and Hispanic children were more than twice as likely as white children to live in poverty.

It is important to note that while people of color are disproportionately poor, the overall majority of poor children are white. In fact, according to Census Bureau (1997) data, 61.7 percent of poor children are white, 32 percent are black, 29.7 percent are Hispanic, and 4 percent are Asian/Pacific Islander (the category Hispanic, as used here, includes Hispanic children across all races; therefore, percentages do not total 100). Many families' experience of poverty is temporary; however, by the early 1990s one out of every twelve children in the United States was continuously poor over a two-year period (Shea, 1996).

In addition to low income levels, many children and their families live without health insurance. In 1996, approximately 30.9 percent of the nation's poor had no health insurance of any kind (Bureau of the Census, 1997). The percentage of all uninsured children was statistically higher in 1996 (14.8 percent) than in 1995 (13.8 percent); this means that 10.6 million children under 18 were without insurance in 1996 (Bureau of the Census, 1997). The percentages of children without health insurance varies considerably by state, ranging from 3.8 percent in Vermont to 18.4 percent in New Mexico and Texas.[38]

Households headed by single mothers comprise by far the poorest demographic group (Seavey, 1996). In 1996, the median income for all female householders (no spouse present) with related children under 18 was only $18,261, compared to the median income of $51,894 for all married-couple households with related children under 18 (Bureau of the Census, 1997). Families with a female householder (no spouse present) accounted for 18.2 percent of all families in 1996; yet they accounted for 54.1 percent of all poor families that year. Indeed, the overall poverty rate for families with children under 18 headed by a female householder (no spouse present) was 41.9 percent in 1996, compared to poverty rates of 20 percent for families with children under 18 headed by a male householder (no spouse present) and 7.5 percent for married-couple families with children under 18 (Bureau of the Census, 1997).

As Dorothy Seavey notes in her 1996 report for Wellesley's Center for Research on Women, *Back to Basics: Women's*

Poverty and Welfare Reform, while discussions of poverty typically focus on people receiving Aid to Families with Dependent Children (AFDC), many poor families do not fit into the category of "the welfare poor." Indeed, while 13.9 million women lived on poverty-level incomes in 1992, only 3.9 million of those women received AFDC (Administration for Children and Families, 1993, cited in Seavey, 1996). In addition to those living at or below the poverty level are millions of people known as the "unofficial poor"—those whose incomes hover just above the poverty line, and the "contingent poor"[39]—those who work in temporary jobs or jobs with unpredictable income, low pay and little or no benefits (Helco, 1994; Spalter-Roth and Hartmann, 1996, both cited in Seavey, 1996).

While it is difficult to calculate precise numbers of people who are unofficially poor (Seavey, 1996), Census Bureau (1997) data indicate that in 1996, 25.8 million people had incomes between 100 and 150 percent of the poverty threshold. While these individuals are not counted in official statistics on people living in poverty, they nonetheless have incomes which are considerably lower than the median per capita income (for example, 150 percent of the poverty threshold for an individual is $11,992.50—only two-thirds of the median per capita income of $18,136).

Even for those living above the poverty level, vast discrepancies exist in the income of males and females. In 1995, among year-round, full-time workers aged 18 and over, males' mean money earnings exceeded females' across all levels of educational attainment (Bureau of the Census, 1997).[40] For instance, male full-time, year-round workers who were high school graduates with no college had mean money earnings of nearly $10,000 more per year ($31,063 for males versus $21,298 for females) than female full-time, year-round workers with the same level of education. In fact, female full-time, year-round workers who were high school graduates earned less on average than their male counterparts with no high school degree ($21,298 for female high school graduates versus $22,454 for males who were not high school graduates). Male workers who were high school graduates had higher average earnings than female workers with associate degrees ($31,063 versus $28,510), and male workers with bachelors degrees had mean money earnings of over $10,000 more than women workers with masters degrees ($51,998 versus $41,676).

These Census Bureau (1997) statistics show that while female workers' mean money earnings increased as their own educational levels increased, they never caught up to the mean money earnings of male workers with the same level of educational attainment. Furthermore, Census Bureau (1997) data indicate that while the female-to-male earnings ratio for full-time, year-round workers reached a new high in 1996, that ratio was still disturbingly low—the real median earnings for women in this group ($23,710) was only approximately 74 percent of the median earnings for such men ($32,144).

Education has an impact not only on earnings, but also on employment rates. For both males and females, higher levels of education are associated with lower unemployment rates (Bureau of Labor Statistics, 1997). In 1996, women aged 16 to 24 with no high school diploma had the highest unemployment rates (28.7 percent), followed by men in this age group without a high school diploma (21.7 percent). Those with a college degree had the lowest unemployment rates—5.2 percent for men and 2.9 percent for women (Bureau of Labor Statistics, 1997). These data, coupled with the data on educational levels and income, show that although increased levels of education correspond to greater gains in earnings for men than for women, obtaining a college degree corresponds to greater gains in employment rates for women than for men. Given the high rate of unemployment and low incomes for women with-

---

Money is my major issue. Money and stress. Actually, money is my stress. I have my baby to take care of, and his father doesn't help us out at all. I put all my money into my daughter and into helping my mother out with the rent and putting food on the table. I don't have anything left over for me.

— Mekeia, age 17
SELF-DESCRIPTION: "African American teen mom"

---

out a high school diploma, it is particularly important for educators, family members, and community members to encourage girls to stay in school, and to strive for postsecondary education.

The discrepancies between adult male and female earnings and unemployment rates are relevant to teen girls for at least two reasons. First, since many children live in female-headed households, their mothers' earnings affect the financial security or insecurity that girls (and boys) experience in their families. In addition, since adolescent girls represent the next generation of adult female workers, the earnings and employment rates of adult women tell us something about what these girls will face when they enter the adult labor force. Given the increases in average earnings that accompany increases in levels of educational attainment, girls should be encouraged to succeed in school and reach the highest levels of education possible. But given the wide discrepancies in average male-to-female earnings at each educational level, there is still much to be done to eliminate wage discrimination against women who have jobs that are comparable to men, and for girls and women to not be channeled into lower paying occupations.

Data on girls' and their families' economic realities have important implications in many areas of girls' lives. The socioeconomic status of families can have significant impact on the academic resources available to their children. Given the inequitable distribution of public school funding across districts, girls who live in poorer communities may attend schools with considerably fewer resources—from up-to-date textbooks, to science, computer, and musical equipment, to adequate school staffing—than girls who live in wealthier communities.

Whereas girls whose families have higher incomes may have considerable choice as to which schools to attend, girls who do not have the financial means to travel to public magnet schools outside their neighborhood (let alone to pay private school tuition) have their choice of schools severely restricted, even if they qualify for admission to schools they would prefer to attend. Further, since students and their families may be expected to pay for field trips, buy athletic equipment for sports activities, and purchase

may be responsible for caring for siblings, their own children, or ill, disabled, or elderly family members, making it difficult to study and, in some cases, to attend school regularly. For girls whose households lack adequate food, heat, and/or electricity, concentration on schoolwork may be challenging, indeed.

Financial concerns can have a profound impact on the quality of girls' health and health care, as well. Access to nutritious food, exercise and sports activities, and quality health care may be compromised by lack of financial resources and comprehensive health benefits. According to *The Commonwealth Fund Survey of the Health of Adolescent Girls* (1997), 44 percent of girls who lacked insurance indicated that they had gone without needed health care. Girls living in poverty may have considerable difficulty obtaining routine gynecological care, contraception, early pregnancy detection, pre- and post-natal care, and abortion services. Indeed, among adolescent mothers under age 15, only 43 percent received prenatal health care in their first trimester (Monthly Vital Statistics Report, 1994).

Further, the average cost of a first-trimester outpatient abortion in the U.S. in 1993 was $296 dollars—in some states the average cost was considerably higher—yet Medicaid covers very few abortions for poor women (Donovan, 1995). For girls who live outside metropolitan areas, the transportation costs involved in reaching clinics, doctors' offices, or hospitals add to these high costs (Sidel, 1996). Indeed, as of 1992, 94 percent of counties in nonmetropolitan areas offered no abortion services (Henshaw and Van Vort, 1994). In states requiring a 24-hour waiting period for abortion procedures, transportation costs may be compounded by the costs of lodging, or doubled for girls who must make two trips.

I'd like someplace where I could just relax. It's hard, because where I live doesn't feel that safe, and so my mother doesn't really want me hanging out outside or going over my friends' apartments. So just a place where we could get together and do stuff that's positive. Not have to worry about guys messing with us or the dealers in the neighborhood or stuff like that.

— Jeanine, age 14
SELF-DESCRIPTION: "black, urban, independent girl"

Economic factors may also affect the safety or danger girls experience in their homes and communities. In neighborhoods where crime rates are high and law enforcement is lacking, girls may be more likely to experience victimization. They may also feel unsafe participating in afterschool, summer, or weekend activities outside their homes. Thus the very girls

materials for classroom and extracurricular activities, girls from poor or working class families may have difficulty participating in these sorts of activities. Given the high costs of daycare, home health care, and elder care, poorer girls whose parents or other caregivers work long hours

who might benefit most from such programs may have the most difficulty participating. Girls who live in buildings with inadequate wiring, smoke detectors, fire extinguishers, plumbing, or pest control may be more prone to danger and disease. Girls whose families do not have insurance may face even greater hardship if they lose their homes or possessions to fire, theft, floods, or other phenomena.

In addition to understanding the potential effects of poverty on girls, concerned adults must also take steps to address its causes. Critical to this endeavor are efforts to eliminate sexist, racist, and classist practices that contribute to wide disparities in educational attainment, wages, types of occupations entered, employment security, access to health and disability benefits, and so on. Adults who wish to advocate for girls can work to make changes in the new welfare laws (discussed in the next section) that target teen mothers. They also need to push for fair wages, and health and disability benefits for all workers and their families, and to support the creation of new stable, well-paying jobs with full benefits for girls' family members.

Since many girls rely on part-time and/or summer employment to make ends meet—according to the Bureau of Labor Statistics (1997), 41.4 percent of high school students reported being engaged in some labor force activity as of October, 1996, and their unemployment rate was 15.6 percent—employers must pay adolescents fair wages, and allow for flexible hours so that students who must work during the school year can focus on their studies. Employers should be encouraged to hire individuals currently receiving welfare, and both educators and employers can resist the channeling of girls and women into lower-paying jobs and career fields. Funders can provide resources to develop and expand job-training programs, especially those that prepare adolescents who are female and/or of color to enter well-paying fields in which their adult counterparts are currently underrepresented. Courts need to set realistic levels of child support and enforce payments from non-custodial parents. All concerned adults can lobby for safe, accessible, and subsidized daycare programs, so that parents and other caregivers can pursue paid employment without compromising the safety of their children.

IMPACTS OF WELFARE REFORM LEGISLATION

New welfare legislation entitled "The Personal Responsibility and Work Opportunity Reconciliation Act of 1996" was signed by President Clinton on August 22, 1996. Although carefully titled to emphasize opportunity, this legislation has far-reaching and troubling consequences for all people living in poverty, and particularly for children, adolescent girls, and immigrant families. Intended to transfer control of welfare from the federal to the state level, and to restrict the amount of time an individual may receive assistance, the legislation provides block grants to each state, places a five-year lifetime limit on payments, and denies most or all assistance to several groups, including legal immigrants, heads of household who do not find jobs within two years, certain teen mothers, and individuals convicted on felony drug charges. The new law has ended AFDC as of 1997 and replaced it with Temporary Assis-

I got pregnant when I was fourteen, and I had my son when I was fifteen. I thought my boyfriend would stay, but he didn't, so we're on our own. Money's a big problem. I worry that my benefits are going to be cut, but I don't have enough for me and my son as it is. My mom isn't really in the picture, so it makes it really tough to be in school and take care of my baby. I miss a lot of school, which I don't want to do, but I need daycare I can count on. I know I'm young, but I want to be a good mother.

– Rochelle, age 16
SELF-DESCRIPTION: "white, heterosexual female"

tance for Needy Families (TANF), which is operated by individual states.

Among the provisions in the new law is a requirement that, in order to receive benefits, unmarried teenage mothers live at home or in an approved adult-supervised setting, and remain in school or a GED or state-approved training program. This provision has serious consequences for both adolescent mothers and their families. While many girls choose to remain at their families' homes to raise their children, this option may be untenable for many others. Research by Boyer and Fine (1992) has found that the majority of teen parents have experienced some form of physical and/or sexual abuse during childhood. Thus, for girls who face abuse in their families, the requirement that they live at home or in a state-approved setting may place them and their children in danger, particularly if their families or other adult supervisors are unsupportive of their pregnancies and motherhood. The provision also discriminates against teen mothers who choose not to be married, but prefer to live with the fathers of their children.

Further, while the legislation requires adolescent girls to stay in school, it does not provide adequately for the daycare that young mothers would require to do so. Therefore, it places a burden on teens' families, often their mothers or other adult female family members, to care for their children while they are at school. By requiring that teenage mothers live at home or in approved adult-supervised settings, this legislation denies benefits to the very young women who need assistance most—those who are raising their children on their own. More disturbing, the new law gives states the option to deny aid even to those teen mothers who do comply with these two regulations.

In addition, the welfare reform legislation allows states to deny additional assistance to subsequent children of teen mothers who are already receiving assistance. While the Clinton Administration has framed this requirement as an "incentive" for teen mothers to avoid having another child, there is no reliable evidence to suggest that this would be the case (Seavey, 1996). In fact, states with the highest teen birth rates have also had the lowest AFDC benefits (Sidel, 1996; Children's Defense Fund, 1995). Further, many who support such a restriction are also those who seek to deny adolescents adequate sexuality education, access to birth control, and the right to a safe and legal abortion. Without the information, support, and resources to prevent or terminate a pregnancy, girls who have another child while already receiving benefits will be doubly disadvantaged. While supporters of limited benefits often speak of increased aid as condoning or rewarding teen pregnancy, refusing mothers additional assistance to care for their children simply increases the likelihood that they will live in poverty, and thus the likelihood that they and their children will lack adequate health care, nutrition, housing, and education.

According to Spalter-Roth and her colleagues' 1995 study for the Institute for Women's Policy Research (IWPR), many of the provisions in the new welfare reform legislation are based on inaccurate assumptions about welfare recipients and teenage girls. Recipients of AFDC have typically been portrayed as unwed teen mothers; as African American; as "able-bodied" but "too lazy" to seek employment; and as dependent on AFDC for many years (Spalter-Roth, et al., 1995). Yet data from the Administration for Children and Families (1996) show that in 1995, teen mothers under 20 years old comprised only seven percent of all adult female AFDC recipients in 1995, and of those, 75 percent were 18- and 19-year-olds.[41] Furthermore, of those families receiving welfare between October 1994 and September 1995, 37.2 percent were headed by African American parent(s), 35.6 percent were headed by white parent(s), 20.7 percent were headed by Hispanic parent(s), 3 percent were headed by Asian parent(s), and 1.3 percent were headed by Native American parent(s) (Administration

for Children and Families, 1996).[42] The proportion of all AFDC recipients who are African American declined from 45 percent in 1969 to 40 percent in 1995, despite a slight increase in the proportion of the overall U.S. population who are African American (Spalter-Roth, et al., 1995).

Contrary to the portrayal of welfare recipients as lazy adults, the vast majority (69 percent) of AFDC recipients in 1995 were children (Administration for Children and Families, 1996). And only nine percent of mothers on welfare in the study by Spalter-Roth, et al., (1995) used benefits without also looking for work, working at paid employment, attending school, or caring for children at home. In their two year IWPR study, Spalter-Roth, et al., also found that:

- Half of all single mothers who spent any time on welfare during the two-year study also worked during that period.
- Forty-three percent of the women studied worked a substantial amount of the time.
- Twenty percent of the women combined work with welfare, and 23 percent cycled between work and welfare.
- The 43 percent of mothers studied who both worked and received welfare earned an average of only $4.29 per hour. Few of these women received health insurance coverage from their employers.
- Twenty-three percent of the mothers receiving welfare were unemployed but actively seeking work during the two year study.
- Seven percent of the mothers receiving welfare had severe disabilities which prevented them from working or seeking employment. These women accounted for one-fourth of the women who neither worked nor looked for work during the two-year study.

Finally, the welfare reform laws target legal immigrants and their families by denying them food stamps and most other welfare benefits. Unfortunately, renewed anti-immigrant sentiment, coupled with damaging stereotypes of the poor and misconceptions of the welfare system, have led to a portrayal of immigrant families as undeserving of public assistance. Given the increasing immigrant population in the United States, many children and adolescents, both girls and boys, will suffer from this legislation. Persuasive lobbying efforts and increased support of immigrants' rights groups are therefore needed to ensure the well-being of all families and their children.

Although the welfare reform law has already been signed, concerned adults can work to amend provisions at the state level that unfairly disadvantage and endanger girls and their children. They can also expand job training programs, and make a conscious effort to hire girls who are entering the workforce. Employers can introduce flex-time so that parents can both work and care for children or attend school. Companies can create jobs that pay fair wages and provide health benefits for workers and their families. Funders can support daycare programs in communities, schools, and workplaces to allow parents with small children to study and work outside the home. Activists should lobby to make benefits available to girls and their families, and help girls and their families obtain continuing education and jobs that will be viable routes for them to move out, and stay out, of poverty.

CONCLUSION

The economic conditions of girls' families can have an important impact on their health, safety, and access to resources that promote their present and future well-being. Even as some economic indicators suggest positive trends in the United States' economy, Census Bureau (1997) data reveal that 36.5 million people lived in poverty in 1996, and 14.4 million people lived in extreme poverty (less than 50 percent of their poverty threshold). Studies show vast gender and race discrepancies in income and poverty rates. Among families with children, those headed by females had poverty rates two times that of those headed by males and over five and one-half times that of married-couple families. According to 1992 figures, black children were most likely to live in poverty (46 percent), followed by Hispanic children (39 percent) and white children (17 percent).

The economic realities of adult women are suggestive of what adolescent girls can anticipate in their futures. While women's incomes rise with increases in their educational attainment, their incomes at each level of education are lower than those of men with less education. For instance, in 1995, women with high school diplomas earned less than men without a high school degree; women with associates degrees earned less than men with high school degrees, and women with masters degrees earned less than men with bachelors degrees. Although the ratio of overall female to male earnings among full-time, year-round workers reached an all-time high in 1996, women's median earnings were only 74 percent of men's. Significant discrepancies also exist among women's income levels: black female-headed families' incomes were 63 percent of white female-headed families, and Hispanic female-headed families' incomes were only 52 percent of white female-headed families in 1996.

An alarming number of children and poor people live without any form of health insurance: in 1996, 30.9 percent of poor individuals lacked health insurance, and 10.6 million children (14.6 percent) were without insurance. Given the high cost of health care, this leaves many girls without access to medical services. Indeed, in one large study of adolescent girls, 44 percent of girls who lacked insurance reported that they had gone without health care when they needed it, and 29 percent lacked a regular physician.

The new welfare reform laws target adolescent mothers, among others. Teen mothers face restrictions on their benefits: they are required to live at home or in a state-approved adult-supervised setting and to remain in school; they may be denied increased benefits if they have additional children while already receiving assistance. These restrictions disadvantage girls who must raise their children on their own. Because the law does not provide adequate funding for daycare, it places an additional burden on girls' family members to care for their children while girls are at school. The new law also discriminates against immigrant girls (and boys) and their families by denying them food stamps and most other welfare benefits.

Girls' economic realities can have a profound impact on their educational opportunities, personal health, access to health care, and safety in their homes and communities. The data in this chapter show that much work needs to be done in terms of modifying the welfare reform law and pressing for the creation of jobs with benefits for girls' family members, fair wages for women, health insurance for all individuals, job training programs for those without requisite skills. Continued efforts are also needed to end the channeling of girls and women into lower-paying occupations.

● Although the median income for all U.S. family households was $43,082 in 1996, approximately 7.7 million families (11 percent) lived in poverty that same year; 36.5 million individuals (13.7 percent) lived in poverty, and 40 percent of the poor, or 14.4 million people (5.4 percent of the population), had incomes of less than one half of their poverty threshold (Bureau of the Census, 1997).

● Among children under 18 years old in 1992, 17 percent of white children, 39 percent of Hispanic children, and 46 percent of black children lived in poverty (Bureau of the Census, 1993).

● Although people of color are disproportionately poor, the overall majority of poor children are white: 61.7 percent of poor children are white, 32 percent are black, 29.7 percent are Hispanic, and 4 percent are Asian/Pacific Islander (Bureau of the Census, 1997).

● Teen mothers under 20 years old comprised only seven percent of all adult female AFDC recipients in 1995, and of those, 75 percent were 18- to 19-year-olds (Administration for Children and Families, 1996).

● Households headed by single mothers comprise by far the poorest demographic group (Seavey, 1996). Families with a female householder (no spouse present) accounted for 18.2 percent of all families in 1996; yet they accounted for 54.1 percent of all poor families that year (Bureau of the Census, 1997).

● The percentage of all uninsured children was statistically higher in 1996 (14.8 percent) than in 1995 (13.8 percent); 10.6 million children under 18 were without insurance in 1996 (Bureau of the Census, 1997). Forty-four percent of uninsured girls surveyed by the Commonwealth Fund reported going without needed health care (1997).

● In 1995, among year-round, full-time workers aged 18 and over, males' mean money earnings exceeded females' across all levels of educational attainment. In 1996, women year-round, full-time workers' median earnings were only 74 percent of comparable male workers' median earnings (Bureau of the Census, 1997).

● Among families with children, those headed by females had poverty rates two times that of those headed by males, and over five and one-half times that of married-couple families (Bureau of the Census, 1997).

● In 1996, black female-headed families' incomes were 63 percent of those of white female-headed families, and Hispanic female-headed families were only 52 percent of those of white female-headed families in 1996 (Bureau of the Census, 1997).

● One in 12 children lived continuously in poverty for a two-year period in the early 1990s (Shea, 1996).

● Although cast in the language of incentive and opportunity, the new welfare reform law threatens the well-being of teen mothers and their children, children living in single-parent households, children of immigrant families, and others. No reliable evidence indicates that the law's so-called incentives would reduce either teen births or girls' likelihood of living in poverty (Seavey, 1996).

ACTIVISM. Heightened efforts are needed to address the incidence and effects of poverty. Girls and their families need greater access to job training; expanded unemployment and disability benefits; quality daycare; and educational opportunities if they are to find and keep jobs.

SOCIETAL AWARENESS. More consciousness-raising is necessary to identify assumptions and practices that stereotype and discriminate against people living in poverty. Education and enlightened policy are needed to challenge the societal racism that underlies the large discrepancies in standards of living between white families and families of color.

MORE RESEARCH. Research is needed to identify the differential impacts of poverty on girls and boys. In particular, research and action are needed to address the implications of the withdrawal of welfare benefits to teen mothers.

FUNDING AND PUBLIC POLICY. Funding is needed to support job training programs for teens, immigrant rights organizations, and quality daycare programs that allow teen parents to work and continue their education. Policies need to counter hiring practices that discriminate against women and girls. Public policy must incorporate an understanding that poverty and related problems are not caused by children and families "at risk," nor is risk an individual phenomenon. Thus, policy discussion should focus on ameliorating social conditions that promote poverty.

Conclusion

I THINK ADULTS SHOULD know that kids know a lot more than people think. Give us a chance, because we have a lot of good ideas and a lot of energy, and we can really make a difference. Sometimes adults are pessimistic, but us kids are optimistic. Let us work on things, and trust us and help us instead of saying, "oh, that won't work, that's just idealistic." Maybe it is, but maybe we need more people to be idealistic, because there are a lot of things in this world that need to be fixed.

—Laurie, age 14

SELF-DESCRIPTION: "black female who lives in the city"

In spite of the many forces that collude to constrain their options, adolescent girls and young women continue to take action, to advocate for themselves and their peers, and to work toward a healthier future. While this report illuminates the many challenges to girls' health and achievement, its examples of girls' resiliency and resistance are inspiring. Promising discussions with girls in schools and youth activist groups reveal that collectively girls can transform not only the conditions of their communities and peers, but also their own sense of strength and possibility (AAUW, 1996a; Pastor, McCormick, and Fine, 1996).

While some girls may, indeed, go underground in adolescence, they also resist, speak out, and struggle to create the terms of their development. In girl-centered magazines, girls share stories, letters, and artwork about the sexism they encounter. In supportive school environments, girls take healthy risks, explore nontraditional roles, excel academically, and explore their own creativity and leadership potential. Through peer education programs and community organizing, girls advocate for one another, their neighborhoods, their families, and their schools. From reproductive rights to animal rights, from education to the environment, girls continue to push boundaries and affect change.

Nowhere was this more evident than in the United Nations Fourth World Conference on Women, held in Beijing in 1995. An emphasis on the rights of the girl-child was put forward at the conference, at the related forum of non-governmental organizations (NGOs), and in the conference's official document, the *Platform for Action.* Girls, themselves, participated in sessions and workshops at unprecedented levels. A youth tent and a youth parade demonstrated just how able girls are to advocate for their own concerns. Following the conference, girls returned home to countries around the world, eager to share their insights with their peers, and to keep in close contact with friends made in Beijing.

Both in the United States and around the globe, girls continue to develop insights, convictions, and talents of their own. But they need and deserve the commitment of adults to support their efforts. Where do we begin? Based on the extensive body of work on girls in the United States reviewed in this report, five overarching conclusions emerge. These understandings should guide adults' efforts to improve girls' lives, and help them to create healthy and satisfying futures:

Girls are multidimensional individuals with diverse perspectives, needs, and developmental contexts. Researchers, policymakers, and people who work directly with girls must be sensitive to the complex interactions of gender with other aspects of their identities, and the communities in which they live. It is especially important to address the experiences and perspectives of girls who tend to be marginalized in research, schools, communities, and programs. This includes girls who are lesbian or bisexual, pregnant or parenting, poor, immigrant, disabled, and/or of color.

Girls can benefit from programs and strategies that highlight their strengths and encourage them to explore meaningful possibilities for their futures. Concerned adults working across the fields of education, health care, athletics, community-based advocacy, and juvenile justice have developed community and school-based programs that support girls who are exploring their identities and talents, considering their options, and preparing themselves for healthy and productive adulthood. Adults who wish to advocate for girls can incorporate the insights gleaned from these efforts into their own work with girls. Programs and policies that foster intergenerational collaboration can be especially effective in developing girls' leadership skills by exposing them to the benefits of mentoring relationships.

Collaboration among adults across a wide range of fields can deepen understandings of girls' needs, and illuminate effective strategies for supporting them. Researchers, educators, health care professionals, policymakers, activists, and funders can share insights gained from their various forms of work with girls. Researchers, policymakers, and funders, in particular, need to learn from the experiences of those involved more directly with girls. Researchers should continue to play a key role in deepening social understanding of girls' needs, and should develop and implement a research agenda informed by the needs and perspectives of girls, their families, and their communities.

Girls need and deserve the awareness, attention, and commitment of a wide range of individuals and institutions to promote their healthy development. While parents and other caregivers continue to play the primary role in supporting girls' development, community members, educators, and other professionals can also help to create safe, supportive environments that nurture and encourage girls to develop and pursue their goals. Partnerships among families, schools, community programs, and cultural organizations can provide opportunities for girls, and let them know that they are valued community members.

Girls have important things to say, and their insights can inform adults who advocate for them. Adults who want to help girls need to collaborate not only with one another, but also with girls themselves. Adults can learn a great deal about girls' experiences by listening to their perspectives, and incorporating their insights into their work. When girls' collaboration is solicited in authentic and meaningful ways, through involvement in the design and implementa-

tion of research and programs, girls can gain leadership skills, develop supportive intergenerational relationships, and experience themselves as active participants in social change.

These broad conclusions can guide those who are concerned about girls and their futures to develop concrete, practical strategies that will promote girls' well-being. Concerned adults can develop and implement strategies that support girls by creating research agendas that focus on what girls need for healthy development; funding programs that support girls; developing and implementing gender-fair educational materials and school practices; encouraging behaviors that promote girls' health; working on policy issues at local, state, and national levels; and engaging girls in safe, meaningful, and fun activities in their communities.

Based on recommendations and successful strategies cited within this report, adults can advocate for girls in myriad ways. (For examples, see "What Do Adolescent Girls Need for Healthy Development," at the end of this report.) Whether by working with girls in families, communities, programs, or schools, developing supportive public policy, conducting research, or funding programs and initiatives on behalf of girls, adults can help girls to deal with the challenges of adolescence and realize their goals. Girls need opportunities to develop their sense of possibility, and to experience themselves as active agents in their own lives. They need the support and collaboration of adults who are committed to girls' entitlement to advocate for themselves. They also need material resources from adults, whether funding, information, transportation, supplies, or office space, to confer with their peers and enact their visions. Girls need continued activism on the part of adults to address the circumstances that limit their options and opportunities.

Since NCRW's *Risk, Resiliency, and Resistance: Current Research on Adolescent Girls* was first published in 1991, research on girls both in the U.S. and around the world has expanded dramatically. The findings reviewed in *The Girls Report* suggest that girls continue to demonstrate resiliency—through activism, academics, sports, and leadership, as well as through relationships with peers and adults. Certain trends are encouraging, including gains in girls' academic achievement levels, increased condom use, broadened athletic opportunities, and declining teen pregnancy and birth rates.

But current research also suggests that young women continue to face many challenges and obstacles to healthy physical, psychological, and social development. Statistics on adolescent girls' victimization, rates of depression, still-high (though declining) pregnancy and birth rates, unhealthy body image, incidence of HIV/AIDS and other STDs, and use of cigarettes, alcohol, and other drugs, are all cause for alarm. Since research suggests that reforms that support girls' needs also tend to benefit boys, attending to these issues will promote the well-being of all youth.

The National Council for Research on Women and its member organizations are deeply committed to developing research, and supporting policy and programming that speak to the complex needs of girls. NCRW encourages those involved in research, funding, education, advocacy, policymaking, and activism, to join its ongoing effort to promote girls' well-being, and to eliminate the many social barriers that threaten girls' healthy development, constrict their options, and dampen their dreams. The resilience of girls in the midst of these challenges speaks to the power and strength of their spirit. Girls deserve and need the respectful support of concerned adults to flourish throughout adolescence, and to have every opportunity to create a happy and healthy future for themselves.

What Do Adolescent Girls Need for Healthy Development?

PARENTS AND OTHER FAMILY MEMBERS WHO:

- Serve as positive role models by showing respect for girls and women, and expressing confidence in girls' aspirations.
- Embrace all aspects of girls' identities—including their sexuality, their perspectives, and their priorities—and provide a respectful context where girls can raise questions and voice their concerns.
- Encourage girls to do well in school by discussing their studies with them, exploring potential areas of interest, supporting their achievements, and becoming involved with girls' schools.
- Encourage girls to explore their strengths and develop their talents in all fields, especially those not traditionally thought of as "female."
- Advocate for equal programs, facilities, equipment, and publicity for girls and boys in school- and community-based athletic programs, and support the involvement of girls who have traditionally not seen themselves as athletes.
- Help girls to respect their bodies and discourage the development of eating disorders by rebutting negative cultural messages about body image, and encouraging healthy behaviors.
- Provide access to non-judgmental information and resources to prevent unwanted pregnancies, and the transmission of HIV/AIDS and other STDs. Offer guidance and support to help girls make healthy decisions about a range of types of sexual activity.
- From a young age, foster girls' sense of entitlement to respectful treatment, and teach them that they can speak out against behaviors of others that hurt them.

- Support girls' involvement in community groups and extra-curricular activities, help them to develop leadership skills, and encourage them to take action to promote constructive social change.
- Raise boys in ways that foster their respect for girls and women.

EDUCATORS AND SCHOOLS THAT:

- Promote gender equity through classroom and school practices, model respect for girls and for people of all cultures, and offer students positive images and balanced information through innovative curricular materials.
- Encourage girls to explore a wide range of subjects and potential careers, especially those in which girls and women are traditionally underrepresented.
- Support and respect girls' efforts to balance school, social, and family challenges.
- Offer girls more leadership opportunities and vehicles for active exploration of their interests and talents.
- Help students to probe issues of gender, race, class, culture, sexuality, and disability, and to challenge attitudes and behaviors that stereotype or discriminate.
- Encourage girls to participate in a wide range of extracurricular activities, including athletic activities, in an atmosphere of respect for girls and women.
- Formulate and enforce publicly stated policies against sexual harassment and discriminatory practices, and protect the rights of students who file harassment claims.
- Offer comprehensive sexuality education programs that promote discussions of sexual health,

provide students with clear, meaningful information and resources, and demonstrate respect for students' diverse sexual orientations.

- Give teachers, counselors, and other school staff the time and space to work together to enhance their effectiveness, and encourage educators to pursue ongoing professional development activities that help them to better meet the needs of diverse student bodies.
- Demonstrate respect for students' cultures and native languages, and work collaboratively with families and communities to understand and support the needs of all students.

ADULT MENTORS WHO:

- Understand and are committed to the communities in which girls live.
- Assist girls in recognizing and confronting the impacts of harmful attitudes and behaviors.
- Address and challenge problematic images of girls and women in the media and school curricula.
- Serve as positive role models—women who are strong, competent, and actively involved in social issues, and men who are supportive and respectful of women and girls.
- Help girls to explore their strengths, develop their skills, achieve in school, and envision a wide range of options for healthy and productive futures.
- Provide a safe context for girls to raise questions, grapple with confusion, voice their concerns, and develop strategies to deal with their concerns.

RESEARCHERS WHO:

- Design studies to learn about girls' strengths, resilience, and the conditions that support their well-being, rather than simply focusing on risks and negative behaviors.
- Understand and present girls as multifaceted individuals who live in diverse social contexts, and have a wide range of needs, perspectives, and experiences.
- Promote more nuanced, layered understandings of the ways that gender interacts with race, ethnicity, sexual identity, socioeconomic status, culture, and disability in shaping girls' identities and social experiences.
- Situate studies of girls' issues in critical analyses of the problematic social practices, inequities, and dominant cultural assumptions that contextualize girls' lives.
- Present data in ways that show the intersections of age, gender, race, social class, and sexuality, rather than offering separate analyses for each category (i.e., youth in general, race comparisons, gender comparisons, etc.).
- Expand research categories to move beyond such practices as characterizing race as only "white," "African American," and "Hispanic/Latino;" oversimplifying notions of "sexual activity" as only heterosexual intercourse; and using narrow concepts of "achievement" as only quantifiable performance on standardized tests.
- Collaborate with advocates and activists in developing research agendas that focus on girls' concerns, and collect data in ways that tap the perspectives of diverse groups of girls and adults.
- Incorporate girls' narratives into research studies, and involve girls in the design, implementation, analysis, and presentation of research so that they can learn new skills, help shape research agendas, and think critically about their own and others' experiences.
- Resist one dimensional portrayals of girls as either passive victims or independent heroes, and instead look at the multiple ways that girls both resist and incorporate problematic societal messages.
- Expand research on "women's issues" (such as rape, battering, harassment, and pregnancy) to incorporate the experiences of adolescent girls.

HEALTH CARE PROFESSIONALS, ADVOCATES, AND OTHER HELPING PROFESSIONALS WHO:

- Demonstrate sensitivity to gender and cultural issues that affect a wide range of girls' behaviors and mental health, including depression, eating disorders, and sexual health practices.
- Challenge economic barriers and social conditions that threaten girls' (and boys') health and safety in their homes, schools, and communities.
- Implement a holistic approach to health by moving beyond the treatment of disease to promote girls' positive feelings about themselves. Encourage girls to reject behaviors that threaten their psychological and physical well-being.
- Provide constructive health education that empowers girls to make choices that are healthy and appropriate for their own lives.
- Encourage girls to critique cultural messages (e.g., images equating extreme slenderness with female attractiveness) and practices (e.g., smoking, unprotected intercourse, drug and alcohol misuse) that may hurt them.
- Provide confidential information and access to reliable contraception, pregnancy and STD testing, and abortion services.
- Help discourage the spread of HIV/AIDS among adolescents by supporting condom distribution and needle exchanges, and providing information about their proper use for HIV/AIDS prevention.
- Listen respectfully to girls' questions and concerns

about sexuality, peer relationships, school experiences, family concerns, and other developmental issues. Provide them with the space and guidance to work through their own solutions.

- Help girls to cope with the effects of victimization, discourage their involvement in criminal activities, and work to eliminate differential treatment of girls in the juvenile justice system.

- Work collaboratively with girls and their families, understanding and respecting their cultural and religious values.

POLICYMAKERS, ACTIVISTS, AND OTHER OPINION LEADERS WHO:

- Understand that support for girls requires social and institutional change, and that a focus on individualistic strategies to raise girls' self-esteem or label girls as "at risk" can mask underlying societal inequities.

- Challenge popular images in school curricula, program materials, and the media that promote gender, racial, and ethnic stereotypes.

- Develop and support programs to counteract messages that promote harmful behavior such as smoking, drug use, unprotected intercourse, and excessive dieting.

- Develop and support affordable, confidential gynecological and other health care programs that are accessible to all girls.

- Support policies and legislation that provide adolescents with access to a wide array of reproductive health options, prevention and treatment of STDs, and sexuality education programs.

- Challenge welfare reform policies that restrict or deny needed benefits to teen mothers and their children.

- Educate the public about the prevalence of violence against girls. Ensure that girls benefit from programs and other advocacy efforts on behalf of women who are survivors of rape, battering, and harassment.

- Expand public awareness of rape to acknowledge the large number of rapes committed by family members and acquaintances, and the high proportion of survivors who are adolescent girls.

- Support teacher training and professional development programs that help educators to cultivate classroom practices that promote girls' achievement. Encourage them to develop and use curricular materials that highlight the work of all women, and men of color, and promote understanding of non-Western perspectives.

- Increase awareness of the impacts of poverty on girls and their families. Expose the racism and sexism that underlie the large discrepancies in income, employ-

ment, and poverty rates between white families and families of color, and between married-couple families and female-headed families.

- Support job training programs for teens and their family members, and provide quality, affordable daycare that allows parents to work and/or continue their education without compromising the well-being of their children.

FUNDERS WHO:

- Support programs in communities, as well as at the state, national, and international level, that promote girls' health, recreation, safety, leadership, and achievement.

- Finance educators, researchers, and advocates working to develop and implement curricula that promote gender equity and cultural awareness.

- Fund innovative teacher and counselor training programs, and continuing education programs that encourage adults in schools to work on gender and cultural issues.

- Fund job training and professional development programs for teens and their families.

- Support the development of quality, affordable daycare programs in workplaces, schools, and communities, and fund elder care and home health care programs so that adolescent girls are released from adult family responsibilities.

- Fund victim services, immigrant rights, and disability rights programs that support girls, their families, and their communities.

- Support programs for girls who may be marginalized in school and community programs, including lesbian and bisexual girls, immigrant girls, girls of color, and girls who are from poor or low-income families.

- Fund community-based health care organizations that provide quality, affordable, preventive health care for girls and their families; accurate and confidential sexuality education for adolescents; and confidential family planning services, abortion services, and services to detect and prevent HIV/AIDS and other STDs, and to offer care for those who live with such diseases.

- Support programs and consciousness-raising efforts that promote healthy behaviors and encourage adolescents to resist such practices as smoking, binge drinking, drug misuse, excessive dieting, and engaging in unprotected intercourse.

- Finance the efforts of schools, programs, and community groups to form partnerships through which concerned adults can share insights and work collaboratively to support the needs of girls.

Looking Ahead: Developing a New Research Agenda

THE RESEARCH DISCUSSED in this report not only informs us about what is known about adolescent girls, but also about what is not yet known. In the last ten years, attention to girls in the research literature has increased, but much work still needs to be done. A review of the research literature reveals several gaps in current knowledge about girls, and points to new directions to pursue.

The National Council for Research on Women (NCRW) calls on researchers and advocates to develop a research agenda that will unearth new understandings about adolescent girls and what is working to support their development. NCRW offers the following guidelines and topics in need of further research as a starting point for shaping such an agenda. These recommendations are based on the findings of the study, and are discussed in more depth in each relevant chapter.

RESEARCH GUIDELINES

The following five broad guidelines can help researchers in designing and conducting research that is supportive of girls' needs:

Research should focus on girls' strengths, progress, and resilience, not just on risks and problems. Researchers should emphasize how girls understand and actively strategize to deal with both the positive and negative aspects of their lives. A focus on girls' assets, rather than deficits, will lead to greater understanding of girls' complex realities and will help to counter negative portrayals of girls as passive, frail, or voiceless.

Researchers should work collaboratively with girls and the adults who advocate for them. Researchers

should conceptualize their research as with and for girls and others in the diverse social contexts in which they live. A collaborative approach involves girls and their advocates in the formulation of research questions and designs, collection and analysis of data, and presentation of findings. This ensures that the research will have practical use, and it enables girls to gain skills for investigating their social worlds and thinking critically about their own lives.

Research should focus on girls in the contexts in which they live in order to illuminate their complex perspectives, priorities, strategies, and identities. While large-scale surveys are helpful for determining the incidence of various behaviors and living conditions, qualitative approaches are also needed to capture important variations across girls' diverse social interactions. Research that takes into account the contexts in which girls live and develop, as well as larger sociopolitical forces, can also help to prevent victim-blaming by focusing public attention on social inequities and the limited resources for girls.

Research should speak to the complexities of girls' social and personal identities as girls themselves define them. Rather than simply comparing males to females or homogenizing girls into static racial groups, researchers should probe the fluid interplay among girls' racial, cultural, social class, gender, and sexual identifications, as well as their social contexts and unique personal experiences and (dis)abilities. Research is needed to better understand the particularities of girls' identities, as well as their shared experiences within and across groups.

Researchers should investigate the impacts of social policy and programs on girls' lives. Researchers should examine the positive and problematic short- and long-term effects of various policies that apply to girls and their families, schools, and communities. Researchers should work with girls, families, and advocates to investigate what types of pro-active policies and programs would be supportive of girls' needs. They should also explore the ways in which girls are involved in supporting and transforming their communities and wider worlds.

TOPICS FOR FURTHER RESEARCH

Several important topics relating to girls have only recently begun to receive research attention, and still others have yet to be researched. Based on extensive discussion with researchers, advocates, educators, activists, and adolescent girls, the National Council for Research on Women has identified the need for studies in the following areas, and recommends that funders provide generous support for these projects. In all studies of girls, researchers should take care to create designs that consider girls not just on an individual level, but also in the context of communities, families, institutions (such as schools or the health care system), and broader sociopolitical phenomena.

Health: How do girls define health, and what do they need to support their healthy development? Researchers need to expand conceptualizations of health as merely the absence of illness. Researchers should explore varying cultural values associated with girls' health, as well as conditions that girls, their families, and those working with them perceive as hindering or fostering their physical health and psychological well-being.

How do physical and psychological health interact with one another in girls' lives? Research is needed to explore the dynamic interplay between physical and psychological aspects of girls' health. Researchers can investigate how girls' decisions and ability to practice health-promoting behaviors impact on their sense of psychological well-being, as well as their physical wellness. They can also examine how girls' sense of psychological strength and entitlement may influence their health-related practices.

What are the effects of social and environmental factors on girls' health? Researchers can move beyond individualistic approaches by examining the health-related impacts of such issues as poverty, environmental problems, community safety, discrimination, social support, unequal access to resources, and the presence or absence of community and school programs. By investigating health at the societal level, as well as an individual level, research can identify needs for social and political reform, rather than simply identifying how girls themselves need to change.

Sexualities: How do girls think about their sexualities, and what helps girls develop positive feelings about their sexual identities? Research that goes beyond tracking incidence of heterosexual intercourse can further understandings of the complexities of girls' decision-making processes and development of sexual entitlement. Research can help to identify factors that facilitate girls' exploration of sexual identities and relationships.

What are the impacts of policy, programs, and resources on girls' sexual development and decision-making? Research is needed to explore how restrictions on sexuality education, access to affordable and confidential gynecological and abortion services, and access to contraception influence adolescents' thinking about sexual options as well as their sexual behavior. Research can also shed light on the ways that adolescents and adult advocates are working to resist and transform such restrictions and the impacts of their strategies.

What kinds of images and messages promote boys' development of respect for girls' sexual entitlement and well-being? Research with boys and their mentors can lead to better understandings of conditions that promote or hinder boys' orientation toward mutuality in intimate relationships and their positive regard for girls' and women's sexual rights.

Schooling: In what ways do schools promote or compromise girls' achievement, educational options, and confidence in their own abilities? Qualitative research on school climates can identify conditions that support girls' academic success and positive feelings about themselves and their schools. Research can also identify inequitable conditions that continue to marginalize girls and/or students who are gay, lesbian, bisexual, immigrant, (dis)abled, or of color. Research should examine classroom practices and curricular materials, as well as after-school programs, sports activities, and collaboration among schools, communities, and families.

How are new curricular initiatives transforming girls' and boys' educational experiences? Research is needed to highlight effective elements of curricula that incorporate nontraditional learning approaches and emphasize the achievements of women and of men of color. Through work with educators and students, researchers should strive to identify what is needed to gain community and school support for new curricular initiatives, as well as the challenges involved in curricular transformation and the ongoing impacts of curricular innovations on girls' and boys' learning and development.

What are the effects of sexual and discriminatory harassment policies, and what steps can be taken to prevent such harassment and discrimination in schools? More research is needed to understand the effectiveness of various harassment policies and programs aimed at fostering respect among all students. Research can illuminate obstacles to implementing such policies and programs, as well as school conditions that promote positive outcomes.

What are the relative merits and limitations of single-sex versus mixed-sex learning environments? In light of recent experimentation with single-sex schools, classrooms, and programs, research is needed to evaluate the positive and problematic outcomes of various approaches. This research should consider not only academic achievement, but also students' attitudes toward schooling, sense of confidence in their abilities, and opportunities for involvement and leadership. Research can point to ways that key elements of various successful learning approaches can be integrated into mixed-sex, public schools so that all students benefit from effective educational practices.

Violence and Victimization: How do girls interpret the violence and victimization they and others experience? Research should not only trace the incidence of various forms of girls' victimization, but also explore how girls understand, name, and resist victimization in their own lives. Research questions should be expanded to consider coercive experiences that do not necessarily involve uses of physical violence. Research should also consider the impact of hostile contexts (such as uninterrupted sexual harassment in schools) on girls' feelings of safety and dignity.

What is needed to prevent victimization of girls, and what can help girls deal with the victimization they witness or experience themselves? Researchers can study the effects of policies and programs aimed at reducing and redressing victimization in the lives of girls and women. They can also

shed light on the availability and effectiveness of victim support services and learn more about the conditions that encourage or discourage girls from using such services. Research is also needed to explore the impact of violence prevention programs, conflict resolution programs, and programs and curricula that foster boys' respect for girls and women.

What can be done to prevent girls from perpetrating violence and other crimes? How can the juvenile justice system do a more effective job of working with girls who have committed crimes? Research efforts should identify the needs of girls who are involved with the juvenile justice system. Researchers should investigate inequities in services and punishment of girls and boys and identify ways that resources can be increased for girls who are marginalized within the criminal justice system, including girls who are pregnant or parenting, (dis)abled, and/or of color.

Economic Realities: How do girls understand and deal with their current economic realities, and what do they envision for their futures? Research is needed to illuminate how girls across a range of socioeconomic statuses think about and use the options available to them. Researchers can also learn more about the impact of wage gaps based on gender and race on girls' expectations for their futures. They can ask girls what they themselves see as their most pressing needs and researchers can also explore how girls' of lower income groups advocate for themselves and their communities within the context of limited resources.

What is the impact of recent welfare reform legislation on girls' lives and opportunities? Since states have developed a wide range of approaches to welfare reform, further investigation is needed to identify the short term and long term effects of various policies and programs. Particular attention is needed to understand the impacts on teen mothers, immigrant girls, and the children of teenagers.

These questions by no means exhaust the potential areas in need of further study. They do, however, suggest several stepping-off points for researchers who wish to direct their work toward the promotion of girls' well-being. As research with and for girls takes on new momentum, the National Council for Research on Women looks forward to ongoing, critical discussion among researchers and other concerned adults who are working to understand and foster the healthy development of all girls.

Notes

1. Progressive health educators and advocates are beginning to use the term "sexually transmitted infections" (STIs) because it is considered more accurate and less stigmatizing than the more commonly used STDs. However, STDs is still more common and is therefore used in this text.

2. While the terms "girls of color" and "people of color" are used in this text, it is important to note that there exists considerable disagreement among activists and scholars about the appropriate terms to use to describe people who are not considered (by themselves and/or the broader society) to be white. On the one hand, some have claimed that the language "of color" seems to suggest that Caucasian people do not have race or "color." Some have also suggested that this term overlooks the many distinctions among people of all different races by dichotomizing "white" and "of color." On the other hand, terms such as "minorities" suggest that Caucasian people are a majority when, in fact, they constitute a minority of the world's population. Terms such as "non-white" are similarly problematic, since they tend to standardize the category whiteness. While the concerns about using the term "of color" are significant, the decision was made to use the term here because, in a racist society, girls (and others) who are not white face discrimination that people who are considered white do not. Thus, there is a need for some term that speaks of groups of people who face such discrimination and marginalization, so that issues of racism can be discussed and problematized. The intention here is not to erase rich and important cultural differences, nor to suggest that Caucasian people do not have race, but rather to acknowledge that some language is needed in order to address these critical issues.

The term "girls with disabilities"—or "girls with (dis)abilities"—is used in this text to refer to girls whose physical, emotional, and/or cognitive needs are typically unmet in the broader society, due to lack of wheelchair access, braille, signers, and so forth, as well as to lack of understanding and tolerance of physical, cognitive, and emotional variation across individuals. While many people experience physical limitations, such as poor eyesight, social institutions and cultural norms accommodate some needs while ignoring others. The term "girls with disabilities" is not intended to suggest that all these girls share common characteristics, but rather to refer to girls who face barriers due to ableism—discrimination against people with disabilities through societal intolerance, stereotyping, discriminatory hiring/educational practices, lack of physical access, etc.

3. Personal communication with Betsy Brill, Executive Director of Girl's Best Friend Foundation, Chicago, Illinois, February 16, 1998. Girl's Best Friend Foundation is currently developing a three-year, assets-based research agenda to learn more about girls' positive developmental experiences and the environments and conditions that keep girls healthy and strong. The research will focus on organizations working with girls from 5 to 18 years old in Illinois.

4. Thanks to Heather Johnston Nicholson at Girls Incorporated for helpful thoughts on this issue. Personal correspondence from Heather Johnston Nicholson to Linda Basch, Nina Sonenberg, and Lynn Phillips, July 21, 1996.

5. Because researchers use various terms to describe race and or ethnic groups in their studies, often without defining them, this report reflects the language used in the studies to which it is referring. While many of the terms, such as "Hispanic" or "Black," are problematic, they have not been replaced with more acceptable terms, such as "Latino/a" or "African American," because it is not clear from the original studies whether such terms would actually be comparable. Readers should note, however, that the broad race and ethnic categories used in many studies do not reflect the many cultural variations within groups. When cultural breakdowns are given in the original studies, these terms are used in this report.

6. Personal communication with Fern Goodhart, Director of Rutgers University's Department of Health Education.

7. Thanks to Heather Johnston Nicholson of Girls Incorporated for clarifying these trends.

8. Personal communication with Donna Shoenfeld, psychologist and health educator at Rutgers University's Department of Health Education.

9. Girls Incorporated's "Girls Re-Cast TV Action Kit" is available at <http://www.girlsinc.org/programs/recast.html>.

10. In this study, smoking was defined as "smoking several cigarettes to a pack or more in the last week"; drinking was defined as "drinking alcohol at least once a month or once a week"; and using drugs was defined as "used illegal drugs in the last month."

11. Low, moderate, and severe depressive symptoms were determined by girls' responses to a series of questions asking them to choose one of three answers (including a positive, a moderately negative, and a severely negative feeling) as to how they had felt in the previous two weeks across 14 different areas. Statements were rated a 1 for moderately negative feelings and a 2 for severely negative feelings. Respondents who scored between 9 and 13 were classified as having moderate depressive symptoms; those scoring 13 or higher were classified as having severe depressive symptoms.

12. The media literacy program, sponsored by the Henry J. Kaiser Family Foundation, may be contacted at 1-800-child-44, or readers may visit their website at <http://www.childrennow.org>. The program is available at no charge by calling the toll-free number.

13. To estimate the ages of those fathers whose ages are not reported, the authors interpolate the unknown fathers' ages from the ages that are known.

14. Personal communication with Michael Males, School of Social Ecology, University of California at Irvine, and Peggy Brick, Director of The Center for Family Life Education, Planned Parenthood of Greater Northern New Jersey, September 30, 1997.

15. Since the data are based on focus groups as well as individual interviews, the exact percentage of respondents who have experienced such pressures cannot be known. This is because some participants in focus groups did not respond aloud to every question, even if they had similar experiences.

16. Personal communication with Peggy Brick, Director of The Center for Family Life Education, Planned Parenthood of Greater Northern New Jersey.

17. In examining the discrepancy in birth rates, readers should note that the base numbers in these two studies are different, since the researchers use different criteria for counting "teen births."

18. Criticisms of the anti-rape movement by writers such as Camille Paglia (1990), Katie Roiphe (1993), and Christina Hoff Sommers (1994) have received particular attention in the popular press.

19. Respondents were asked two general questions about abuse (Have you ever been sexually abused? and Have you ever been physically abused?) and allowed to use their own definition of abuse in answering the questions. They were also asked if a date or a boyfriend had ever forced them to have sex against their will or when they did not want to. Since findings of other studies (i.e., Phillips, 1995) have suggested that young women often resist using terms such as "abuse" when thinking about or describing their experiences, these results may still understate the extent of abuse among adolescent girls.

20. These statistics are considered by many to be more accurate than those of the U.S. Department of Justice studies due to the still-conservative definitions and methodologies used by the Bureau of Justice Statistics (Koss, 1993; Koss & Cook, 1993; Sanday, 1996).

21. As researchers at the Wellesley Center for Research on Women point out, these statistics may be influenced by cultural norms surrounding definitions of rape, since sexual victimization of girls (as opposed to older women) is more likely to be reported and accepted as rape. This may be because it is more difficult to claim that a young girl "asked for it." Personal communication with Susan McGee Bailey, Sumru Erkut, and Nan Stein, January 6, 1998.

22. See note 11.

23. Personal communication among Heather Johnston Nicholson, Linda Basch, Nina Sonenberg, and Lynn Phillips, July 21, 1997.

24. Personal communication between NCRW and Harilyn Rousso of Disabilities Unlimited Consulting Services, September 19, 1994. Cited in National Council for Research on Women, Sexual Harassment: Research and Resources, p.31.

25. See note 16.

26. It should be noted that much of this is small base effect.

27. All performance differences reported by the National Center for Education Statistics in the National Assessment of Educational Progress (NAEP) are statistically significant.

28. It is important to note that unlike many national achievement exams that test representative samples of all elementary and secondary school students, the SAT is generally taken only by students who believe they will apply for admission to college.

29. Personal communication with Linda Burnham, Executive Director of the Women of Color Resource Center, Berkeley, California, February 27, 1998.

30. Personal Communication with Janet Kann, Senior Research Scientist, Wellesley Center for Research on Women, March 6, 1998.

31. The author wishes to thank Nina Sonenberg for sharing information about these programs.

32. Personal communication with Michelle Fine, social psychologist at CUNY Graduate Center and expert witness in school race and gender desegregation cases, February 27, 1998.

33. Anne Connors, NOW-NYC President, and Karen Baker, NOW-NYC Vice-President of Public Information in letter to the editor, Ms. Magazine, March/April 1997, p. 9-10.

34. Personal communication with Susan Cote, Director of Counseling and Health Education, Kent Place School, Summit, New Jersey.

35. Thanks to researchers from the Wellesley Center for Research on Women for clarifying this point. Personal communication, January 6, 1998.

36. The majority of Cuban Americans in the High School and Beyond sample were recent immigrants, rather than children of the cohort who arrived in the United States immediately following the Cuban revolution.

37. These statistics include families with and without children.

38. These percentages represent averages of the three years' percentages, rather than the percent of the average numbers (Bureau of the Census, 1998).

39. As discussed in the next section, the Personal Responsibility and Work Opportunity Reconciliation Act of 1996 ended AFDC as of 1997. This program has been replaced by Temporary Assistance for Needy Families (TANF), which is operated by the states rather than the federal government.

40. Year-round, full-time workers are defined as those working at least 35 hours per week for a period of 50 to 52 weeks per year (Bureau of the Census, 1997).

41. These data refer to the age of the mothers of youngest child in household.

42. These statistics refer to "AFDC families by race of natural or adoptive parent." Percentages do not total 100 because the race of 2.2 percent was unknown. (Administration for Children and Families, 1996).

Bibliography of Works Cited

Abma, J.C., Chandra, A., Mosher, W.D., Peterson, L.S., and Piccinino, L. (1997). "Fertility, Family Planning, and Women's Health: New Data from the 1995 National Survey of Family Growth." National Center for Health Statistics, *Vital and Health Statistics 23 (19)*.

Acosta, R.V. and Carpenter, L.J. (1996). "Women in Intercollegiate Sport: A Longitudinal Study—Nineteen-Year Update 1977-1996." Brooklyn, NY: Department of Physical Education, Brooklyn College.

Administration for Children and Families. (1993). *FY '92 Characteristics and Financial Circumstances of AFDC recipients*. Washington, DC: U.S. Department of Health and Human Services.

Administration for Children and Families. (1996). *Characteristics of AFDC Recipients: FY 1995*. Washington, DC: U.S. Department of Health and Human Services.

Administration for Children and Families. (1998). *Characteristics of AFDC Recipients: FY 1997*. Washington, DC: U.S. Department of Health and Human Services.

Alan Guttmacher Institute. (1994). *Sex and America's Teenagers*. New York: Author.

American Association of University Women. (1991). *Shortchanging Girls, Shortchanging America*. Researched by Greenberg-Lake. Washington, DC: American Association of University Women Educational Foundation.

American Association of University Women. (1992). *The AAUW Report: How Schools Shortchange Girls*. Researched by the Wellesley Center for Research on Women. Washington, DC: American Association of University Women Educational Foundation.

American Association of University Women. (1993). *Hostile Hallways: The AAUW Survey on Sexual Harassment in America's Schools*. Conducted by Louis Harris and Associates. Washington, DC: American Association of University Women Educational Foundation.

American Association of University Women. (1995). *Growing Smart: What's Working for Girls in Schools*. Researched by Hansen, S., Walker, J., and Flom, B. Washington, DC: American Association of University Women Educational Foundation.

American Association of University Women. (1996a). *Girls in the Middle: Working to Succeed in School*. Researched by Cohen, J. and Blanc, S., and Research for Action, Inc. Washington, DC: American Association of University Women Educational Foundation.

American Association of University Women. (1996b). *The Influence of School Climate on Gender Differences in the Achievement and Engagement of Young Adolescents*. Researched by Lee, V.E., Chen, X., and Smerdon, B.A. Washington, DC: American Association of University Women Educational Foundation.

American Association of University Women. (1998). *Separated by Sex: A Critical Look at Single-Sex Education for Girls*. Washington, DC: American Association of University Women Educational Foundation.

Bailey, S.M. (1996). "Shortchanging Girls and Boys." *Educational Leadership* 53 (8): 75-79.

Bauer-Maglin, N. and Perry, D., eds. (1996). *Bad Girls/Good Girls: Women, Sex, and Power in the Nineties*. New Brunswick: Rutgers University Press.

Bennett, K.P. (1986). "Study of Reading Ability Grouping and Its Consequences for Urban Appalachian First Graders." Ph.D. diss. Cincinnati, OH: University of Cincinnati.

Benson, P. (1990). *The Troubled Journey*. Minneapolis: The Search Institute.

Benson, P. (1997). *All Kids Are Our Kids: What Communities Must Do to Raise Caring and Responsible Children and Adolescents*. San Francisco: Jossey-Bass.

Block, J.H. (1984). "Psychological Development of Female Children and Adolescents." In *Sex Role Identity and Ego Development*, pp. 126-42. San Francisco: Jossey-Bass.

Boyer, D. and Fine, D. (1992). "Sexual Abuse as a Factor in Adolescent Pregnancy and Child Maltreatment." *Family Planning Perspectives* 24 (1): 4-11.

Bridgeman, B. and Wendler, C. (1989). *Prediction of Grades in College Mathematics Courses as a Component of the Placement Validity of SAT Mathematics Scores*. New York: College Board.

Brick, P. and colleagues. (1996). *The New Positive Images: Teaching Abstinence, Contraception, and Sexual Health*. Hackensack, NJ: Planned Parenthood of Greater Northern New Jersey.

Bureau of the Census. (1990). *Census of the Population and Housing, 1990.* Washington, DC: U.S. Government Printing Office.

Bureau of the Census. (1993). *Dynamics of Economic Well-Being: Labor Force, 1992-1993: A Perspective of Low-Wage Workers.* Washington, DC: U.S. Government Printing Office.

Bureau of the Census. (1997). *March Current Population Survey.* Washington, DC: U.S. Government Printing Office.

Bureau of Justice Statistics. (1992). "Child Rape Victims." *Crime Data Brief,* NCJ-147001. Washington, DC: U.S. Government Printing Office.

Bureau of Justice Statistics. (1996). "Child Victimizers: Violent Offenders and Their Victims." NCJ-158625. Washington, DC: U.S. Government Printing Office.

Bureau of Justice Statistics. (1997). *Sex Offenses and Offenders.* Washington, DC: U.S. Government Printing Office.

Bureau of Labor Statistics. (1997). Labor Force Statistics from the Current Population Survey, Tables 1 and 2. Washington, DC: U.S. Government Printing Office.

Center for Women Policy Studies. (1995). *Girls Talk About Violence: Summary of Preliminary Findings.* Washington, DC: Center for Women Policy Studies.

Centers for Disease Control and Prevention. (1992). *1992 National Health Interview Survey—Youth Risk Behavior Supplement.* Washington, D.C.: U.S. Department of Health and Human Services. Tabulations by Child Trends, Inc.

Centers for Disease Control and Prevention. (1993a). "Cigarette Smoking: Attributable Mortality and Years of Potential Life Lost—United States." *Morbidity and Mortality Weekly Report* 42: 645-649.

Centers for Disease Control and Prevention. (1993b). *Facts About Adolescents and HIV/AIDS.* Washington, D.C.: U.S. Department of Health and Human Services, Public Health Service. October, 1993.

Centers for Disease Control and Prevention. (1993c). "Youth Risk Behavior Surveillance—United States, 1993." 44: SS-1. Washington, D.C.: U.S. Department of Health and Human Services, Public Health Service.

Centers for Disease Control and Prevention. (1995a). "State Specific Pregnancy and Birth Rates Among Teenagers—United States, 1991-92. *Morbidity and Mortality Weekly Report* 44 (37): 677-684.

Centers for Disease Control and Prevention. (1995b). "Youth Risk Behavior Surveillance—United States, 1993." *Morbidity and Mortality Weekly Report* 44: SS-1.

Centers for Disease Control and Prevention. (1996a). *Facts About Women and HIV/AIDS.* Washington, D.C.: U.S. Department of Health and Human Services, Public Health Service.

Centers for Disease Control and Prevention. (1996b). *HIV/AIDS Surveillance Report* 8 (2). U.S. Department of Health and Human Services, Public Health Service.

Centers for Disease Control and Prevention. (1997). *HIV/AIDS Surveillance Report* 9 (2). Washington, D.C.: U.S. Department of Health and Human Services, Public Health Service.

Child Trends, Inc. (1996). *Facts at a Glance.* Washington, DC: Child Trends, Inc.

Child Trends, Inc. (1997). *Facts at a Glance.* Washington, DC: Child Trends, Inc.

Children's Defense Fund. (1995). *The State of America's Children Yearbook, 1995.* Washington, DC: Children's Defense Fund.

Cole, N.S. (1997). *The ETS Gender Study: How Females and Males Perform in Educational Settings.* Princeton, NJ: Educational Testing Service.

Cole, P. and Putnam, F. (1992). "Effect of Incest on Self and Social Functioning: A Developmental Psychopathology Perspective." *Journal of Counseling and Clinical Psychology* 60 (2): 174-184.

College Board Online. (1997). "Table 18." Princeton, NJ: Educational Testing Service.

Committee on Ways and Means, U.S. House of Representatives. (1994). "1994 Green Book: Overview of Entitlement Programs." Washington, DC: U.S. Government Printing Office.

Commonwealth Fund. (1997). *The Commonwealth Fund Survey of the Health of Adolescent Girls.* Conducted by Louis Harris and Associates. New York: Commonwealth Fund.

Costello, C. and Krimgold, B.K. (1997). *The American Woman: 1996-97: Where We Stand.* New York: W.W. Norton & Company.

Donovan, P. (1995). *The Politics of Blame.* New York: Alan Guttmacher Institute.

Duncan, M.C., Messner, M.A., and Williams, L. (1991). "Coverage of Women's Sports in Four Daily Newspapers." Los Angeles: Amateur Athletic Foundation of Los Angeles.

Dweck, C.S., Davidson, W., Nelson, S., and Enna, B. (1978). "Sex Differences in Learned Helplessness, II: The Contingencies of Evaluative Feedback in the Classroom," and "III: An Experimental Analysis." *Developmental Psychology* 14 (3): 268-276.

Dweck, C.S., Goetz, T.E., and Strauss, N.L. (1980). "Sex Differences in Learned Helplessness, IV: An Experimental and Naturalistic Study of Failure Generation and Its Mediators." *Journal of Personality and Social Psychology* 38: 441-452.

Egan, J. (1997). "The Thin Red Line." *New York Times Magazine.* July 27: 20-25.

Erkut, S., Fields, J.P., Sing, R., and Marx, R. (1996). "Diversity in Girls' Experiences: Feeling Good About Who You Are." In *Urban Girls: Resisting Stereotypes, Creating Identities,* B.J. Ross Leadbeater and N. Way, eds. New York: New York University Press.

Federal Bureau of Investigation. (1992). *Crime in the United States.* Washington, DC: U.S. Department of Justice.

Federal Bureau of Investigation. (October 1996). 1995 *Crime in the United States.* Washington, DC: U.S. Department of Justice.

Federal Bureau of Investigation, Uniform Crime Reporting Program. (December 1993). *Age-Specific Arrest Rates and Race-Specific Arrest Rates for Selected Offenses,* 1965-1992. Washington, DC: U.S. Department of Justice.

Federal Bureau of Investigation. (1990). "Total Arrest Trends, Sex, 1980-1989." *Uniform Crime Report.* Washington, DC: U.S. Department of Justice.

Feminist Majority Foundation's Task Force on Women and Girls in Sports. (1995). *Empowering Women in Sports.* Arlington: Feminist Majority Foundation.

Fine, M. (1988). "Sexuality, Schooling, and Adolescent Females: The Missing Discourse of Desire." *Harvard Educational Review* 58 (1): 29-53.

Fine, M. (1991). *Framing Dropouts: Notes on the Politics of an Urban Public High School.* Albany: State University of New York Press.

Fine, M., Genovese, T., Ingersoll, S., Macpherson, P., and Roberts, R. (1994). "White Li(v)es: Looking for a Discourse of Male Accountability." In *Unmasking Social Inequalities: Victims and Resistance,* M. Lykes, A. Banuazizi, R. and Liem, eds. Philadelphia: Temple University Press.

Fine, M. and McPherson, P. (1995). "Hungry for an Us." *Feminism and Psychology* 5 (2): 181-200.

Fine, M. and Zane, N. (1991). "Bein' Wrapped Too Tight: When Low-Income Women Drop Out of High School." In *Dropouts from School: Issues, Dilemmas, and Solutions,* L. Weis, E. Farrar, and H.G. Petrie, eds. Albany: State University of New York Press.

Finkelhor, D. and Dziuba-Leatherman, J. (1994). "Victimization of Children." *American Psychologist* 49 (3): 173-183

French, S.A. and Perry, C.L. (1996). "Smoking in Adolescent Girls." *Journal of American Medical Women's Association* 51 (1&2): 25-28.

French, S.A., Perry, C.L., Leon, G.R., and Fulkerson, J.A. (1994). "Weight Concerns, Dieting Behavior, and Smoking Initiation among Adolescents: A Prospective Study." *American Journal of Public Health* 84: 1818-1820.

French, S.A., Story, M. Dawnes, B., Resnick, M.D., and Blum, R.W. (1995). "Frequent Dieting in Adolescents: Psychosocial and Health Behavior Correlates." *Journal of Public Health* 85: 695-701.

Gallup Organization, Inc. (1997). *Teens and Technology.* Princeton, NJ: Gallup Organization.

Gilligan, C. (1982). *In a Different Voice.* Cambridge: Harvard University Press.

Gilligan, C. and Brown, L.M. (1992). *Meeting at the Crossroads: Women's Psychology and Girls' Development.* Cambridge: Harvard University Press.

Gilligan, C., Lyons, N.P. and Hanmer, T.J. , eds. (1990). *Making Connections: The Relational Worlds of Adolescent Girls at Emma Willard School.* Cambridge: Harvard University Press.

Gilligan, C., Ward, J., and Taylor, J. , eds. (1988). *Mapping the Moral Domain: A Contribution of Women's Thinking to Psychological Theory and Education.* Cambridge: Harvard University Press.

Girls Incorporated. (1992). *Past the Pink and Blue Predicament: Freeing the Next Generation from Sex Stereotypes.* New York: Girls Incorporated.

Girls Incorporated. (1995). *Recasting TV: Girls' Views. A Nationwide Survey of School-Age Children.* Conducted by Louis Harris and Associates. New York: Girls Incorporated.

Girls Incorporated. (1996a). *Prevention and Parity: Girls in Juvenile Justice.* New York: Girls Incorporated.

Girls Incorporated. (1996b). "Responding to the Impact of Violence on Girls: A Community Needs Assessment for Girls Incorporated Affiliates." Working paper. Indianapolis: Girls Incorporated.

Girls Incorporated. (1997a). "Girls and HIV/AIDS Fact Sheet." Indianapolis: Girls Incorporated.

Girls Incorporated. (1997b). "Girls and Sports." Indianapolis: Girls Incorporated.

Girls Incorporated. (1997c). "Stamp Out Smoking." Indianapolis: Girls Incorporated.

Gross, G. (1997). "Girls Gleefully Claim a League of Their Own." *New York Times,* August 4: A1.

Haag, P. (1998). "Single-Sex Education in Grades K-12: What Does the Research Tell Us?" in *Separated by Sex: A Critical Look at Single-Sex Education for Girls.* Washington, DC: American Association of University Women Educational Foundation.

Haffner, D. (1990). *Sex Education 2000: A Call to Action.* New York: Sex Information and Educational Council of the U.S.

Hancock, L. And Kalb, C. (1996). "A Room of their Own: Public Schools Try Single-Sex Classes." *Newsweek,* June 24.

Harter, S., Waters, P.L., Whitesell, N.R., and Kastelic, D. (1997). "Level of Voice among High School Females and Males: The Role of Relational Context, Support, and Self Worth." Unpub. ms.

Henry J. Kaiser Family Foundation. (1996). *Kaiser Family Foundation Survey on Teens and Sex: What They Say Teens Today Need to Know, and Who They Listen to.* Conducted by Princeton Survey Research Associates. Menlo Park, CA: Henry J. Kaiser Family Foundation.

Henshaw, S.K. and Van Vort, J. (1994). "Abortion Services in the United States, 1991 and 1992." *Family Planning Perspectives* 26: 100-106.

Irwin, C. and Shafer, M. (1991). "Adolescent Sexuality: The Problem of a Negative Outcome of a Normative Behavior." Paper prepared for the Cornell University Medical College Conference, "Adolescents at Risk: Medical and Social Perspectives." Cornell University, February 1991.

Jaffee, L. And Mahle-Lutter, J. "Adolescent Girls: Factors Influencing Low and High Body Image." *Melpomene Journal* 14 (2): 14-22.

Johnston, L.D., O'Malley, P. and Bachman, J. (1997). *The National Survey Results on Drug Use from the Monitoring the Future Study, 1975-1997.* Ann Arbor, MI: University of Michigan.

Kahn, A.S., Mathie, V.A., and Torgler, C. (1994). "Rape Scripts and Rape Acknowledgment." *Psychology of Women Quarterly* 18: 53-66.

Kann, L., Warren, C.W., Harris, W.A., Collins, J.L., Williams, B.I, Ross, J.G., and Kolbe, L.J. (1996). "Youth Risk Behavior Surveillance—United States, 1995." In Center for Disease Control Surveillance Summaries, *MMWR* 45: SS-4.

Koff, E., Rierdan, J., and Stubbs, M. (1990). "Conceptions and Misconceptions of the Menstrual Cycle." *Women and Health* 16 (3-4): 119-136.

Kolstad, A. and Owings, J. (1986). *High School Dropouts: What Changes Their Minds about School.* Washington, DC: Office of Educational Research and Improvement, U.S. Department of Education.

Koss, M.P. (1993). "Rape: Scope, Impact, Interventions, and Public Policy Responses." *American Psychologist* 48 (10): 1062-69.

Koss, M.P. and Cook, S.L. (1993). "Facing the Facts: Date and Acquaintance Rape Are Significant Problems for Women." In *Current Controversies on Family Violence*, R.J. Gelles and D.R. Loseke, eds. Newbury Park, CA: Sage, pp. 104-119.

Landry, D.J. and Forrest, J.D. (1995). "How Old Are U.S. Fathers?" *Family Planning Perspectives* 27 (4): 159-165.

Leadbeater, B.J. Ross and Way, N. , eds. (1996). *Urban Girls: Resisting Stereotypes, Creating Identities.* New York: New York University Press.

Lee, V.E., Croninger, R.G., Linn, E., and Chen, X. (1996). "The Culture of Sexual Harassment in Secondary Schools." *American Educational Research Journal.*

Lee, V. and Marks, H. (1990). "Sustained Effects of the Single-Sex Secondary School Experience on Attitudes, Behaviors, and Values in College." *Journal of Educational Psychology* 82 (3): 578-592.

Lindberg, L.D., Sonenstein, F.L., Ku, L., and Martinez, G. (1997). "Age Differences Between Minors Who Give Birth and Their Adult Partners." *Family Planning Perspectives* 29 (2): 61-66.

Linn, E., Stein, N.D., Young, J., and Davis, S. (1992). " Bitter Lessons for All: Sexual Harassment in Schools. In *Sexuality and the Curriculum*, J. Sears, ed. New York: Teachers College Press.

Lips, H.M. (1989). "Gender-Role Socialization: Lessons in Femininity." In *Women: A Feminist Perspective*, J. Freeman, ed. Mountain View, CA: Mayfield Publishing Company.

Males, M.A. (1993). "School-Age Pregnancy: Why Hasn't Prevention Worked?" *Journal of School Health* 63 (10): 429-432.

Males, M.A. (1995). "Adult Involvement in Teenage Childbearing and STD." *Lancet* 346: 64-65.

Males, M. and Chew, S.Y. (1996). "The Ages of Fathers in California Adolescent Births, 1993." *American Journal of Public Health* 86 (4): 565-568.

Mann, J. (1994). *The Difference: Growing Up Female in America.* New York: Warner.

McDonnell, L.M. and Hill, P.T. (1993). *Newcomers in American Schools: Meeting the Educational Needs of Immigrant Youth.* Santa Monica, CA: Rand.

McKenna, T. and Ortiz, F. (1988). *The Broken Web: The Educational Experience of Hispanic American Women.* Berkeley: Floricanto Press.

McMillen, M., Kaufman, P., and Whitener, S. (1994). *Dropout Rates in the United States, 1993.* Washington, DC: National Center for Education Statistics, U.S. Department of Education.

Melpomene Institute. (1996). "Study Shows Girls' Body Image is a Black and White Issue." St. Paul, MN: Melpomene Institute.

Miller, K.S., Clark, L.F., and Moore, J.S. (1997). "Sexual Initiation with Older Male Partners and Subsequent HIV Risk Behavior among Female Adolescents." *Family Planning Perspectives* 29 (5): 212-214.

Miller, C.L. (1987). "Qualitative Differences among Gender-Stereotyped Toys: Implications for Cognitive and Social Development in Girls and Boys." *Sex Roles* 16 (9/10): 473-487.

Minnesota Women's Fund. (1990). *Reflections of Risk: Growing Up Female in Minnesota. A Report on the Health and Well-Being of Adolescent Girls in Minnesota.* Minneapolis, MN: Minnesota Women's Fund.

Monaco, N.M. and Gaier, E.L. (1992). "Single Sex versus Coeducational Environment and Achievement in Adolescent Females." *Adolescence* 27: 579-594.

Moore, K.A., Miller, B.C., Glei, D., and Morrison, D.R. (1995a). *Adolescent Sex, Contraception, and Childbearing: A Review of Recent Research.* Washington, DC: Child Trends, Inc.

Moore, K.A., Miller, B.C., Sugland, B.W., Morrison, D.R., Glei, D.A., and Blumenthal, C. (1995b). *Beginning Too Soon: Adolescent Sexual Behavior, Pregnancy, and Parenthood. A Review of Research and Interventions.* Washington, DC: U.S. Department of Health and Human Services.

Moore, K.A., Sugland, B., Blumenthal, C., Glei, D. and Snyder, N. (1996). *Adolescent Pregnancy Prevention Programs: Interventions and Evaluations.* Washington, DC: Child Trends.

Mosher, W. and Aral, S. (1991). "Testing for Sexually Transmitted Diseases among Women of Reproductive Age: United States, 1988." *Family Planning Perspectives* 23 (5): 216-221.

Ms. Foundation for Women. (1994). *Body Politic: Transforming Adolescent Girls' Health. A Report of the 1994 Proceedings of the Healthy Girls/Healthy Women Research Roundtable.* New York: Ms. Foundation for Women.

NARAL Foundation. (1995). *Sexuality Education in America: A State-by-State Review.* Washington, DC: NARAL Foundation.

NARAL Foundation. (1997). *Who Decides? A State-by-State Review of Abortion and Reproductive Rights.* Washington, DC: NARAL Foundation.

National Center for Education Statistics. (1991). *Digest of Educational Statistics, 1990.* Washington, DC: U.S. Department of Education.

National Center for Education Statistics. (1993). *America's High School Sophomores: A Ten-Year Comparison.* Washington, DC: Office of Educational Research and Improvement, U.S. Department of Education.

National Center for Education Statistics. (1997a). *The Condition of Education, 1997,* NCES 97-388. Washington, DC: Office of Educational Research and Improvement, U.S. Department of Education.

National Center for Education Statistics. (1997b). *National Assessment of Educational Progress 1996, Mathematics Report Card for the Nation and the States.* Washington, DC: Office of Educational Research and Improvement, U.S. Department of Education.

National Center for Health Statistics. (1976). *Monthly Vital Statistics Report, 25 (10).*

National Center for Health Statistics. (1994). *Monthly Vital Statistics Report.*

National Center for Health Statistics. (1996). Unpublished work tables prepared by the Mortality Statistics Branch, Division of Vital Statistics.

National Center on Addiction and Substance Abuse. (1996). *Substance Abuse and the American Woman.* New York: National Center on Addiction and Substance Abuse.

National Council for Research on Women. (1991). *Risk, Resiliency, and Resistance: Current Research on Adolescent Girls.* New York: National Council for Research on Women.

National Council for Research on Women. (1994). "Sexual Harassment. A Look at a Disturbing Trend Among Teens." *IQ* 1 (1). New York: National Council for Research on Women.

National Council for Research on Women. (1996). "Beyond Beijing: Who's Doing What to Turn Words Into Action." *IQ* 2 (1). New York: National Council for Research on Women.

National Council for Research on Women. (1998). "Women and Girls in Science, Math and Engineering." *IQ* 2 (2). New York: National Council for Research on Women.

National Federation of State High School Associations. (1993). *Sports Participation Survey.* Kansas City, MO: National Federation of State High School Associations.

National Federation of State High School Associations. (1996). *The National Federation of State High School Associations Handbook, 1995-1996.* Kansas City, MO: National Federation of State High School Associations.

National Institute of Mental Health. (1993). *Eating Disorders.* NIH Publication No. 93-3477. Washington, DC: U.S. Department of Health and Human Services.

National Organization for Women. (1996). *Legislative Update.* Washington, DC: National Organization for Women Action Center.

National Science Board. (1996). *Science and Engineering Indicators–1996.* NSB-96-21. Washington, DC: U.S. Government Printing Office.

National Victim Center. (1992). *Rape in America: A Report to the Nation.* Arlington, VA/Charleston, SC: National Victim Center.

National Women's History Project. (1997). "Ideas for Program." <http://www.nyhp.org>

Nolen-Hoeksema, S. (1990). *Sex Differences in Depression.* Stanford, CA: Stanford University Press.

Office of National AIDS Policy. (1996). *A Report to the President.* Washington, DC: Office of National AIDS Policy.

Office on Smoking and Health, National Center for Chronic Disease Prevention and Health Promotion. (1994). *Preventing Tobacco Use Among Young People: A Report of the Surgeon General.* Washington, DC: U.S. Government Printing Office.

Ooms, T. (1997). *Involving Boys and Men in Teen Pregnancy Prevention: A background paper.* Prepared for a roundtable meeting on February 11-12, 1997, cosponsored by the Family Impact Seminar and the National Campaign to Prevent Teen Pregnancy.

Orbach, S. (1982). *Fat Is a Feminist Issue II.* New York: Berkley Publishing Group.

Orenstein, P. (in association with the American Association of University Women). (1994). *SchoolGirls: Young Women, Self-Esteem, and the Confidence Gap.* New York: Anchor Books.

Paglia, C. (1990). *Sexual Personae: Art and Decadence from Nefertiti to Emily Dickinson.* New Haven: Yale University Press.

Pastor, J., McCormick, J., and Fine, M. (1996). "Makin' Homes: An Urban Girl Thing. In *Urban Girls: Resisting Stereotypes, Creating Identities,* B.J. Ross Leadbeater and N. Way, eds. New York: New York University Press.

Pedersen, S. (1996). "Girls Who Hurt (Themselves)." *Sassy* 9: 70-72.

Phillips, L. (1993). "Using/Losing Her Voice: Consent, Coercion, and Sexual Silences." Paper presented at the Annual Ethnography and Education Conference. Philadelphia, Pennsylvania, March.

Phillips, L. (1996). "Constructing Meanings in Hetero-Relations: Young Women's Experiences of Power and Desire." Paper presented at the XIVth biennial meetings of the International Congress of Psychology. Montreal, Quebec, August 18-22.

Phillips, L. (1997). *Unequal Partners: Exploring Power and Consent in Adult-Teen Relationships.* Hackensack, NJ: Planned Parenthood of Greater Northern New Jersey.

Phillips, L. (forthcoming). *Flirting with Danger: Sexuality and Danger in Young Women's Hetero-Relations.* New York: New York University Press.

Pipher, M. (1994). *Reviving Ophelia: Saving the Selves of Adolescent Girls.* New York: Ballantine Books.

Postrado, L.T., Weiss, F.L., and Nicholson, H.J. (1996). *Predictors of Initiation of Sexual Intercourse for Young Teen Women: A Causal Model from the Girls Incorporated Preventing Adolescent Pregnancy Project.* Indianapolis: Girls Incorporated National Resource Center.

President's Council on Physical Fitness and Sports. (1997). *Physical Activity and Sport in the Lives of Girls: Physical and Mental Health Dimensions from an Interdisciplinary Approach.* Minneapolis: The Center for Research on Girls and Women in Sport.

Quintero, E. and Rummel, M.K. (1995). "Voice Unaltered: Marginalized Young Writers Speak." In *Children and Families "at Promise": Deconstructing the Discourse of Risk*, B.B. Swadener and S. Lubeck, eds. Albany: State University of New York Press.

Reid, P.T. (1985). "Sex-Role Socialization of Black Children: A Review of Theory, Family, and Media Influence." *Academic Psychology Bulletin* 7: 201-212.

Rhodes, J.E. and Davis, A.B. (1996). "Supportive Ties between Nonparent Adults and Urban Adolescent Girls." In *Urban Girls: Resisting Stereotypes, Creating Identities*, B.J. Ross Leadbeater and N. Way, eds. New York: New York University Press.

Rierdan, J. and Koff, E. (1991). "Depressive Symptomatology among Very Early Maturing Girls." *Journal of Youth and Adolescence* 20: 415-525.

Roffman, D. (1996). "Reinventing Sex: Transforming Our Vision of Sex and Sexuality." Presentation at the 6th annual Sexuality Conference of Planned Parenthood of Central Pennsylvania, York, Pennsylvania, March 21, 1996.

Roiphe, K. (1993). *The Morning After: Sex, Fear, and Feminism on Campus.* Boston: Little, Brown and Company.

Rotheram-Borus, M.J., Dopkins, S., Sabate, N., and Lightfoot, M. (1996). "Personal and Ethnic Identity, Values, and Self-Esteem among Black and Latino Adolescent Girls. In *Urban Girls: Resisting Stereotypes, Creating Identities*, B.J. Ross Leadbeater and N. Way, eds. New York: New York University Press.

Sadker, M. and Sadker, D. (1986). "Sexism in the Classroom: From Grade School to Graduate School." *Phi Delta Kappa* 67 (7): March.

Sadker, M. and Sadker, D. (1994). *Failing at Fairness: How America's Schools Cheat Girls.* New York: Charles Scribner and Sons.

Sanday, P.R. (1996). *A Woman Scorned: Acquaintance Rape on Trial.* New York: Doubleday.

Schneider, M. (1997). "Sappho Was a Right-On Adolescent: Growing up Lesbian." *Journal of Lesbian Studies* 1 (1): 69-85.

Schupak-Nauberg, E. and Nemeroff, C.J. (1993). "Disturbances in Identity and Self-Regulation in Bulimia Nervosa: Implications for a Metaphorical Perspective of 'Body as Self.'" *International Journal of Eating Disorders* 13 (4): 335-347.

Sears, J. (1992). *Sexuality and the Curriculum: The Politics and Practices of Sexuality Education.* New York: Teachers College Press.

Seavey, D.K. (1996). *Back to Basics: Women's Poverty and Welfare Reform.* Wellesley, MA: Wellesley College Center for Research on Women.

Selingo, J. and Naughton, J. (1997). "New Federal Guidelines Seek to Define Pay Equity for Men's and Women's Coaches." *Chronicle of Higher Education*, November 14: A45-46.

Shakeshaft, C. and Libresco, A. (1992). "Single Sex vs. Mixed Sex: What's Best for Females?" Unpublished ms. New York: Hofstra University School of Education.

Shea, M. (1996). "Dynamics of Economic Well-Being: 1991-1993." *Current Population Reports.* Washington, DC: Bureau of the Census.

Sidel, R. (1996). *Keeping Women and Children Last: America's War on the Poor.* New York: Penguin Books.

Siegel, D.L. (1995). *Sexual Harassment: Research and Resources.* New York: National Council for Research on Women.

Silin, J. (1992). "School-based HIV/AIDS Education: Is There Safety in Safer Sex?" In *Sexuality and the Curriculum: The Politics and Practices of Sexuality Education*, J. Sears, ed. New York: Teachers College Press.

Sommers, C.H. (1994). *Who Stole Feminism? How Women Have Betrayed Women.* New York: Simon & Schuster.

Sorensen, A.B. and Hallinan, M.T. (1987). "Ability Grouping and Sex Differences in Mathematics Achievement." *Sociology of Education* 60 (2): 63-72.

Spalter-Roth, R., Burr, B., Hartmann, H., and Shaw, L. (1995). *Welfare that Works: The Working Lives of AFDC Recipients.* Washington, DC: Institute for Women's Policy Research.

Stein, N. (1992). *Secrets in Public: Sexual Harassment in Public (and Private) Schools.* Wellesley, MA: Wellesley College Center for Research on Women.

Stein, N. (1995). "Sexual Harassment in Schools: The Public Performance of Gendered Violence." *Harvard Educational Review* 65 (2).

Stein, N., Marshall, N.L., and Tropp, L.R. (1993). *Secrets in Public: Sexual Harassment in Our Schools.* Wellesley, MA: Wellesley Center for Research on Women and NOW Legal Defense and Education Fund.

Stein, N. and Sjostrom, L. (1994). *Flirting or Hurting: A Teacher's Guide on Student-to-Student Sexual Harassment in Schools (Grades 6 through 12).* Washington, DC: National Education Association and Wellesley College Center for Research on Women.

Steiner-Adair, C. (1990). "The Body Politic: Normal Female Adolescent Development and the Development of Eating Disorders." In *Making Connections: The Relational Worlds of Adolescent Girls at the Emma Willard School*, C. Gilligan, N.P. Lyons, and T.J. Hanmer, eds. Cambridge: Harvard University Press.

Story, M., French, S., Resnick, M., and Blum, R. (1995). "Ethnic/Racial and Socioeconomic Differences in Dieting Behaviors and Body Image Perceptions among Adolescents." *International Journal of Eating Disorders* 18 (2): 173-179.

Sullivan, A.M. (1996). "From Mentor to Muse: Recasting the Role of Women in Relationship with Urban Adolescent Girls." In *Urban Girls: Resisting Stereotypes, Creating Identities*, B.J. Ross Leadbeater and N. Way, eds. New York: New York University Press.

Sullivan, M. (1990). *The Male Role in Teenage Pregnancy and Parenting: New Directions for Public Policy.* New York: Vera Institute of Justice.

Swadener, B.B. (1995). "Children and Families 'at Promise': Deconstructing the Discourse of Risk." In *Children and Families "at Promise:" Deconstructing the Discourse of Risk*, B.B. Swadener and S. Lubeck, eds. Albany: State University of New York Press.

Swadener, B.B. and Lubeck, S. (1995). "The Social Construction of Families 'at Risk': An Introduction." In *Children and Families "at Promise:" Deconstructing the Discourse of Risk*, B.B. Swadener and S. Lubeck, eds. Albany: State University of New York Press.

Swan, A.V., Creeser, R., and Murray, M. (1990). "When and Why Children First Start to Smoke." *International Journal of Epidemiology* 19: 323-330.

Thompson, B.W. (1992). "A Way Outa No Way: Eating Problems in African-American, Latina, and White Women." *Gender and Society* 6 (4): 546-561.

Thompson, Sharon. (1995). *Going All the Way: Teenage Girls' Tales of Sex, Romance, and Pregnancy.* New York: Hill and Wang.

Thorne, B. (1993). *Gender Play: Girls and Boys in School.* New Brunswick, NJ: Rutgers University Press.

Todd, A.L. (1996). "Razor's Edge: Teenage Girls Who Cut and Burn Themselves." *Seventeen*, June: 140-143.

Tolman, D.L. (1996). "Adolescent Girls' Sexuality: Debunking the Myth of the Urban Girl." In *Urban Girls: Resisting Stereotypes, Creating Identities*, B.J. Ross Leadbeater and N. Way, eds. New York, NY: New York University Press.

Tolman, D.L. and Higgins, T.E. (1996). "How Being a Good Girl Can Be Bad for Girls." In *Bad Girls/Good Girls: Women, Sex, and Power in the Nineties*, N.B. Maglin and D. Perry, eds. New Brunswick, NJ: Rutgers University Press.

United Nations. (1995). *United Nations Human Development Report 1995.* New York: United Nations.

U.S. Department of Commerce, Bureau of the Census. (1990). *Poverty in the United States, 1988 and 1989.* Series P-60, No. 171. Washington, DC: U.S. Government Printing Office.

U.S. Department of Commerce, Bureau of the Census. (1993). *Current Population Survey*, October. Washington, DC: U.S. Government Printing Office.

U.S. Department of Education. (1992). *1992 Trends in Academic Progress.* Washington, DC: U.S. Government Printing Office.

U.S. Department of Education. (1994). *Dropout Rates in the United States, 1993.* Washington, DC: U.S. Government Printing Office.

U.S. Department of Education. (1997). "The Condition of Education: 1997." *Digest of Educational Statistics.* Washington, DC: U.S. Government Printing Office.

U.S. Department of Health and Human Services. (1989). *National Adolescent Student Health Survey: A Report on the Health of America's Youth.* Atlanta: Centers for Disease Control.

U.S. Department of Health and Human Services. (1994). *Division of STD/HIV Prevention: 1994 Annual Report.* Atlanta: Centers for Disease Control.

U.S. Department of Health and Human Services. (1997). "1995 National Survey of Family Growth." Summarized in *Teen Sex Down, New Study Shows*, May 1, 1997.

U.S. Department of Justice. (1994). *Crime Data Brief*, NCJ-147001, June 1994. Washington, DC: Bureau of Justice Statistics.

U.S. Merit Systems Protection Board. (1988). *Sexual Harassment in the Federal Government: An Update.* Washington, DC: U. S. Government Printing Office.

Ward, J.V. (1996). "Raising Resisters: The Role of Truth Telling in the Psychological Development of African American Girls." In *Urban Girls: Resisting Stereotypes, Creating Identities*, B.J. Ross Leadbeater and N. Way, eds. New York: New York University Press.

Waters, M.C. (1996). "The Intersection of Gender, Race, and Ethnicity in Identity Development of Caribbean American Teens." In *Urban Girls: Resisting Stereotypes, Creating Identities*, B.J. Ross Leadbetter and N. Way, eds. New York: New York University Press.

Weitzman, L.J., Birns, B. and Friend, R. (1986). "Traditional and Nontraditional Mothers' Communication with Their Daughters and Sons." *Child Development* 56: 894-898.

Wilson Sporting Goods Company and The Women's Sports Foundation. (1988). *The Wilson Report: Moms, Dads, Daughters, and Sports.* Los Angeles: Diagnostic Research, Inc.

Women's Environment and Development Organization. (1996). *Beyond Promises: Governments in Motion One Year After the Beijing Women's Conference.* New York: Women's Environment and Development Organization.

Women's Environment and Development Organization. (1997). *Promise Kept, Promise Broken? A Survey of Governments on National Action Plans to Implement the Beijing Platform.* New York: Women's Environment and Development Organization.

Women's Sports Foundation. (1989). *Minorities in Sports: The Effect of Varsity Sports Participation on the Social, Educational, and Career Mobility of Minority Students.* New York: Women's Sports Foundation.

Zill, N., Nord, C.W., and Loomis, L.S. (1995). *Adolescent Time Use, Risky Behavior, and Outcomes: An Analysis of National Data.* Rockville, MD: Westat, Inc.

Resource Guide

THIS RESOURCE SECTION of the Girls Report contains descriptions of programs and publications that address the needs of adolescent girls. Although the majority of entries are examples of activities sponsored by member centers of the National Council for Research on Women, and include programs, publications, grants, and services, we have also included the resources of a few collaborating organizations because of the relevance of their programs. The following organizations have contributed to the resource section and can be found on the pages listed:

American Association of University Women Educational Foundation

1111 Sixteenth Street, NW
Washington, DC 20036

Contact: Karen Sloan Lebovich, Director
Phone: (202) 728-7613
Fax: (202) 463-7169
Website: http://www.aauw.org

The American Association of University Women (AAUW) Educational Foundation is a national membership organization of 135,000 college graduates dedicated to promoting equity and education for girls. Since 1888, nearly 6,000 women from more than 100 countries have received fellowships and grants from the Educational Foundation, which offers direct support to women for scholarly research, advanced graduate study, and community action projects.

Publications

Shortchanging Girls, Shortchanging America (1991)
Based on a survey of 3,000 4th through 10th graders, the study found that as girls get older, they experience a "signficantly more dramatic drop in self-esteem levels than boys." The resulting gap between the self-esteem levels of girls and boys, and the corresponding decrease in girls' interest in math and science, has national implications.

The AAUW Report: How Schools Shortchange Girls
by Susan McGee Bailey, et. al. (1992). An examination of how girls in grades K-12 receive an inferior education to boys in America's schools. Shortchanging is a joint publication of the AAUW Educational Foundation and National Education Association.

Girls in the Middle: Working to Succeed in School (1996)
A study of middle-school girls and the range of their behaviors identified in the classroom. Girls in the Middle identifies specific traits such as: "speaking out," voicing one's views openly; "doing school," modestly achieving the expectations of the adults; and, "crossing borders," assuming the difficult position as a negotiator between groups.

Separated by Sex: A Critical Look at Single Sex Education for Girls (1998)
Examination of the findings of the foremost educational scholars on single sex education in grades K-12 to discover if girls learn better when they are separated from boys. The report, including a literature review and a summary of a forum convened by the AAUW Educational Foundation, considers what roles single-sex classes and schools should play in national educational reform.

AAUW Educational Foundation Community Action Grants

Contact: AAUW Educational Foundation, 2201 N. Dodge Street, Iowa City, IA 52243-4030

Phone: (319) 337-1716

Grant are offered through AAUW branches, states, and collaborating organizations for programs on non-degree research projects that promote education and equity for women and girls. Projects funded in the past include: math and science camps for girls, curriculum development programs, and mentoring programs. Currently, grants range from $500 to $5,000.

Abigail Quigley McCarthy Center for Research on Women College of St. Catherine

2004 Randolph Ave.
St. Paul, MN 55105

Contact: Catherine Lupori, Interim Director
Phone: (612) 690-6000
Fax: (612) 690-6736

This center sponsors annual awards for research, writing, and creative work that focuses on women; supports a national grant for research; and promotes student leadership.

Programs

The Legacies Project
This program has trained college students to work in public and private elementary schools and learn how to be good mentors. Students present programs (e.g., skits or poster demonstrations) on "remarkable women" at local schools during March, Women's History Month. In 1998, with a grant from the AAUW, the program created additional mentoring opportunities and made it possible to include local high school girls as co-presenters.

Opportunities and Initiative Fund Program
Small grants are given to students who need support for individual and group projects, particularly for girls off-campus. One recent grantee's project provided basic reading lessons for girls 7-14. The students, mostly Hmong and Latina, learned how to advance their reading skills, write poems and stories, and create art projects related to reading.

Barnard Center for Research on Women Barnard College

3009 Broadway, Room 101
Barnard Hall
New York, NY 10027-6598

Contact: Leslie J. Calman, Director
Phone: (212) 854-2067
Fax: (212) 854-7491
Website: http://www.barnard.columbia.edu/learning.html#CENTER_FOR_RESEARCH

Through public programs, conferences, lectures, films, and seminars, the Barnard Center for Research on Women generates and publicizes advanced research in feminist scholarship and attracts to Barnard outstanding women in public life.

Conference
24th Annual Conference: The Scholar and The Feminist
The 24th Annual conference (November, 1998) will explore the virtues of single-sex education both at the K-12 and college levels.

Center for the American Woman and Politics
Eagleton Institute of Politics
Rutgers University
191 Ryders Lane
New Brunswick, NJ 08901-8557

Contact: Debbie Walsh, Acting Director
Phone: (732) 932-9384
Fax: (732) 932-6778
Website: http://www.rci.rutgers.edu/~cawp/

The Center's programs include: seminars for scholars and practitioners, national conferences for women public officials, and public leadership education programs for students. CAWP's research about women in politics has given convincing evidence of why it matters that more women are elected at every level – proof that women bring new issues to the public agendas and open up government to the fresh ideas of different voices. The center is a national clearinghouse for information about women in politics and for analysis of the women's political movement.

Programs
NEW Leadership
The National Education for Women's Leadership (NEW Leadership) is an initiative of the Center for the American Woman and Politics (CAWP) to empower and educate young women to take on public leadership roles. NEW Leadership began in 1991 with the support of the W.K. Kellogg Foundation. Currently, NEW Leadership programs are held in New Jersey and across the country in conjunction with regional partners.

NEW Leadership is built on a five-part curriculum which includes: 1) teaching students about women's historical and contemporary participation in politics and policymaking; 2) connecting students with leaders who are making a difference in the public sphere; 3) exploring leadership in a diverse society; 4) building leadership skills; and 5) practicing leadership through action.

New Leadership Summer Institute
The heart of NEW Leadership is a week-long residential summer institute. Students hear from women in a variety of roles in politics and policy making, learn from educators in the field of women and politics, participate in hands-on building workshops, and discuss their own concepts of leadership. After participating in the institute, students are eligible to compete for leadership grants which allow them to develop projects on their home campuses. These projects

enable students to put their ideas about leadership into action.

Center for Education of Women
Women in Science and Engineering Program
University of Michigan
330 East Liberty
Ann Arbor, Michigan 48104-2289

Contact: Carol Hollenshead, Director
Phone: (734) 998-7225
Fax: (734) 998-6203
Website: http://www.umich.edu/~cew/women.html

Founded in 1964, CEW offers administrative internships, annual competitive scholarships to support women with educational interruptions, and small emergency grants for students. CEW's library contains material on educational resources, career planning, employment trends, and the history and status of women. The Center's Women in Science and Engineering program conducts programs and research focusing on increasing women's participation in science, mathematics, and engineering.

Programs
Future Science: Future Engineering
The program hosts 7th and 8th grade Michigan girls for two one-week sessions at the University of Michigan during the summer. Activities aim to demonstrate to them that "science and mathematics can be fun, challenging and rewarding." The objectives of this model are to provide participants with hands-on experiences in selected fields; to illustrate how science is practiced; to expose them to the working world of a research scientist and to women and minority role models; to build their confidence; to provide interaction with girls their own age with similar interests; and to introduce them to the variety of careers in science, engineering and mathematics and assist with their planning for high school and college.

Center for Research on Women and Gender
The University of Illinois at Chicago
1640 West Roosevelt Road, Fifth Floor
Chicago, Illinois 60608-6902

Contact: Alice Dan, Director
Phone: (312) 413-1924
Fax: (312) 413-7423
Website: http://www.uic.edu/depts/crwg/outline.htm

The Center for Research on Women and Gender (CRWG), founded in 1991, promotes collaborative, multidisciplinary research related to women and gender, particularly in the areas of work, health, and culture.

Programs
Action Research on Institutional Change
Toward Gender Equity
The Center works collaboratively with several organizations to facilitate institutional change in government and schools so that they provide better services to girls and women. One

project, the Voices for Girls Project, aims to provide technical assistance to city and county departments in order to provide girl-specific programs. The Center is also a member of the Illinois Gender Equity Commission (IGEC) which has surveyed state school systems regarding their compliance with Title IX. The IGEC now works to provide resources and training to schools interested in fostering gender equity.

Research Information Network on Women and Girls in Illinois
An internet-based resource created to serve the audience of policymakers, service providers, funders, and researchers who want to contribute to bettering the lives of women and girls in Illinois. With the support of Chicago Community Trust, the Center is creating this network which will provide easy-to-use access to research findings and reports about girls and women in Illinois with a focus on the following areas: health and aging, employment and poverty, education and training, caregiving and family issues, and violence and safety.

Publication
Mapping a Path for Evaluation
A practical, easy-to-use guide to evaluating your project or organization. Produced as a collaborative effort between Girl's Best Friend Foundation and the UIC Center for Research on Women and Gender, this guide uses evaluation of programs for girls as examples to lay out the basic principles and benefits of evaluation to any non-profit.

The Center for Study of Women in Society University of Oregon
340 Hendricks Hall
1201 University of Oregon
Eugene, Oregon 97403-1201

Contact: Sandra Morgen, Director
Phone: (541) 346-5015
Fax: (541) 346-5096
Website: http://darkwing.uoregon.edu/~csws/

CSWS was founded at the University of Oregon in 1983 as a multidisciplinary research center that generates, supports, and disseminates research on gender and on all aspects of women's lives. An important goal is to work with the university community and with regional, national, and international networks to create conditions that facilitate excellent research and to make connections between education and research, public policy, and advocacy.

Programs
Research Initiatives and Research Interest Groups
CSWS currently has 3 named research initiatives: Women in the Northwest, Women's Health and Aging, and the Feminist Humanities Project. CSWS also sponsors 13 research interest groups comprised of faculty, students, and community affiliates whose work is supported by the group or done in collaboration with the group. Scholarship about girls is included in a number of outreach projects including a study of welfare reform in Oregon, a study of emergency contraception, a study of girls and popular culture and the "Girls Groups".

The Girls Group
A project funded by the CSWS with the following goals: develop information about community resources for girls, determine how well we are meeting their needs, stimulate the development of partnerships and projects for girls and people who want to work with them, and to develop collaborative funding proposals. The project involves University of Oregon staff and students, local organizers, parents, teens, and others committed to improving the lives of girls.

Conference
Girls, Generations and Globalization
On February 27-28 1998, CSWS hosted a conference designed to expand the research agenda about girls nationally and internationally. CSWS also supported a companion conference "Success in the Middle". The conference's mission was to equip middle-school girls with the tools they need to thrive as they cross the threshold from pre-teen to teenager. High school age girls/young women helped organize the conference and facilitate groups.

Center for Women Policy Studies
1211 Connecticut Avenue, NW
Suite 312
Washington, DC 20036

Contact: Leslie Wolfe, President
Phone: (202) 872-1770
Fax: (202) 296-8962

The Center is a national non-profit multiethnic and multicultural feminist policy research and advocacy institution. Founded in 1972, the Center addresses cutting-edge issues that have significant implications for women and girls.

Research
Violence Against Women and Girls
The Center has conducted preliminary research into the connection between the physical and sexual victimization of girls and girls' increasingly violent behavior. The Center recently published "Victims No More: Girls Fight Back Against Male Violence." In addition, the Center convened a Summit on Girls and Violence and plans to publish a report on the findings in mid-1998.

Programs
Stop Acquaintance Rape (StAR)
The StAR project is intended to heighten public awareness about acquaintance rape and to create a public intolerance of this crime, which disproportionately affects girls and young women. The project's major focus this year will be the publication of an issue-defining paper on acquaintance rape.

Education and Economic Equity
This program focuses on access to post-secondary education for women and girls and gender bias on the Scholastic Achievement Test (SAT). The SAT project, which has produced landmark research showing that sex bias results in the SAT's underprediction of women's first-year college

grades, conducts public education on strategies to respond to the testing bias.

Douglass College, Rutgers University

125 George St.
Dean's Office, College Hall
New Brunswick, NJ 08901

Contact: Barbara Shailor, Dean of College
Phone: (732) 932-9721
Fax: (732) 932-8877

Douglass College was founded in 1918 as the New Jersey College for Women by Mabel Smith Douglass. It is part of the statewide university system of Rutgers University. It enrolls approximately 3,000 undergraduate women, which makes it the largest women's college in the nation.

Programs
Douglass Science Institute Program Series
Part of the nationally recognized Douglass Project for Rutgers Women in Math and Science and Engineering, the Douglass Science Institute Program Series (DSI) is a summer residential science enrichment program at Douglass College serving 9th through 12th grade young women in New Jersey. In one- and two-week sessions, young women explore biology, chemistry, computer science, engineering, marine science, mathematics and physics through hands on laboratory activities, field trips, and sessions with women scientists and engineers. The purpose of the DSI Program Series is to encourage young women to persist in mathematics and science courses in high school.

Douglass Science Career Exploration Day
This is an annual event held at Douglass College for 11th and 12th grade young women who are interested in exploring careers relating to mathematics, the sciences, and engineering. The program features outstanding guests from the scientific community who speak about their fields.

Douglass Science Weekend Academy
The Douglass Science Weekend Academy offers young women in 9th and 10th grades in central New Jersey the opportunity to explore life and physical sciences and mathematics through labs and workshops. Held three consecutive Saturdays on the Douglass College campus, the program features hands-on activities led by high school teachers, Rutgers faculty and undergraduate women in the sciences.

Annual Women's Conference at Douglass College
The Annual Women's Conference is a weekend program for achieving high school seniors who are interested in attending Douglass College. Planned by first-year students at Douglass, the Conference includes issues workshops, discussions with undergraduates, and programs focused on themes selected by students.

Shaping a Life
All first-year students at Douglass College enroll in "Shaping a Life", an interdisciplinary course focusing on women's lives. Based on biography, autobiography, and oral history, the course explores the ways women's lives are shaped in American society. The course introduces students to a diverse array of prominent women--scientists, artists, business professionals, public leaders--at weekly presentations followed by small group discussions. Through "Shaping a Life", students engage in technology-based research activities, sharpen their critical thinking skills, and begin to explore their educational and long term goals.

Girls Scouts Go to College
Each year, Senior Girl Scouts spend the day at Douglass College, meet Douglass undergraduates, and learn about life at the college.

Girls Career Institute
Co-sponsored by Douglass College and the New Jersey State Federation of Women's Clubs, this annual one-week residential program for high school students provides an introduction to college life in a series of workshops with career women and undergraduates.

The Douglass College Sisterhood Program
The Douglass College Sisterhood program links undergraduates with 7th and 8th graders in a local city school to introduce them to campus life and provide motivation for higher education. The pairing of Douglass students with the middle school young women provides a personal connection to the college world.

Institute for Women's Leadership
Douglass College, Rutgers University

Ruth Dill Johnson Crockett Building
162 Ryders Lane, 3rd Floor
New Brunswick, NJ 08901

Contact: Mary S. Hartman, Director
Phone: (732) 932-1463
Fax: (732) 932-4739

The Institute for Women's Leadership at Douglass College, Rutgers University, was founded in 1991 as the nation's first university-based center dedicated to examining and fostering women's leadership. Building on a history of educating achieving women, Douglass College has joined other distinguished women's programs and women's research centers at Rutgers in forming this Institute to initiate research and develop programs and strategies to speed women's emergence as leaders.

Programs
IWL Scholars Program in Women's Leadership and Social Change
An interdisciplinary program that prepares undergraduate students to be informed, innovative, and socially responsible leaders. The program includes a concentrated academic sequence including one course specific to the student's field of study, an interdisciplinary seminar, and a supervised two-semester practicum.

Publication
Powerful Women Talk Leadership

Powerful Women Talk Leadership is a book of interviews with prominent women leaders. Scheduled for release by Rutgers Press in January, 1999, the book explores why and how women lead, analyzes the barriers women face as leaders, describes how these obstacles were addressed by the women, and includes personal reflections on leadership geared to the next generation of women leaders.

Feminist Press at the City University of New York
City College, Wingate Hall
Convent Ave. at 138th Street
New York, NY 10031

Contact: Florence Howe, Publisher and Director
Phone: (212) 650-8890
Fax: (212) 650-8893

Since 1970, the Feminist Press has published fiction and non-fiction that challenges stereotypes and illuminates the ideas, experiences, and feelings of women of all ages, cultures, races, and social classes. Its list includes fiction classics, original literature, anthologies, interdisciplinary texts, original and rediscovered memoirs by significant women writers and activists, and children's books that feature brave, intelligent heroines.

A Selection of Publications
of Interest to Young Adults
Brown Girls, Brownstones
by Paule Marshall

Allegra Maud Goldman
by Edith Konecky

The Changelings
by Jo Sinclair

Biographies
Black Foremothers
by Dorothy Sterling

Journey Toward Freedom
The Story of Sojouner Truth
by Jaqueline Bernard

Five College Women's Studies Research Center
Dickinson House
Mount Holyoke College
South Hadley, MA 01075

Contact: Gail Hornstein, Director
Phone: (413)-538-2922
Fax: (413) 538-2082
Email: fcwsrc@persephone.hampshire.edu

The Five College Women's Studies Research Center is a collaborative project of the women's studies programs at Amherst, Hampshire, Mount Holyoke, and Smith Colleges and the University of Massachusetts at Amherst. Founded in 1991, the Center provides visiting residencies for feminist scholars, artists, and teachers at all levels of the educational system, and for community organizers and political activists, both local and international. The Center is committed to broadening the base of feminist scholarship, forging partnerships between academics and activists, and supporting research that can be useful to the diverse realities of women's lives.

Program
The Communities Project
The goal of the Communities Project is to encourage the development of partnerships between the more than 350 women's studies faculty at the Five Colleges and local human service providers and teachers, thus bringing together the best work done in both the field and the academy on issues affecting women and girls' lives.

Program Components:
Dinner Symposia
These dinners offer a space for the presentation of information on specific topics and dialogue with others concerned with similar issues. Speakers are drawn from community activists, Five College faculty, and human service providers.

Critical Issues Seminars
This program offers individuals from the Five Colleges and a wide variety of community groups an opportunity to participate in multi-session seminars on issues pertinent to the lives of women and girls. Participants discuss readings, meet with guest speakers engaged in current research, and share their personal and professional perspectives.

Women's Research Roundtables
Roundtables convene community agencies with faculty from the Five Colleges working on the issues related to the health needs of women and girls. Health is conceived broadly, including the impact of violence, welfare reform, and psychosocial aspects of disease.

Community Associate Program
This is a visitors program designed for local activists, community organizers and teachers interested in conducting research projects on women's lives. Once selected, each associate is provided with an office at the Center, faculty privileges at the computer centers and libraries at all five colleges, a free e-mail account and internet access, and the use of athletic facilities at Mount Holyoke College. Associates become part of a diverse research community and have the opportunity to enhance their research experience through work with a faculty partner, participate in a specially designed monthly seminar, attend Center events and present their research publicly at a "Works-in-Progress" session.

Girls Incorporated
120 Wall Street, 3rd Floor
New York, NY 10005

Contact: Isabel Carter Stewart, National Executive Director
Phone: (212) 509-2000
Fax: (212) 509-8708

Girls Incorporated National Resource Center

441 West Michigan Street
Indianapolis, IN 46202

Contact: Heather Johnston Nicholson,
Director of Research and Resources
Phone: (317) 634-7546
Fax: (317) 634-3024
Website: http://www.girlsinc.org

Girls Incorporated is a national youth service, research and advocacy organization that inspires all girls to be strong, smart and bold. The first Girls Incorporated clubs were in the Northeast mill towns in the 1860's; in 1995 it celebrated 50 years as a national service organization and now provides afterschool education at over 1,000 sites in 32 states. In the past 15 years, Girls Incorporated has invested more than $20 million in understanding the strengths and needs of girls and developing an effective programmatic response.

Programs

**Acting You: A Girls Incorporated Workbook
On Improvisation and Theater Games**
Developed in 1982, Acting You is an alternative type of theater for girls. It is a process that taps the creativity and inspiration of each participant to develop self-confidence and promote the ability to express personal experience in a meaningful manner.

Career Action Center
The Career Action Center facilitates and connects girls ages 6-18 to ideas, resources, and concrete plans for a challenging and interesting career.

Discovery: A Leadership Program for Girls and Women
Together, girls ages 9 to 11 and women in their communities explore the concept of leadership and the history and culture of girls and women as leaders. They practice leadership skills and undertake a community action project. This program was developed in collaboration with the Minneapolis YWCA.

Eureka!
This four-week summer intensive course and school year continuation program is conducted on a college campus with a year-round follow-up at the Girls Incorporated affiliate. The course introduces middle-school girls to five program areas: science, math, sports, personal development, and career orientation.

Friendly PEERsuasion
Friendly PEERsuasion was developed by Girls Incorporated to convince girls to avoid using harmful substances. Participants in the 12- to 14-year-old age group are trained to become peer leaders for 6- to 10-year-olds. The experience of teaching reinforces the PEERsuaders' commitment to avoiding drug and alcohol use.

Girl Power/Health Power
This program introduces girls ages 9 to 12 to personal responsibility for health care, including nutrition, physical fitness, reproductive health, and avoiding substance use.

Girls Dig It
This program introduces girls ages 12 to 14 to the disciplines of the humanities--history, art, and American Studies--through hands-on engagement with archeology.

Keeping Healthy/Keeping Safe
This program is an overview of sexuality education and emphasizes integration of HIV/AIDS prevention into programming for girls and young women.

Operation SMART (Science, Math and Relevant Technology):
Girls Incorporated developed Operation SMART to sustain girls' interest and participation in science, math and relevant technology. This comprehensive program includes components for girls ages 6 to 18.

Poetry Writing
The goal of the national poetry writing program is to introduce girls and young women ages 6 to 18 to the pleasures and challenge of writing poetry.

Preventing Adolescent Pregnancy Program, Growing Together
This program offers parents and daughters the opportunity to practice positive communication skills, including dealing with sexual information and values.

Will Power/Won't Power
Girls ages 12-14 learn assertiveness skills and analyze peer and social pressures in this active program designed to encourage young teens and to delay engaging in sexual intercourse.

Taking Care of Business
This is a structured program designed to increase young women's educational opportunities and career planning skills as well as their motivation and resources to avoid early pregnancy.

Health Bridge
This is a cooperative health promotion program and delivery system for girls and young women ages 12-18.

Action for Safety
Based on the principles and practices of the Center for Anti-Violence Education, Inc., Action for Safety is a gender-specific, anti-violence program for girls ages 9 to 11. As girls learn verbal and physical techniques to avoid violence, they also gain an understanding of their rights and limitations.

Steppingstones
This is a basic motor skills development and fitness appreciation program for girls ages 6 to 8. Participants develop body management and manipulative skills that they may later apply to formal movement, including games, sports, dance, gymnastics, and aerobic exercise.

Bridges
This program builds directly upon Steppingstones, offering fun-filled activities, that develop basic sports skills in softball, tennis, basketball and soccer for girls 9 to 11. Bridges provides

leadership exercises to enhance girls' interest in sports as an integral part of their lives.

Sports Unlimited
This program introduces teen women to a variety of lifelong sports that they choose, while teaching the importance of nutrition and physical fitness.

Teen Connections
This health and action program for teen women links health education and leadership development in Girls Incorporated centers with methods to improve the quality of health resources and availability and access to them in your community.

Publications
Past the Pink & Blue Predicament: Freeing the Next Generation from Sex Stereotypes
A report reviewing and summarizing research about gender. It discusses ways that boys and girls differ and ways they do not, dispelling long-held myths.

What's Equal? Figuring Out What Works for Girls in Co-ed Settings
A resource for parents and educators committed to creating a non-sexist learning environment for girls.

It's My Party: Girls Choose to Be Substance Free
This document provides a summary of the Girls Incorporated Friendly PEERsuasion program, outlining the research, results and policy recommendations.

Prevention and Parity: Girls and Juvenile Justice
This publication addresses key issues that affect the ways which the juvenile justice system can meet girls' needs—the nature and extent of young women's involvement, specific factors that place young women at risk, variables, or issues, in treatment and effective programs.

Girls Re-Cast TV Action Kit
This collection of action cards contains individual, interactive and group activities to teach girls to watch TV actively and critically.

Re-Casting TV: Girls Views
Summary and excerpt from the poll commissioned by Girls Inc. and conducted by Louis Harris and Associates, Inc. This 1995 survey asked more than 2,000 kids in grades 3-12 their opinions about TV and gender stereotypes.

No Turning Back:
Milestones for Girls in the Twentieth Century
Edith Phelps, former national executive director of Girls Incorporated, recounts the tradition of action taken by women on behalf of girls in the twentieth century. Phelps gives an inside look at an astonishing period of social change and upheaval.

Luann Becomes a Woman
This educational booklet featuring Luann and her friends, illustrated with cartoon strips by nationally syndicated cartoonist Greg Evan, explains menstruation as a natural and positive event.

Holding Our Own:
A Handbook for Girls and Women Exploring Leadership.
Girls Incorporated and the YWCA of Minneapolis Prevention of Sexual Intercourse for Teen Women aged 12 to 14. The Prevention Researcher, 4(1), 10-12 Postrado, L.T., Weiss, F.L. & Nicholson, H.J. (1997)

Friendly PEERsuasion Against Substance Use:
The Girls Incorporated Model and Evaluation.
Drugs and Society.
12(1/2), 7-22 Weiss, F.l. & Nicholson, H.J. (1998).

Affiliated Girls Incorporated Organizations
Kid-Ability
Kid-Ability is a program developed and distributed by Girls Inc. of Omaha. It includes comprehensive guides, journals and videos for kids, parents, and volunteers covering pertinent information about self-protection and sexual abuse prevention for children. Available through Girls Incorporated of Omaha

Choices: A Teen Women's Journal for Self-Awareness and Personal Planning
Making Choices: Life Skills for Adolescents
A series of curricula, guides and journals developed to help navigate the realities of adolescent development, parenting, career and life planning and the school to work transition. Published by Advocacy Press: Santa Barbara, CA. Proceeds of Advocacy Press Support the programs of Girls Incorporated of Santa Barbara.

Henry A. Murray Research Center
Radcliffe College
10 Garden Street
Cambridge, MA 02138

Contact: Anne Colby, Director; Jackie James, Asst. Director
Phone: (617) 496-8140
Fax: (617) 496-3993

The Murray Center of Radcliffe College was founded in 1976 as a center for research on changing lives of women. The Center offers staff assistance for data users; seminars and conferences on methods for using existing data; research grants to doctoral students and post doctoral scholars; and a visiting scholars-in-residence program. The Murray Center staff researchers work in areas of cognitive, social, and personality development. The data archive includes not only computer-accessible quantitative data but also qualitative materials such as case histories, open-ended interviews, and responses to project tests. Many of the data sets are longitudinal in design, following the same people over many years.

Recent Research:
Dana Nurge, Block Dissertation Award, 1996-1997
Topic: An Ethnography of Female Gangs, Drugs, and Violence in Boston

Lorrie K. Sippola, Visiting Scholar, 1996-1997
Topic: Care and Justice, Moral Dimensions of Adolescents' Relations with Friends and Peers

Gail Melson, Visiting Scholar, 1996-1997
Topic: The Peaceable Kingdom: The Significance of Animals in the Lives Of Children

Institute for Research on Women and Gender
Stanford University

Serra House
Stanford, CA 94305-6905

Contact: Laura L. Carstensen, Director
Phone: (650) 723-1994
Fax: (650) 725-0374

Founded in 1974, the Institute for Research on Women and Gender supports scholarship on women and gender and organizes educational programs to make such work accessible to a broader public. The Institute sponsors interdisciplinary research, seminars, lectures, conferences, and publishes a working paper series, completed research, and a quarterly newsletter. Employment , education, law, literature, art, health, poverty, and families have been recurring concerns. Stanford's Institute fosters major interdisciplinary research on women and gender and involves the wider community in its activities.

Program
Girls and Gangs

Contact: Belinda Smith Walker, Acting Executive Director of Girls and Gangs
Phone: (626) 440-0057
Fax: (626) 440- 0214

This is a project of the Los Angeles Associates of the Institute for Research on Women and Gender at Stanford University. Girls and Gangs is a task force of individuals from public and non-profit organizations serving girls throughout Los Angeles County. Its mission is to develop a support program for girls in the county detention system to build constructive lives when they return to society. Its first goal is to develop a support program for girls leaving Camp Scott, the only detention facility in L.A. County solely for girls.

International Center for Research on Women (ICRW)

1717 Massachusetts Ave., NW
Suite 302
Washington, DC 20036

Contact: Geeta Rao Gupta, President
Phone: (202) 797-0007
Fax: (202) 797-0020
Email: ICRW@igc.org
Website: http://www.icrw.org

Founded in 1976, ICRW is a private, non-profit organization dedicated to promoting social and economic development with women's full participation. ICRW generates quality, empirical information, and provides technical assistance on women's productive activity, their reproductive and sexual health and rights, their status in the family, their leadership in society, and their management of environmental resources. In 1998, ICRW will be launching three new studies on adolescents.

Programs
Adolescent Sexuality and Fertility in India
Provides technical assistance to four research institutions in India which are undertaking a research program on adolescent reproductive health to help inform the design of services.

Publications
Health Consequences of Adolescent Childbearing
In Developing Countries
This is a working paper which examines the health consequences of adolescent childbearing that accesses a number of studies, focusing on such indicators as maternal morbidity, physical growth during pregnancy, birthweight, and prematurity in infants. A discussion of programmatic efforts to reduce poor health consequences of childbearing by adolescents is also included.

The Costs of Adolescent Childbearing
In Latin America and the Caribbean
This working paper explores the implications–social and economic–of adolescent childbearing on mothers and children and results of four studies are discussed, with attention given to the design of social policy.

Adolescent Sexual and Reproductive Behavior:
Evidence for India
A report on the existing research of sexual and reproductive behavior. The review points out the gaps in knowledge of adolescent sexual and reproductive behavior, explores the knowledge and attitudes among this population in India, and calls for more social science research to determine how health and information services can be structured to respond to the needs of adolescents.

Vulnerability and Opportunity:
Adolescents and HIV/AIDS in the Developing World,
Findings from the Women and AIDS Research Program
This report synthesizes the findings from the first phase of ICRW Women and AIDS Research Program which supported 17 studies in Africa, Asia and the Pacific, and Latin America and the Caribbean. The report argues that factors that influence sexual risk are: lack of information and services, social, cultural, and economic forces that result in gender differences in sexual experiences, expectations, and the ability of youth to adopt HIV/STD preventive behaviors.

The Nutrition and Lives of Adolescents in Developing
Countries: Findings from the Nutrition of Adolescent Girls
Research Program
Findings from eleven studies on the nutritional status of adolescents in the broader context of their lives—health, education, activities, and self-perceptions.

The National Council for Research on Women

11 Hanover Square, 20th Floor
New York, NY 10005

Contact: Linda Basch, Executive Director
Phone: (212) 785-7335
Fax: (212) 785-7350
Email:ncrw@ncrw.org
Website: http://www.ncrw.org

Established in 1981, NCRW is a working alliance of centers and individuals actively involved in feminist research, policy analysis, advocacy, and innovative programs for women and girls. Through its member centers, affiliates, events, and publications, the Council links a community of scholars and practicioners and fosters collaboration among researchers, advocates, policymakers, and national and international organizations. The Council's constituencies include the academic community, government, media, business, public policy and non- profit institutions, and the general public.

Publications
Risk, Resiliency, and Resistance:
Current Research on Adolescent Girls
Debra Schultz, (1991)
This report, an overview of current research and appendixes of model programs and key scholars which points to the wealth of resources available for linking feminist scholarship to grassroots change on behalf of girls.

Sexual Harassment:
Research and Resources, 3rd Edition (1995)
This expanded report of NCRW's Sexual Harassment Information Project summarizes the wealth of research and resources on sexual harassment, including teen on teen sexual harassment, current legal and scholarly interpretations, patterns of behavior of the harassed, myths about harassers, anti-harassment policies and procedures, and efforts needed to bring about significant change.

Who Benefits, Who Decides? (1995)
The report documents what is known about funding for women and girls—and the lack of it. Topics include: perceptions of social change, discussion of the roles of research in philanthropy, issues affecting women's and girl's organizations, models of successful funding, and suggestions for expanding potential sources of support.

IQ Sexual Harassment: What's Going On? A Look at a Disturbing Trend Among Teens
This report exposes a troubling element in today's culture–sexual harassment among children and teens. Perspectives, a section within IQ, traces the core theme through brief interviews with key researchers, policy specialists, and practitioners.

IQ Immigration: Women and Girls Were Do They Land?
The girls section of this edition addresses gender equity for immigrant girls and takes a special look at a self-esteem building program for immigrant Filipina girls.

IQ Philanthropy: Do Universal Dollars Reach Women and Girls?
According to 1994 Foundation Center figures, of the leading foundations, only 5.3 percent of funding in 1992 was specifically tagged for women and girls. The figures show a mere flicker of improvement, up only two-tenths of one percent from 1989. Over 90 percent of foundation dollars go to "universal or "generic" programs, in spite of increasing evidence that these dollars do not trickle down to meet the needs of women and girls.

IQ: Beyond Beijing: After the Promises of the UN Conference on Women: Who's Doing What to Turn Words into Action?
The girls section of this edition of IQ highlights the contributions of young female activists who took part in the Beijing Conference, as well as some of the ongoing projects generated by the experience in Beijing.

IQ: Women and Girls in Science, Math, and Engineering
This publication presents an overview of recent debates, funding, and the opportunities and obstacles faced by girls and women in various scientific fields.

Newcomb College Center for Research on Women
Tulane University
New Orleans, LA 70118

Contacts: Beth Willinger, Director;
Crystal Kile, Program Coordinator
Phone: (504) 865-5238.
Fax: (504) 862-8948
Website: http://www.tulane.edu/~wc

Established in 1975, Newcomb promotes research and teaching about women's lives and feminist perspectives through library, archival and on-line research, course work, and public lectures.

Programs
IMAGINE - Internet Mastery as Girls' Imagination-Nurturing Engine
This program fosters the Internet presence of women and girls and increases girls' Internet skills. This 20 hour summer camp program helps girls explore through readings and the Internet how young women are represented in the heavily sexualized contemporary consumer youth cultures; to identify and examine alternative images and role models; and to become empowered to represent themselves and to set and enunciate goals for their futures. Over the course of the program, girls will go through a series of guided exercises in order to become adept at basic and intermediate Internet communication and research skills. Students will be encouraged to construct personal webpages that represent their lives and goals for the future, and which contain links to online resources containing information to help them overcome the obstacles they face and to reach these goals. The process of critical thinking, self-evaluation, goal-setting and technologically mediated creative self-expression is designed to support the girls as they develop as peer-counselors, role models

and community leaders. Girls participating are residents of a public housing community in New Orleans.

Northwest Center for Research on Women
University of Washington
Imogen Cunningham Hall, Box 351380
Seattle Washington, 98195

Contact: Angela Ginorio, Director
Phone: (206) 543-9531
Fax: (206) 685-4490

The Northwest Center for Research on Women (NCROW) was established in 1980 by scholars at the University of Washington to promote, disseminate, and support feminist research by and about women. NCROW has focused on bringing women into academic areas from which they traditionally have been excluded. Furthermore, is committed to making academia more inclusive and to recasting knowledge about women in society. The Center strongly supports the interaction of scholars and facilitates their research on women that focuses on the integration of women of color into the curriculum and women in science and technology.

Programs
Rural Girls
The Northwest Center for Research on Women's comprehensive program for rural girls created a partnership among all players influencing a student's decision to pursue science, engineering and mathematics (SEM) careers. Students, teachers, counselors, parents and community members come together to actively participate in creating an environment conducive to rural girls' science and math achievement. The summer part of the program includes: 1) The Summer Science Program for Rural High School Girls, 2) the Summer Science Institute for Rural High School Teachers, and 3) the Summer Workshop for Counselors in Rural High Schools. In addition to the summer programs, each school-based group participate in ongoing activities during the school year, including a Long-Term research Project (LTRP), an Internet science club and two working meetings.

The NOW Legal Defense and Education Fund
99 Hudson Street, 12th Floor
New York, NY 10013

Contact: Kathryn Rodgers, Executive Director
Phone: (212) 925-6635
Fax: (212) 226-1066
Website: http://www.nowldef.org

NOW LDEF was established in 1970 as a national advocacy organization for women and girls and to be a resource for women's rights organizations, attorneys, and legislators. NOW LDEF's docket of over fifty cases includes economic rights and the needs of low income women, sexual harassment in the workplace and in the schools, reproductive freedom, family law, and violence against women. NOW LDEF publishes legal resource kits on sexual harassment in the workplace, schools, and housing, pregnancy and parental leave, stalking, domestic violence and child custody, violence against women, and a guide to court watching in domestic violence and sexual assault cases. The organization also provides technical assistance and legal analysis on legislation that affects women.

Referral Assistance
NOW LDEF's Intake Department maintains a national referrals database listing organizations across the country that can provide direct assistance, legal representation, and information to young women and girls. Young women and girls can contact the NOW Legal Defense and Education Fund's Intake Department for information and referrals on a range of issues, including: domestic and dating violence, sexual abuse and assault, child sexual abuse and incest, and sexual harassment in the workplace, schools, and housing.

Southwest Institute for Research on Women
University of Arizona
Douglass Building, Room 102
Tuscon, AZ 85721

Contact: Janice Monk, Executive Director
Phone: (520) 621-7338
Fax: (520) 621-1533

The Southwest Institute for Research on Women (SIROW) was established in 1979 with a grant from the Ford Foundation. Arizona, Colorado, New Mexico, Utah, and West Texas comprise the SIROW region. SIROW also collaborates with El Colegio de la Frontera Norte, Mexico. SIROW's goals are to develop collaborative inter-institutional and interdisciplinary research focusing on southwestern problems or populations of interest to scholars in the southwest; to identify, coordinate and disseminate research on women in the southwest; to link researchers with community organizations and policy makers; to support undergraduate and K-12 education about and for women.

Program
Women in Science and Engineering Project
SIROW offers a suite of programs under this project which offers: an annual "expanding your horizon" conference for junior high-school girls, mentoring for undergraduates, job shadowing/mentoring for high school girls, and scholarships for gifted girls in science.

The Wellesley Centers for Women
The Center for Research on Women
Stone Center for Developmental Services and Studies
Wellesley College
106 Central Street
Wellesley, MA 02181-8259
Contact: Susan McGee Bailey, Director
Phone: (781) 283-2507
Fax: (781) 283-2504
Website: http://www.wellesley.edu/wcw/nrwsub.html

The Wellesley Centers for Women builds on the strengths and accomplishments of its two partners, the Center for Research on Women and the Stone Center for Developmental Services and Studies, by facilitating the development of new research, increasing efficiency, and expanding the Centers' outreach. It also unites the two Centers in a joint mission to educate, inform and expand the ways we think about women in the world. At the Centers, questions come out of women's diverse experiences, and fuel positive change with the power of new knowledge that benefits women, men and children.

Research/Programs

The Social Competency Program of the Reach Out to Schools Project

by Jean H. Krasnow, Pamela Seigle, Roberta Kelly (1993). This program is based on the understanding that improving the nature and quality of classroom relationships is the key to increased social and academic success for children. As a practical application of Stone Center theory, this program emphasizes the central role of relationships to student growth and development.

Raising Competent Girls: An Exploratory Study of Diversity In Girls' Views of Liking One's Self

by Sumru Erkut, Fern Marx (1995). This exploratory project is a study of middle school girls' understanding of what it means for a girl to like herself and what advice they would give new parents on how to raise their baby girl so that she will grow up to have a positive regard for herself.

Raising Competent Girls: One Size Does Not Fit All

by Sumru Erkut, Fern Marx, Jacqueline Fields, Rachel Sing (1996). This is a study of middle-school girls' self-evaluations based on questionnaire and focus group interview data from 31 African-American, 47 Caucasian, 40 Chinese-American, and 19 Puerto Rican middle-school girls in the greater Boston area.

Publications

Bullyproof: A Teacher's Guide on Teasing and Bullying for Use with Fourth and Fifth Grade Students

by Lisa Sjostrom and Nan Stein (1996). The guide contains eleven sequential lessons. Class discussions, role plays, case studies, writing exercises, reading assignments, art activities, and nightly homework combine to give students the opportunity to explore and determine the fine distinctions between "teasing" and "bullying." Children gain a conceptual framework and a common vocabulary that allows them to find their own links between teasing and bullying and, eventually, sexual harassment.

The AAUW Report: How Schools Shortchange Girls

by Susan McGee Bailey, et. al. (1992). An examination of how girls in grades K-12 receive an inferior education to boys in America's schools. Shortchanging is a joint publication of the AAUW Educational Foundation and National Education Association.

Girls in Schools: A Bibliography of Research on Girls in U.S. Public Schools (Kindergarten through Grade 12)

by Susan McGee Bailey (1992). Books, reports, and journal articles included in this bibliography are listed under topic headings to facilitate use by readers interested in a wide range of subjects. Among the more than 25 topics included are sex and gender socialization, teen pregnancy and parenting, vocational education, sexual harassment, and women in educational leadership.

Sexism in Special Education: The Case of Individual

Education Plans by Ruth E. Nemzoff (1992). This talk explores Individual Education Plans, which mandate parent and specialist involvement, creating an individualized plan to foster maximum learning for a disabled child. Nemzoff concludes that, in this planning process, mother's voices are invalidated as a result of sex bias.

Books for Boys and Girls Today: An Annotated Bibliography of Non-Sexist Books for Infants, Toddlers and Preschoolers

by Carrie Spillane, and Maureen Crowley (1996). This list of books for infants, toddlers, and preschoolers also includes publisher information for each book.

Bullying and Sexual Harassment in Elementary Schools: It's Not Just Kids Kissing Kids

by Nan Stein (1997). A review of research on gender-based bullying (U.S., international, and preliminary research results); connections to sexual harassment in elementary schools is also analyzed.

Becoming a Woman: Considerations in Educating Adolescents About Menstruation

by Margaret L. Stubbs, Jill Rierdan, Elissa Koff (revised 1988). In this paper, the authors review their findings on the psychological significance of menstruation and offer recommendations for improving menstrual education for both girls and boys.

How Schools Can Stop Shortchanging Girls (and Boys): Gender-Equity Strategies (1993)

by Kathryn A. Wheeler. This manual is designed to foster gender-equitable learning environments by linking educational research and practice. It includes the following: (1) an introduction to the issue, including a summary of How Schools Shortchange Girls, (2) gender bias self-assessment instrument, (3) research-based strategies to promote gender equity, and (4) resources for teachers.

Sex Education and Sex Stereotypes: Theory and Practice

by Margaret L. Stubbs (1989). This paper addresses the gap between theory and practice in the application of principles of sex equity to sex education. One means of closing this gap is offered in the paper's discussion of sex-equitable menstrual education.

Body Talk

by Margaret L. Stubbs (1990). "Body Talk" is a set of four pamphlets designed to help early adolescents find answers to their questions about puberty growth.

Menstruation: Fact and Fiction, (1990)
by Jill Rierdan, Sally A. Hastings. This paper examines how women writers of award-winning short fiction describe menstruation in comparison to how psychologists examine this aspect of women's lives in research literature.

Audiotapes
Interweaving of Biological and Environmental Factors in Predicting Girls' Success on the Math SAT's, (1996 Audiotape)
by Beth Casey. Dr. Casey presents research which traces the origins of gender differences in spatial and mathematical skills. She also discusses a theoretical model for how environmental and biological factors can interact to influence gender difference in the development of both spatial and math abilities.

"Possible Selves" and School Motivation in Early Adolescent Girls
by Carol Goodenow (1995 Audiotape). An overview of Goodenow's research on girls' motivations and school performance. The multi-method study involves 7th- and 8th-grade students from diverse districts known to have above-average drop-out rates.

Looking In, Looking Out: Faculty and Students Reflect on Gender-Equity Issues in Their School System (1995 Audiotape)
by Kathryn A. Wheeler. The speaker's presentation is a case study of one school system's efforts to raise awareness and determine perceptions of gender bias through the use of a district-wide survey. The design, administration, and analysis of student and faculty questionnaires are discussed.

Gender Equity and Educational Policy: The Cases of U.S. and Australia
by Susan McGee Bailey, Lyn Yates (1993 Audiotape). The speakers discuss the need for gender-equitable education for girls and boys, and their work towards instituting new policies to eliminate gender bias in the classroom.

Young Women's Christian Association of The USA
350 Fifth Avenue, Suite 301
New York, NY 10118

Contact: Prema Mathai-Davis, National Executive Director
Phone: (212) 273-7800
Fax: (212) 979-6829
Website: http://www.YWCA.org

The Young Women's Christian Association (YWCA) is a women's orgnization committed to working toward the empowerment of women and the elimination of racism through a variety of services and programs, advocacy, and public policy initiatives. At present the YWCA serves 2 million girls, women, and their families in 4,000 locations across the country. Activities include special programs for peer counseling; teen pregnancy prevention, exercise and education programs for those who have had breast cancer; programs for young mothers and victims of domestic abuse; women's resource centers; career counseling and job search information; support groups, classes, and services for seniors, refugees, and other groups with special needs. Current advocacy emphasis is on equity, economic security, youth, child care and health care. The YWCA is a member of World YWCA, uniting more than 80 national YWCA's worldwide.

Programs
YWCA/Nike Sports Program
This program which targets girls of diverse backgrounds ages 9-14 provides as an alternative to negative influences such as teens to negative influences such as teen pregnancy or becoming involved with gangs or drugs. The program has been a great success in providing girls with the opportunity to discover their true potential, make friends, and have fun.

Peer Education in Sexuality and Health (PACT)
This program is a health promotion and pregnancy prevention program for teens that uses high school students as peer educators. The overall goal of the peer approach program is to empower teens, both male and female, to make informed decisions about their sexual behavior, thereby reducing the incidence of unwanted teen pregnancies, STDs, and HIV/AIDS. The PACT program recognizes that teens turn to their peers for validation of their feelings about their own sexuality. By providing teens with accurate information, they are better able to disseminate the information and make responsible, safe decisions.

TechGIRLS
Raises girls' interest, confidence and competence in the crucial area of technology, while helping to develop critical thinking and problem solving skills. The initiative gives girls 9-13 a chance for hands-on exploration of difference technologies with the encouragement of women established, and college women emergent in the field of technology. Our goal is to broaden girls' knowledge and interests, to help girls to develop the confidence to use technology tools in whatever profession they pursue, and to discover links between enjoyable technology project and acedemic subjects such as science and math.

TechGIRLS Day
An annual hands-on technology day of fun and learning for girls and their college mentors. Activities designed for girls of varying ages and levels of expertise will entice, encourage, and challenge both girls and mentors to try out different equipment and new ideas. The girls will engage in Internet scavenger hunts, design on the computer, and explore electronic and robotics.

TechGirls Clubs
This program will give girls a chance to invent, design, and present their own work in the context of learning life skills. Individual and group projects will help develop communication, critical thinking, time management and presentation skills.

Educational Testing Service
Princeton, NJ 08541
Phone: (609) 921-9000

Educational Testing Service (ETS), a leader in educational research and testing, is the world's largest private non-profit educational assessment and measurement institution. Since 1947, ETS has provided education, government, and business with measurement tools. ETS has made a major commitment to linking assessment with instruction, a commitment that puts new emphasis on the diagnostic and formative roles of assessment.

Publication
Willingham, W., and Cole, N. S. (1997). Gender and Fair Assessment. Hillsdale, NJ: Lawrence Erlbaum.
A comprehensive compilation of information about gender and achievement from K12 through postsecondary education. Includes information from PSAT, SAT, ACT, GRE, the National Assessment of Educational Progress, and many other standardized assessments (as well as non-test indicators of achievement such as grades).

Girl's Best Friend Foundation
900 North Franklin
Suite 608 Chicago, Illinois 60610

Contact: Betsy Brill, Executive Director
Phone: (312) 266-2842
Fax: (312) 266-2972
Email: gbf@ix.netcom.com

Girls Best Friend Foundation is a Chicago-based family organization dedicated to advancing policies and programs that have an impact on the lives of Illinois girls. The foundation makes grants to non-profit organizations, maintains an archive and information clearinghouse, and sponsors programs designed to educate non-profits, funders, and policymakers about issues facing girls. The goal of the foundation is to help develop and sustain programs that ensure girls' self-determination, power and well being. Issues the Foundation addresses in its grantmaking include reproductive health and sexuality, gender bias and racial discrimination, sports, arts, violence against women and girls, girls' civil rights and human rights, equity and opportunity for girls.

Publication
Mapping a Path for Evaluation: A Planning Guide
A publication produced in collaboration with the University of Illinois at Chicago, Center for Research and Gender. This practical guide uses evaluation of programs for girls to lay out the basic principles, practices and benefits of evaluation for any non-profit.

International Network for Girls
NGO Committee on UNICEF, TA-24A
UNICEF House 3 UN Plaza,
New York, NY 10017

Contact: Mary Purcell, Co-Chair, Working Group on Girls
Phone: (212) 824-6394
Fax: (212) 824-6466
Website: www.ngo.org/INFG/wgg.html
Established in 1993 the NGO Working Groups on Girls (WGGs) are two Working Groups based in New York and Geneva, affiliated with the NGO Committee on UNICEF and the NGO Committee on the Status of Women. Comprising more than 100 international NGOs and their affiliates in nearly 100 countries, the WGGs work to further the rights of girls worldwide in all areas of their lives.

Programs
International Network for Girls (INfG)
INfG consists of 400 NGOs to date in nearly 90 countries who work with or on behalf of girls. The objective of the INfG is to share information and resources, to help build national and regional alliances to advocate for the rights of girls and support governments in meeting their commitments to work with existing networks and coalitions, and to work at the global level to make sure that girls' issues are addressed and acted upon.

INfG served as official NGO Task Force at the March 1998 Commission on the Status of Women (CSW) meeting where the WGGs presented a progress report on Girls, (see below) organized several panels, including "Listen to Girls" event in which 15 adolescent girls from 7 global regions talked about the situations in their countries to government delegates and NGOs; and held daily caucus meetings to lobby for strengthening language in the final Commission resolutions on girls.

Past activities have included: preparation of position papers, organization of daily caucuses, and lobbying at the Beijing Women's Conference and Prepcoms for a separate chapter on Girls (Section L) in the Platform for Action; creation of an International Network for Girls.

Publication
Clearing a Path for Girls:
NGOs Report from the Field on Progress since Beijing.
Based on responses to a survey from 248 NGOs in 87 countries, the report evaluates government action on behalf of girls based on commitments made in Section L of the Platform for Action; assesses the areas of most and least progress for girls in their countries; describes community-based NGO programs.

Ms. Foundation for Women
120 Wall Street, 33rd. Floor
New York, NY 10005

Contact: Brigette Rouson, Program Officer
Phone: (212) 742-2300
Fax: (212) 742-1653

The Ms. Foundation for Women has been working to promote institutional and adult support for girls over the past several years. In 1991, determined to raise public awareness of the complex realities of girls lives and help develop programs aimed at fostering girls' health, strength and resiliency, the Foundation launched the National Girls Initiative, a series of efforts to serve the needs and amplify the voices of girls. In 1997 Ms. provided $1.7 million in grants to 14 groups representing diverse cultures, settings and approaches, nationwide.

Programs

Take our Daughters to Work
In 1992, the Foundation conceived and initiated "Take Our Daughters to Work Day", a groundbreaking national public campaign designed to bring public attention to the unique needs of adolescent girls.

The Collaborative Fund for Healthy Girls/Healthy Women
Established in 1995, the Collaborative Fund seeks to organize 15-20 grantmakers who will capitalize a $4.2 million Fund and jointly regrant over $2 million to help develop and support innovative girls programming over the next several years.

Grantees Include:
The AIDS and Adolescents Network of New York (AANNY), founded in 1987, is a women-led organization that works to unite youth service providers, educators, parents and young people together to fight adolescent HIV/AIDS and address related sexual health issues.

The Center for Young Women's Development, is a community- based peer directed organization established in 1993, to address the lack of youth sensitive services, leadership opportunities and advocacy for the poor, young women (ages 13-19) who have been living on their own, out of school, and/or working in the street economies.

Cool Girls, Inc., Atlanta. Founded in 1989, is dedicated to the self empowerment of girls in low income communities, with an emphasis on public housing. Components of the program are:

> **Cool Scholars:** a program that collectively assists girls by offering tutoring three times weekly, providing a supplemental math program, creating opportunities to inventory assets and explore career options, preparing for college through campus visits, and directing attention to admission processes, implementing culturally-based esteem building to foster academic excellence.

> **Cool Sisters:** a mentoring program, developed as a means to establish one-on-one relationships with each girl, for the purpose of role modeling, mentoring, guidance and friendship.

> **Girls Club:** a program considered to be the heartbeat of Cool Girls Inc. Through a 4-6 week training modules focusing on life skills, early pregnancy prevention, conflict resolution, self-esteem, cultural awareness with attention to challenges of racism, sexism, and poverty condition, the girls interact with peers and develop a sense of oneness with the group.

Publications

Programmed Neglect: Not Seen, Not Heard
A survey report documenting the dearth of holistic girls programming in the U.S.

Body Politic: Transforming Adolescent Girls Health
A Report of the 1994 Proceedings of the Healthy Girls/Healthy Women Roundtable

---

ELECTRONIC RESOURCES

The following websites are among the many clearinghouse resources for women and girls:

National Organization for Women
http://www.now.org/home.html
> National Organization for Women's Homepage has a search engine which allows for research by subject (e.g., sexual harassment, global feminism). The site also has links to chapter and state contacts, press releases, N.O.W. Times, and Internet resources for women.

Women's Web
http://www.sfgate.com/examiner/womensweb.html
> This site contains news, links to Internet resources for women, and forums for discussion.

Women's Resources Project
http://sunsite.unc.edu/cheryb/women/wshome.html
> This site has links to women's web resources listed by subject (e.g., art, health, sexuality) and links to national and international women's studies programs.

Feminist Curricular Resources Clearinghouse
http://www.law.indiana.edu/fcrc.html
> This is a clearinghouse for resources related to teaching feminism and law. It includes syllabi, reading lists, bibliographies, an index by topic, and an index by author.

Voices Of Women
http://www.voiceofwomen.com/
> This is a journal and resource guide with articles, a calendar of events, a directory of women-friendly businesses, a web marketplace, and links.

The following websites are a few of the many for girls, teenagers, and young adults:

Teen Voices Online
http://www.teenvoices.com/
> This is a teen magazine for adolescent girls. *Teen Voices* encourages its audience to participate by writing and submitting their own book and music reviews.

Club Girl Tech
http://girlstech.com/
> This site encourages girls to write articles and book reviews. It contains positive news articles about girls and a search engine to help the viewer find other websites for girls.

Girls Power
http://www.health.org/gpower
> This is a site to help give girls a positive self-image.

A Girls World
http://www.agirlsworld.com
> This is an online clubhouse for girls to share experiences, ideas, and opportunities.

American Girl Magazine
http://www.americangirl.com/ag/ag.cgi
> This is a web magazine for teenage girls. It has articles as well as forums for girls to share ideas, information, and volunteer experiences.

Femina
http://femina.cybergrrl.com
> This is an excellent annotated and searchable database of websites of interest to young women.